ANDOVER:
WARREN F. DRAPER,
MAIN STREET.
1869.

TO

PROFESSOR EDWARDS A. PARK

IT IS FITTING

That these Pages should be Dedicated.

Most of them were written at his suggestion, and were first printed in that Library of Sacred Literature of which he is an editor and founder. And while there is a manifest fitness in inscribing

THE THEOLOGY OF THE GREEK POETS

with the name of one of the brightest ornaments of American Literature and Theology, the Author takes great pleasure in this public recognition of a personal friendship which began when we were members of the same College Faculty, and which years of intimacy in kindred pursuits, though in different spheres, have been continually strengthening.

PREFACE.

Natural Theology may be contemplated from two different points of view, and so may be seen in two different aspects. We may look at it from the standing-point of our own observation and reason in the light of modern science and of Christianity; or we may consider it as it has been developed in the literature and history of heathen nations, and as it appeared to the eyes of those who were destitute of the Christian revelation. Treated in the former way it is, or may be, a science. Indeed, Natural Theology is the science of sciences, the grandest and most comprehensive of them all, embracing within its scope many departments of physical and mental science, and from the loftiest heights in the wide realm of philosophy looking up to the loftier heights, and peering out into the wider realms, of faith. Observed and studied in the latter way it is, or may be, a history. Indeed, it is properly the consummate flower and fruit of all history, and the widest and highest sphere of the philosophy of history.

This volume is intended as a humble contribution to Natural Theology in both these forms. The first chapter is a contribution to the science, or rather to the argument and illustration of the science; the other chapters furnish facts and materials for the history.

The first chapter does not aspire to originate any new kind of argument, but only to furnish new illustrations of the argument which was wielded with such overwhelming power by Bishop Butler in his day, and to carry it out to larger and more positive results. Starting with the assumption that God is in nature and in history, the aim is to show, by the numerous familiar and striking analogies which pervade them, that the same God is in the Bible and in the church. Or starting, as the Christian will prefer to do, and may legitimately do, with the persuasion that God is the author of the Bible, and Christ the head of the church, the aim of the chapter is to show, by the resemblance in the style of thought and expression, that the same God is the author of nature — to prove, by the similarity in the principles and methods of administration, that the same Christ is also head over all things in the material and the moral world. With what success the argument has been conducted, the reader will judge for himself. The conclusion admits of being carried out to a still further result, of being carried up to a still higher consummation. The Scripture teaches that Christ is not only head over all things, but head over all things *to the Church*, that is, for the *benefit* of the Church. And it was my original plan and intention to follow the first chapter, which is entitled, "The Head of the Church Head over all things," by a second chapter in proof of the proposition that he is also Head over all things for the benefit of the Church. If God, or Christ, or, as the Christian would say, God in Christ, does govern both the Church and the world, we should presume that he would govern the world for the sake of the Church — the lower for the sake of the higher; the material for the sake of the spiritual; the temporal for the sake of the eternal. And it was the design of this contemplated second chapter to show, by an observation and induction of facts in the history of nature and the history of mankind, that as the earth was manifestly being made and prepared for man during all the ages before he was placed upon it, and all the lower forms of existence now minister to him, so all the ages of human history prior to the Christian era were preparatory to the introduction of Christianity, and the progress of society and the march of history since all tends to the gradual establishment and final consummation of this highest form of the civilization of man and of the kingdom of God. But this range of thought was soon found to be too wide to leave room for the other contents of the volume, and too extended also for me to hope that I should be able, with all my other duties, to discuss it to my own satisfaction or that of my readers. The chapter was therefore dropped out of the plan, though hints and fragments bearing on it — raw materials for it — will be found scattered through the volume.

The other chapters of the work present Natural Theology in its historical aspect, and that only in quite a limited field. And since they occupy by far the larger part of the whole, on the principle of the ancient logicians, *a potiori nomen fit*, these chapters have given its title to the volume, "The Theology of the Greek Poets." In this part also an additional chapter was contemplated, viz. a chapter on The Theology of Euripides. This would perhaps have rendered the plan more complete. But it would have swelled the volume beyond the size desired; and other engagements have interfered with the writing of it within the time contemplated. Moreover, we should have found in Euripides few, if any, new doctrines, and few essentially different modes of statement or illustration. He adds less to the theology of the Greek poets than to their rhetoric, ethics, and politics. Indeed the theology of the Greeks, like their dramatic poetry, degenerates in his hands. We should find in him more philosophy but less faith, more of speculation, subtilty, and refinement, but more, also, of scepticism in religion and scoffing at the gods. The theology of the Greek poets culminates in Aeschylus, whose faith in the providence and government of the gods seems to have been strengthened or inspired with enthusiasm by the triumphant issue of the Persian wars, in which he was a heroic actor. With Sophocles, as we have remarked in the concluding pages of the chapter on that poet, theology is already becoming an aesthetic element, a beautiful idea, a harmonious song. Euripides took no active part either in war, or politics, or the religion of the state; but, shunning society, sad of countenance, a hater of laughter, a hater also of women, and almost an enemy of the gods, he breathes out scoffing and scorn in his sentiments as freely and forcibly as he excites terror in his plots.

Some of my readers will perhaps think that I discover in Homer, Aeschylus, and Sophocles anticipations of Christian truths of which they had no knowledge. But we *ought* to see in these old poets more than they themselves were fully conscious of, because we can see their life and times in the light of subsequent history, their theology in the light of a brighter, purer, and better religion; just as with the help of modern glasses we can see the very same heavenly bodies which the ancient star-gazers observed in new aspects and relations, and even discover in the speculations of some ancient philosophers nearer approximations than they were aware of to the Copernican system of astronomy.

Others will perhaps object, on the other hand, that I assume too much for the Christian religion. To such I have only to say, that Christianity is, at least, a fact; and it is not to be ignored or set aside. It is the grand, significant, culminating, dominant fact, hitherto, of the world's history, and to assume that it does not hold that place in the world by right were as unhistorical and unphilosophical as to ignore its existence. As scholars and philosophers, not less than as Christians, we have a right to assume just the contrary. And it is no part of the design of this volume to apologize for Christianity, or even to defend it, but only to illustrate its true place in literature and history.

The chapters of this book have all appeared as Articles in the Quarterlies, and are reprinted now at the request of many pupils and other friends. Besides Professor Park, to whom the work is dedicated, I cannot refrain from expressing my especial obligations to Professor H. B. Smith, of the Union Theological Seminary, in whose Theological Review two of the Articles were first printed, for encouragement and co-operation in giving them to the public in the form in which they now appear. If, as my friends have encouraged me to hope, this republication shall conduce to a more enlightened view of the relations between knowledge and religion, and so to the honor of Him who is the Author of both, my object will have been accomplished.

CONTENTS.

I.

THE HEAD OF THE CHURCH HEAD OVER ALL THINGS.[1]

The Head of the church is likewise "head over all things"—sovereign alike in the kingdom of nature, the kingdom of providence, and the kingdom of grace. He is "God over all"—the God of nature, of providence, and of grace. This is evidently a doctrine of revelation, directly asserted in many passages,[2] and clearly implied in the whole tenor of Scripture.

It is my present design to show that reason teaches the same doctrine—that a rational and candid examination and comparison of the kingdoms of nature, providence, and grace will lead us to the conclusion that they have the same head. My arguments will be drawn from analogy, "that powerful engine which," as has been well said, "in the mind of a Newton discovered to us the laws of all other worlds, and in that of Columbus put us in full possession of our own"; and which, it might have been added, in the mind of a Butler disclosed to us the indissoluble ties that pervade the economy of the natural and spiritual worlds. The analogies which run through nature, providence, and grace are such as, if not to establish the proposition, yet to create a strong presumption, that they have the same head,

[1] Reprinted from the Biblical Repository, Vol. xii. No. 31, July 1838.
[2] Eph. i. 22; Rom. ix. 38.

and are in fact but different provinces of the same empire, distinct departments of the same government.

The principle involved in this argument is so fully elucidated by Butler in his "Analogy," as to be familiar to the memory and convincing to the judgment of every reader of that great work. He has left little for those who come after him to do, but to gather new instances of analogy, and thus furnish fresh illustrations of the principle and additional confirmations of the argument. This field of investigation, which Butler merely opened to our view, is as boundless as the universe; its treasures and wonders will be exhausted only when the plan of God's universal government is fully developed and perfectly understood. Into this field my readers are now invited, with the promise that, if they discover nothing new, they shall be conversant with themes that cannot fail to be interesting to the admiring student of the divine works.

1. The first analogy which I shall mention respects the qualifications for entering into the kingdoms, whether to explore or to enjoy them. In all three alike, these qualifications are humility and faith.

Without a humble and teachable spirit we are unprepared to investigate the question before us. On the outermost walls and gates of each of the kingdoms which we are about to examine and compare, on every side, is inscribed the motto: "Let no man enter here, save in the garb of humility." Bacon was the first to discover and apply this analogy. "The kingdom of men founded in science," he says, "is like the kingdom of heaven; no man can enter into it, except in the character of a little child." A child-like humility and docility was the key by which he opened the vestibule of nature, and in his "Novum Organum" he committed the same key into the hands of subsequent philosophers, and commended it to them as alone capable of unlocking every chamber and cloister in the spacious temple. It need scarcely be remarked that the same key is necessary and adequate to unlock the mysteries of providence and of revelation.

The book of nature, the book of providence, and the book of grace are severally dedicated to children. None but those who have the simplicity and docility, the humble and inquiring disposition of little children are permitted to read them. If others make the attempt, they cannot understand, still less relish their contents.

Without a figure, they who would study the system of nature, providence, or grace must come disposed and prepared, not to determine how things should be, but to inquire how things are; not to dogmatize and dictate, but to learn and obey; not to reason *a priori*, but to observe and infer. And they who would live happily under either system must have a contented and submissive spirit, and wear the apparel of humility and modesty.

Faith in its essential elements sustains a relation to each of the three kingdoms akin to that which humility sustains. It is the passport for admission. Not a step can be taken in the study of nature or the observation of providence, any more than in the knowledge of revelation, without a belief in the divine veracity, in other words, a belief that God will fulfil his tacit promise by maintaining a uniformity in his laws and plans of operation. It confers the right of citizenship. No man can be a useful or happy citizen in the kingdom of nature, providence, or grace without combining with the intellectual belief just mentioned a heartfelt confidence in the power, wisdom, and goodness of the Supreme Ruler of the universe.

Hence it is that true science and true religion mutually aid each other. Pure Christianity begets the confiding modesty yet eager hope of the philosopher; and sound philosophy fosters the humility and faith of the Christian. The philosopher believes anything with evidence, nothing without; and so does the Christian. The Christian feels himself to be merely a humble inquirer at the oracles of God, with no authority to dictate, no power to control; and so does the philosopher. The proud and dogmatizing spirit of many of the old Greek philosophers was not more unchristian than it was unphilosophical; accordingly their knowledge of nature and providence was as crude as their notions of religion. The same spirit as exhibited by the modern schools of *a priori* reasoning is not more unphilosophical than it is unchristian; accordingly while most philosophers of the observing school have been believers in revelation, scepticism has made sad havoc among those of the school of reasoners *a priori*. The humble, inquiring, and believing philosophy of Socrates made him almost a Christian without a revelation. The proud, dictating, and dogmatizing philosophy of the German Neologist makes him an infidel in spite of revelation. We know not whether the modesty of Newton partakes more largely of true religion or of sound philosophy. We know that Voltaire in his arrogance and conceit was neither a philosopher nor a Christian. The humble believer, — he it is in every age that discovers the truths, beholds the wonders, and enjoys the blessings of nature, providence, and grace — he alone possesses the clue that will conduct him through the labyrinth of the divine works. To return to the figure with which this head was introduced, humility and faith, not exactly in their Christian forms, but in their essential elements, are the passports for admission and the qualifications for citizenship alike in the kingdom of nature, the kingdom of providence, and the kingdom of grace. This analogy, so interesting in itself, it was peculiarly appropriate and important that we should notice at the commencement of our inquiries. But we must not linger about the walls ; let us enter the kingdoms in the spirit of humble and believing inquirers, and we shall find secondly, that

2. They are all governed by general laws. This is a characteristic feature of the divine government. Human governments multiply statutes, and strive, but strive in vain, to enact an express law for every specific case. Each day gives birth to an unforeseen emergency, and calls for a new enactment. With the increase of population and national prosperity the difficulty of legislation increases till the uninterrupted exercise of legislative wisdom is insufficient to provide for the ever-varying interests and relations of the people.

Suppose now some lawgiver should arise who could comprise every specific right and duty and interest and relation in one simple, comprehensive law. How would he throw into the shade the far-famed lawgivers of antiquity and the boasting legislators of the present day. But Lycurgus and Solon may rest in peace in their glory, and our representatives in the legislative hall need indulge no fear of being superseded in their functions and prerogatives. Such a legistator never has arisen and never will appear.

Yet it is by such laws that the kingdoms of nature, providence, and grace are governed. Take for examples the law of gravitation, the law of society, and the law of love.

The first regulates the relations and movements of every world and every atom in the material universe. The falling pebble and the rising mote, the descending rain and the ascending fog, the revolving planet, the eccentric comet, and the central sun, are alike subject to its sway.

The second regulates the relations and movements of every individual in society. Not a human being but feels the power of the social principle attracting him towards other human beings. None are so high as to be independent of the principle; none so low as to escape its all pervading influence.

In like manner, the third regulates the relations and movements of every Christian in the church. However different their denominations and forms and ceremonies, however diverse their rank or talent or dress or deportment may be, just so far as they are Christians all their thoughts and feelings and words and actions are controlled by one general law — the law of love. Thus the material, the social, the spiritual universe each has one general law, all-pervading, all-controlling, and all-comprehensive.

And these laws bear a mutual analogy not only in their universality, but in their nature. They are all laws of attraction, of association, of union. There is a bond of society and of holy brotherhood in the natural as well as the moral world. It requires no very lively imagination to see in the planet and its satellites the emblem of a harmonious and happy family; in the solar system a larger circle of affectionate friends and neighbors; in those groups of solar systems which revolve perhaps about some common centre, so many well-regulated and well-governed nations; and in the universe of worlds, all circling around the central throne of God, a counterpart of what the human race would be, did they but yield as perfect obedience to the law of their social and moral nature as the heavenly bodies render to the law of gravitation. What is holy love but a principle of attraction, a law of gravitation in the spiritual world, which unites individual Christians into particular churches, particular churches into the church universal, the church on earth to the spirits of the just made perfect in heaven, the whole general assembly and church of the First-born, to the innumerable company of the angels, and all holy beings fast to the throne of the Most High.

Knit like the social stars in love,
Fair as the moon, and clear
As yonder sun enthroned above,
Christians through life appear.

And in the future life, when the repelling and disturbing power of selfishness will be annihilated, how strong will be the bond, how exquisite the harmony, how beautiful and blissful the union and sympathy that pervades the church triumphant — the holy universe.

3. The laws in each kingdom are self-executing. This is another characteristic analogy which pervades the various departments of the divine government.

In human governments it is usually quite as difficult to execute the laws as to make them. The executive does not always understand them, sometimes wilfully misinterprets or fails to execute them; and even when the agents of the government are well disposed and efficient men, they are utterly incapable either of securing perfect obedience to the laws or of punishing every instance of disobedience. The man who should devise a code of laws that would execute themselves would be an unrivalled benefactor to his species, and would acquire for himself an imperishable renown.

Such, now, are the laws of nature, providence, and grace. They are inwrought into the very constitution, stamped on the forehead, graven upon the heart, of the subject; "I will put my law in their inward parts, and write it upon their hearts." Such is the decree of heaven promulgated in relation to the kingdom of grace, and the realms of nature and providence are governed according to the same decree. Every subject yields obedience to the law from the necessity of his nature, or if, in the exercise of free-agency, he disobeys, he cannot help the self-infliction of the penalty. Every man must obey the laws of his physical nature, or injure his health and shorten or destroy his life. He must obey the laws of his social nature, or torture himself while he wrongs and provokes others. He must obey the laws of his moral and spiritual being, or conscience condemns and passion rages and consumes the offender.

Take the laws already specified, the law of gravitation, the law of society, and the law of love. Obedience to each secures order and harmony, safety and beauty. Disobedience is immediately and inevitably followed by disorder, confusion, and ruin. "The wreck of matter and the crush of worlds" which would attend a suspension of the law of attraction is but a type of the jarring and collision of fiercer elements and the wreck and ruin of dearer interests which are consequent upon a suspension of the social principle and the law of love. On the other hand, the harmonious and beautiful order of the material universe as it is, is an emblem fit of the harmony, peace, and happiness that would pervade the spiritual world on condition of perfect obedience to the law of social reciprocity and universal benevolence.

> "There's not an orb which thou behold'st
> But in his motion, like an angel sings
> Still quiring to the young-eyed cherubims,—
> Such harmony is in immortal souls;
> But while this muddy vesture of decay
> Doth grossly close it in, we cannot hear it."

4. There is a striking analogy in the degree and manner of sovereignty exercised in each of the kingdoms.

Does God make one creature an animalcule to float in the minutest drop of spray, and another a great whale to traverse the boundless ocean; one a reptile to crawl in the dust, another a lion to roam the monarch of the forest, and a third an eagle to soar above the clouds; the zoöphyte scarcely to be distinguished from the senseless plant, and man to bear the image of his Maker and exercise in part the sovereignty of the universal Lord —without consulting at all the wishes of his creatures?

In like manner, his providence has cast one man's lot in the wilderness, a wandering savage, and another's in the city, amid luxury and refinement; has exalted one to sit king on a throne, and doomed another to toil a slave in the mines; has taught one to range the universe, "borne on thought's most rapid wing," and left another to confine his views to his native valley and his necessities to the supply of his bodily wants; and he has done all this without consulting the preference of the individuals concerned.

That a similar sovereignty is exercised in the kingdom of grace need scarcely be stated, for it forms a standing objection to the administration of that realm. There, too, "it is not of him that willeth nor of him that runneth, but of God that showeth mercy." The angels sin, and are all thrust down to the realms of darkness and despair. Man rebels, and an atonement is provided for his salvation. Yet only a part of mankind are destined to obtain eternal life, while the remainder are left to perish in their sins. Some are born to live and die heathen, while a Christian birth-right and inheritance fall to the lot of others.

There is no democracy, no levelling, no fear of distinctions, in any part of God's government; and it is most unreasonable and inconsistent that they who have always recognized the exercise of absolute sovereignty in some parts of his government should be surprised to discover the same sovereignty in other parts, and that they who find no fault with the principle in nature and providence should consider the same principle an insuperable objection to the administration of divine grace.

There is an analogy also as to the manner in which, or the principle on which, the sovereignty is exercised. "I thank thee, O Father, Lord of heaven and earth," says Christ, "that thou hast hid these things from the wise and prudent, and hast revealed them unto babes; even so, Father, for so it seemed good in thy sight." In like manner Paul says, in relation to his own times: "Ye see your calling, brethren, how that not many wise men after the flesh, not many mighty, not many noble are called; but God hath chosen the foolish things of the world to confound the wise, and God hath chosen the weak things of the world to confound the mighty, and base things of the world and things which are despised hath he chosen, yea, and things which are not, to bring to nought things which are."

The great principle involved in both these passages is that the heirs of earthly good are not usually chosen to inherit spiritual blessings. And it is a principle, which pervades every department of God's government, that he seldom lavishes all his favors upon the same individuals. The treasures of nature, of providence, and of grace are all infinite, yet they are meted out with a sparing and a discriminating hand.

How liberal has nature been in the provision of her gifts, yet how parsimonious in the distribution of them. The sum total is beyond calculation, the dividend is usually small. Through the whole range of animals how rarely are strength and agility combined, beauty and melody blended, cunning and courage united. The gaudy plumage of the peacock, and the sweet voice of the nightingale never meet. The strength and ferocity of the lion do not co-exist with the cunning of the fox or the reason of man.

So Providence rarely allots learning to the king or rank to the scholar. He takes health and peace away from both, and makes them the portion of the obscure and illiterate peasant. The healthy are not usually the wealthy, nor the wealthy the wise. Solomon stands almost alone as at once the greatest, the richest, and the wisest man in his kingdom; and he was in many things only a "wise fool." God has given to tropical climes beauty and fertility, but he has also given them the tempest and the tornado. He has doomed the inhabitants of temperate climes and mountainous regions to toil and fatigue, but he has rewarded them by "health, peace, and competence." In like manner divine grace has made exhaustless provision for our spiritual wants. Heaven was emptied of its choicest treasure and brightest glory to procure gifts for men; yet these gifts are not lavished upon those who have already full hands and surfeited hearts. The gospel was committed, not to the wise at Athens, the great at Rome, or the Rabbis at Jerusalem, but to the fishermen of Galilee. It was preached unto the poor, and embraced by the humble and unlearned. It is the poor and hungry, the weeping and mourning, the despised and persecuted, that inherit the Christian beatitudes. If you would find the abodes of virtue and piety, you must go, not where

"the spicy breezes
Blow soft o'er Ceylon's isle,
And every prospect pleases,
And only man is vile;"

but to New England's rock-bound coast and Iceland's frozen shores, the rugged mountains of Scotland, or the inaccessible fastnesses of the High Alps.

5. There is the same necessity for active exertion in each of the three kingdoms. Divine sovereignty and human agency run parallel through nature, providence, and grace. It is the law of the kingdom of grace: "Work out your own salvation with fear and trembling, for it is God who worketh in you both to will and to do of his good pleasure." It is the law of providence: "God helps those that help themselves"; and the law of nature: "The sunshine and the plough cover the valleys over with corn." "The blessing of the Lord, it maketh rich," — naturally, intellectually, spiritually rich, — but not without "the hand of the diligent."

He who would explore the mysteries of nature, providence, and grace must study hard; and he must labor hard who would secure and enjoy their blessings. In the sweat of his face man eats his bread. This life gives us nothing without great labor,[1] and strait is the gate and narrow the way that leads to life everlasting. We must agonize to enter the kingdoms of nature and providence as well as the kingdom of heaven; all alike suffer violence and the violent take them by force.

The divine agency may be more or less secret and inscrutable, and we may not be able to discern the connection between the means required of man and the end to be accomplished, yet both are absolutely essential to the accomplishment of the end. We cannot discover the manner of divine and human co-operation, yet it is an obvious fact that without that co-operation we can put forth no successful effort of body, mind, or heart; transact no important business in the natural or the spiritual world; secure no valuable interest for time or eternity. The Creator's efficiency and the creature's responsibility, absolute dependence and entire free-agency, run parallel throughout the natural and the moral universe.

6. There is the same apparent mixture of good and evil, order and confusion, light and darkness, in each of the three kingdoms.

Look where you will in this world, you see a checkered scene. The eye of man never rests on a spot of unmixed good or unmixed ill. Not a creature exists within the whole range of our observation that does

[1] Τῶν γὰρ ὄντων ἀγαθῶν καὶ καλῶν οὐδὲν ἄνευ πόνου καὶ ἐπιμελείας Θεοὶ διδόασιν ἀνθρώποις. — Xenophon, Memorabilia, ii. 1. 28.

Nil sine magno
Vita labore dedit mortalibus. — Horace, Sat. 9, Lib. i.

not drink a cup of mingled sweet and bitter. What animal ever lived and died without experiencing both pleasure and pain? Man, does he receive good at the hand of Providence, and does he not also receive evil? Nor is there a just man on earth that doeth good and sinneth not. Natural good and natural evil, providential good and providential evil, spiritual good and spiritual evil everywhere commingle. Like opposite polarities, the existence of the one always indicates the existence of the other.[1]

Are there "wars and fightings" in the spiritual world? So there are in society. So there are in the animal kingdom. There is war everywhere on earth; there *was* war in heaven once. Natural, civil, and ecclesiastical history are severally histories of alternate war and peace, battles and truces, cruel oppressions and cruel sufferings. "The whole creation groaneth and travaileth in pain together."

Does slavery exist in human society? So it does among the lower animals. White ants, like white men, capture their colored brethren, and doom them to involuntary, perpetual servitude.[2] And slavery exists in the spiritual world, too.[3]

[1] Plato in his Phaedo, speaking of pleasure and pain, says: "If any person pursues and receives the one, he is almost always under a necessity of receiving the other, as if both of them depended from one summit." — Phaedo, iii.

[2] See Natural History of Insects, Family Library, No. viii. chap. 7. "The legionary ant is actually formed to be a slave-dealer, attacking the nests of other species, stealing their young, rearing them, and thus by shifting all the domestic labors of their republic on strangers, escaping from labor themselves. This curious fact, first discovered by Huber, has been confirmed by Latreille, and is admitted by all naturalists. The slave is distinguished from his master by being of a dark ash color, so as to be entitled to the name of negro (Formica fusca)."

[3] Rom. vi. 16: "His servants (δοῦλοι, slaves) ye are, to whom ye obey." John viii. 34; 1 Pet. v. 8; Eph. ii. 2.

Are there earthquakes in nature? There are also moral and spiritual earthquakes — convulsions which shake society and the church to their foundations, and threaten to destroy their very existence.

Some churches sometimes exhibit a most lovely spectacle of order and harmony and peace. Such was the state of the church at Jerusalem in its infancy, when no man claimed or sought anything as his own, none gloried in wealth, and none suffered from poverty; "and they continued daily with one accord in the temple, and breaking bread from house to house, did eat their meat with gladness and singleness of heart, praising God, and having favor with all the people." But it was not always so with the church at Jerusalem or other apostolic churches. It was not long before Paul was under the necessity of rebuking the church at Corinth for such disorders as were "not even named among the Gentiles," and pronouncing the members "carnal" because of "envyings, strifes, and divisions among them." There was envy and jealousy, cowardice and treachery, in the chosen band of Christ's apostles. And none need be told, for every eye hath seen and every ear hath heard, how much there now is in the church of that strife which is accompanied with "confusion and every evil work."

In like manner there is here and there a regular and cheerful family, an orderly and quiet community, a peaceful and happy nation. But how often does confusion succeed order in these very families and communities and nations; or if not in the same, how does it prevail in others around them? Someman prospers and the bad only suffer; but how often times the good the tables are turned and the order reversed; and oftener still "one event happeneth to all."

In like manner in the natural world there are deserts amid tropical verdure, and oases amid deserts. There is an Etna in fertile Sicily, and a Vesuvius threatening the rich fields and blooming villages and beautiful bay of Naples. The tempest breaks in upon the sunshine, the earthquake succeeds the calm, and the blazing meteor, the streaming comet, and the appearing and disappearing star seem to disturb the harmony of the higher heavens. Throughout the divine economy strange disorder and confusion are set over against exquisite order and harmony.

It is a common complaint of deists that there is obscurity in the Bible, and mystery in the whole scheme of grace. But is there no obscurity in the deist's bible, no mystery in the divine economy which the deist acknowledges? Had the economy of grace been all light and brightness, it would have been too unlike the constitution and course of nature to be referable to the same author. Now, where in God's works is there not obscurity and mystery? I may find such a spot in another world, but I never have in this. There is light everywhere, but only enough to make the darkness visible; and the more light there is, the more we are sensible of the darkness; just as the larger the sphere illumined by a lamp in the open air at midnight, the more extensive is the concavity of darkness by which it is enveloped. There never has been a day in this world which did not answer in some respects to the description of the prophet: "It shall come to pass in that day that the light shall not be clear nor dark — not day nor night." There is light enough in nature, providence, and grace, severally, to guide us in all matters of practical utility or necessity, but if you would explore further, you enter the region of darkness. If you look downwards, you can only penetrate the surface, only examine a few scratches in the rind of the earth. If you look around you, every mineral is a cabinet of wonders, every plant a natural labyrinth, every animal a microcosm of mysteries, and of every element it may be said, as of the wind, "thou canst not tell whence it cometh, nor whither it goeth." If you turn your eye upwards, the stars twinkle very far, but you know not how far, above your head, their dimensions and velocities are very great, but how great in most cases none can tell, while as to the specific purposes which they are made to subserve you are left to mere conjecture.

And the deist's new testament, the book of providence, is there less mystery in that than in the New Testament of our Lord and Saviour Jesus Christ? Then why all those murmurings and repinings of which the mouths of worldlings and the books of infidels are full?

It is this mixture of good and evil, order and confusion, light and darkness, which gives such a color of plausibility to the most opposite views of our world. Voltaire looks only at the dark side of the picture, and uses the following language of complaint: "Who can without horror consider the whole world as the empire of destruction? It abounds with wonders; it abounds also with victims. It is a vast field of carnage and contagion. Every species is without pity pursued and torn to pieces through the earth and air and water. ..... In man there is more wretchedness than in all the other animals put together. He loves life, and yet he knows that he must die. If he enjoys a transient good, he suffers various evils, and is at last devoured by worms. This knowledge is his fatal prerogative; all other animals have it not. He spends the transient moments of his existence in diffusing the miseries he suffers, in cutting the throats of his fellow creatures for pay, in cheating and being cheated, in robbing and being robbed, in serving that he might command, and in repenting of all he does. The bulk of mankind are a crowd of wretches equally criminal and unfortunate, and the globe contains rather carcasses than men. I tremble on the review of this dreadful picture to find that it contains a complaint against providence itself, and I wish I had never been born."

Paley looks chiefly at the bright side of the picture, and says: "It is a happy world, after all. The air, the earth, the water, teem with delighted existence. In a spring noon or a summer's eve, on whichever side I turn my eyes, myriads of happy beings crowd upon my view. Swarms of new-born flies are trying their pinions in the air. Their sportive motions, their wanton mazes, their gratuitous activity, their continual change of place without use or purpose, testify their joy and the exultation which they feel in their newly-discovered faculties. ..... If we look to what the waters produce, shoals of the fry of fish frequent the margins of rivers, of lakes, and of the sea itself. These are so happy that they know not what to do with themselves. ..... A child is delighted with speaking without knowing anything to say, and with walking without knowing where to go. The young are happy in enjoying pleasure; the old are happy when free from pain." Halyburton, in the midst of affliction and in full view of death, looks on the same side and exclaims: "Oh, blessed be God that I was born. I have a father and mother and ten brothers and sisters in heaven, and I shall be the eleventh. Oh, there is a telling in this providence, and I shall be telling it forever. If there be such a glory in his conduct towards me now, what will it be to see the Lamb in the midst of the throne! Blessed be God that ever I was born."

Now, were not the present such a mixed state of things as I have described, different views might be taken of it, but not views diametrically opposite, yet both apparently just and true. And God makes use of this very mixture of good and evil to test and develop and form character. There is such a preponderance of good in nature as to furnish presumptive evidence of the goodness of its author, but such a mixture of evil as to give scope for the development of a heart of unbelief and discontent. There is such a preponderance of order and justice in the providential government of this world as to create a presumption that God is just, but such a mixture of disorder and injustice as to afford a strong argument for a future state. There is such a preponderance of light in the Bible as to satisfy a reasonable mind of its truth and sacredness, but such a mixture of darkness as to let the perverse heart wonder and cavil and despise and perish. It would seem as if God intended in this universal analogy to present us everywhere with the most sensible and striking proof that he reigns alike in the realms of nature, providence, and grace, and that we are now living in a state of trial, the issue of which will be a state of unmixed good or unmixed ill in another world. But this leads me to a seventh analogy:

7. In nature, providence, and grace alike, God brings good out of evil, order out of confusion, light out of darkness.

It has been already intimated that character is better tested and developed in a mixed state. There can be no trial of faith in a world of such effulgent light as enforces belief; no trial of patience where there are not ills to provoke impatience. And reason accords with revelation in pronouncing the trial of these virtues to be more precious than that of silver and gold.

None could avoid admiring a state of perfect order. Voltaire, though he might have been of a discontented spirit, would not have vented his feelings in such loud and eloquent complaints had no disorders or evils met his eye; and though Paley might have been benevolent and cheerful, and Halyburton pious at heart, yet they could have given comparatively little evidence of such a character had they never seen anything but goodness and happiness in the world around them. In such a world the three men could never have seen themselves so clearly, or exhibited so conspicuously to others the radical difference in their characters.

But more than this is true. A mixture of good and evil is essential to the formation of a highly excellent or deeply depraved character by beings constituted as we are. Our physical, intellectual, and moral powers are all strengthened by severe trial and discipline, and to this feature of our own constitution the structure of the world around us is nicely adapted. It is in no small degree a world of barrenness and thorns, a world of obscurity and mystery, a world of temptation and sin. We may and do perfect our natures by struggling with, and overcoming, such obstacles. Physical strength is derived, not from the easy chair in the parlor, but from ploughing and hoeing the earth, swinging the axe, or belaboring the anvil. Intellectual power and acumen are not received without effort in the nursery or the lecture-room, but acquired by delving in the mines and separating the gold from the ore. Moral and religious principle becomes firm and decided, not in the select circle of virtue and piety, but in the wide world of temptation and sin. Thus the natural and spiritual worlds resemble, and conspire with each other in the development and formation of character in the only way adapted to our constitution and state of probation, that is, by such a mixture of good and evil as shall leave us at full liberty to choose a right or a wrong course, and furnish us at once the means which are necessary to aid our progress in the way of our choice, and the obstacles, the removal of which by continued effort is necessary to develop our powers and confirm our habits.

In the same manner, and probably for the same end, the sciences have exerted alternately good and bad influences on religious character. Like the three kingdoms of which they constitute the history and the philosophy, they are partly light and partly darkness, and they have alternately obscured and illustrated the evidences of revealed religion. Now they have raised objections, and now they have removed those objections, and furnished contrary and corroborating evidence. Such has been the history of every science, theology not excepted. Accordingly different men have found in the same science, one nutriment for his faith, and another support for his scepticism; one the means of perfecting his excellences, another of deepening his depravity.

Another way in which good is brought out of evil in all the departments of the divine government, is by the increased value which good acquires, or seems to acquire, by contrast with evil. The fertile field never appears so rich as when contrasted with the barren desert. How does the hungry and thirsty, weary and wayworn traveller through the interminable prairie or the boundless Sahara revel in the shades and fountains, and fruits and flowers of the wooded island or the verdant oasis. None but he who has suffered a long confinement in the narrow streets and infected atmosphere of a populous city knows the luxury of life in the fresh, green country.

It is so with providential good. If you are ever grateful for health, it is when you have visited a hospital and had your heart wrung with sympathy for the afflicted and distressed inmates; and if you ever enjoy the blessings of health with a keen, a peculiar relish, it is when you have yourself just risen from a bed of painful and protracted sickness. You set the highest value upon your knowledge when you view it in contrast with the ignorance of others, or perhaps with your own former ignorance. It is so with spiritual good. When the Christian looks "at the rock whence he was hewn, and the hole of the pit whence he was digged," and sees others still cleaving to the hardness of impenitence and sinking in the mire of pollution, then it is that he sings the loudest, most enrapturing song of praise to his God and Redeemer. Heaven is the traveller's resting-place and the pilgrim's home; the warrior's peace and the runner's goal; perpetual health to the diseased and eternal life to the dying; confirmed holiness to the sinner and perfected bliss to the miserable; and through eternity the joys of the redeemed will be enhanced and their notes of praise swelled immeasurably by contrast with the sins and miseries of earth, and the deeper sin and misery of the lost.[1]

But evil is also made, throughout the divine government, the direct means of preventing a greater evil or accomplishing a greater good. The volcano is often a terrible scourge to its immediate vicinity, but it gives vent to those internal fires which would otherwise shake continents and lay waste nations. France in the last century was a political and moral volcano. Anarchy and infidelity broke out there in such frightful ravages and convulsions as to put an effectual check upon the risings and heavings of other nations, and to furnish a safeguard to society and the church in every subsequent age of the world. And who can say that our world is not the vent of sin for the moral universe, designed to exert a conservative influence over thousands of worlds and myriads of intelligent beings through endless ages.[2]

The lightning and the tempest often ravage the earth and destroy human life, but they also purify the atmosphere and prevent it from becoming fatal on a larger scale. So the judgments of heaven reform individuals,

[1] The songs of the redeemed in the Revelation are chiefly songs of deliverance in view of the dreadful and final overthrow of the wicked. In making such representations, the ministers of the gospel and the sacred writers are often charged with a fiendish delight in the miseries of others. But it is nothing more than that joy and gratitude which we always and necessarily feel in contrasting our enjoyments with our deserts, our present happiness with our former misery, or our own weal with the woe of others.

[2] That the influence of the fall, together with the scheme of recovery, is not confined to our world, is clear from such passages as the following: Luke xv. 10; Col. i. 20; 1 Cor. iv. 9; Eph. iii. 20. That it should affect all moral beings accords with all our ideas of moral influence, and to suppose that it does, gives new grandeur to the scheme of moral government and to the plan of redemption.

purify churches, correct social habits, and improve national character.

The modern Italian derives subsistence and pleasure from the surface of the lava that entombed Herculaneum and Pompeii; Europe owed the revival of letters not a little to the destruction of Constantinople; and the Gentile world were indebted to the persecution of the church at Jerusalem for the general propagation of the gospel. Indeed if there is any truth in natural, political, and ecclesiastical history, convulsions have been a principal means of fertilizing and beautifying the surface of the earth; revolutions, of reforming and advancing society; and persecutions, of purifying and enlarging the church. Who is not struck with the peculiar wisdom that originated this plan of operation, and the symmetry that extended it to every department of the divine government?

Slavery, that scourge of Africa and curse and disgrace of the nations that have sanctioned it, has it done no good? To say nothing of the conversion and salvation of thousands that would otherwise have lived and died in heathenism, what else has produced, or could have produced, that unparalleled sympathy and excitement in behalf of Africa which has led so many white missionaries to breathe her pestilential airs and lay their bones on her burning sands; and what else has sent back so many of her own sons, civilized, enlightened, and redeemed, to build up nations on her coasts and spread the blessings of knowledge, society, and religion through the countless heathen tribes of the interior? And who can tell to what new heights of heroic and philanthropic virtue the friends of liberty and humanity may yet rise in the struggle to remove this curse, and what new elements of Christian gentleness, patience, and faith this despised race may yet infuse into the national character and life.

And the evil one himself, has he not been the means of doing good? He too has occasioned a sympathy in behalf of his wretched victims through all the heavenly hosts, and "there is joy in heaven over one sinner that repenteth, more than over ninety and nine just persons that need no repentance." When he drove on his slaves to crucify the Son of God, he helped to execute a scheme which the angels desire to look into, and which all holy beings will study and contemplate with ineffable wonder, love, and joy forever and ever.

The animal kingdom, which is sometimes represented as a mere scene of carnage and cruelty, is a scheme of comprehensive wisdom and goodness; and the existence of carnivorous and venomous animals, so far from a blemish, is the wisest and best and most wonderful part of the scheme. Venomous animals rarely attack other species except for purposes of defence or subsistence. Now what more effectual means of defence against the larger animals could be devised than their venomous bite or sting; and what other way of destroying their smaller prey would be so sudden, so easy, and attended with so little pain?

The destruction of many animals is absolutely necessary to prevent such a multiplication of them as would exhaust vegetation, and subject not only the whole animal kingdom, but man himself, to a lingering, torturing death by famine. Now, how profound, how superhuman, is the wisdom which makes this necessary destruction the means of subsistence and happiness to another class of animals that execute it in a manner far less painful to the victims than the slow tortures of famine, disease, or old age. But for the comforts of society, the pleasures of intellect, and the hopes and fears of immortality, it would be better for man to die in the same way. As it is his reason which exempts him from the scheme of animal destruction, so it is his rational and immortal nature only which renders it desirable that he should be exempted. Thus, without any loss on the whole, but rather the reverse, to the herbivorous tribes, the happiness of the carnivorous species is clear gain to the sum total of animal enjoyment.[1]

Now it is a doctrine of Christian theology that the sum total of moral as of natural good is enhanced by the existence of evil. We cannot see so clearly how this result is effected in the moral as in the natural world, hence there is some dispute as to the manner; but as to the fact there can be no doubt.[2] The Bible implies it,[3] and we see enough of the process to satisfy a reasonable mind. The sins and temptations of a wicked world give occasion for the exercise of some virtues which could not otherwise exist, and discipline other virtues to a degree of strength and perfection which they could not otherwise attain. Earth, with all its barrenness and thorns and briars, is the very soil for faith and patience and charity and heroism and martyrdom to bloom in and bear their precious harvest of golden fruit.

Without the existence of evil there could not be the luxury, to us unequalled, of contemplating our deliver-

[1] For authority and more extended discussion on this subject, the reader may refer to Paley's Natural Theology, chap. 26, and Buckland's Bridgewater Treatise, chap. 13.

[2] Theologians of all parties agree that evil is in some way, or for some reason, incidental to the best system.

[3] Rom. iii. 5–7; v. 20; xi. 11, 12, 32, 33, etc.

ance and praising our deliverer. The beauties of the Redeemer's character and the glories of redemption could have been exhibited only in a theatre of sin and misery. Other worlds may owe their continued allegiance to our apostasy, their further progress in knowledge and holiness to our folly and guilt; and the holy universe will understand the nature, perceive the beauty, and enjoy the pleasures of holiness far more than if sin and misery had never existed.

As in the natural world destruction and pain afford the means of subsistence and pleasure, so in the spiritual world sin and misery furnish nutriment to holiness and happiness; and as the happiness of carnivorous animals is clear gain without any loss to the herbivorous, so without doing the wicked any wrong the Head of the church will by their means greatly enhance the holiness and happiness of his people, while he makes a matchless display of his own wisdom and goodness. Thus he causes the wrath of the elements and animals and men and devils to praise him, and to work together for the good of the universe; and we only need clearer eyes, larger minds, and better hearts to see every apparent evil in every department of the divine government producing real good.

> "All nature is but art unknown to thee;
> All chance, direction which thou canst not see;
> All discord, harmony not understood;
> All partial evil, universal good."

8. The order of proceeding in nature, providence, and grace alike is gradual. The processes are never hurried, often exceedingly slow. The growth of the plant, the animal, the man, is by almost imperceptible gradations. Human character and condition are formed and

decided by steps equally gradual. And the same is true of the Christian character and state.

Look at the same law of order on a larger scale. The work of creation occupied six natural days according to the common understanding of the sacred record. According to the interpretation of many philologists and the records of geology many thousand years were occupied in preparing the earth to be a suitable habitation for man. How slow is the process of civilization, and the progress of society. All Europe was overrun with savage tribes from its first peopling till the supremacy of the Roman empire, and the larger part of it remained in a savage state till after the Reformation. It was only within a century that government began to be administered for the good of the people; and, according to the analogy of past history, many and many a year must roll away before this will become the end of all government.

We need not be surprised, then, at the slow progress of revelation and spiritual renovation. The human race lived two thousand years without any written revelation, and two thousand years more had elapsed before the canon of Scripture was completed. A third period of two thousand years has almost passed away, and not one fourth of the human race bear so much as the Christian name. Not one fourth of these have the Bible in their own tongue and are able to read it; and of these again, not one fourth probably are real and spiritual Christians. Yet the process has been ever going on, and is destined to go on till the world is converted.

There is the increasing twilight, the gradual dawn, and the slowly advancing day alike in nature, providence, and grace. Everywhere, in everything in our world, infancy, childhood, youth, manhood, succeed each other by almost imperceptible stages.

9. This law of order is not only gradual but progressive. There is a gradual process of improvement or advancement alike in nature, providence, and grace: "First the blade, then the ear, then the full corn in the ear." "The path of the just is as the shining light, that shineth more and more unto the perfect day." These similes rest on the analogy between the natural and the spiritual worlds of which I am speaking; and exhibit the order of everything which we see under the divine government. If "order is heaven's first law," progression is its second, and no less universal than the first. Particular illustrations without number will be suggested from the similes of the Bible, from the parables of our Lord, and from every reader's own observations and reflections. We will confine our attention to the following of a more general nature.

According to the first chapter of Genesis the order of creation was as follows: first inorganic matter, then successively grass, the herb yielding seed, the fruit tree yielding fruit, reptiles, the monsters of the deep, the fowls of the air, the beasts of the field, the cattle after their kind, and man in the image of God. There is obviously a constant progress from good to better, from less perfect to more perfect forms of organization and modes and ranks of existence. Now whether geology presents us with a record of this same creation, as some maintain, or, as others hold, carries us back to an earlier series of creative acts succeeding each other at long intervals, all agree that it exhibits the same general law of progression from the rudest mineral up, through successive stages, to the most perfect animal — from mere chrystalization to vegetation, from improving vegetation to dawning sensation, from advancing sensation to commencing sagacity or intelligence, and from rising intelligence to reason and moral sense,[1] where the progression ceases to be transferred from one species to another, but will go on in the same species through the countless stages of improvement to which man is destined during an endless existence.[2]

It cannot be denied that there has been a progression

[1] "Geology shows us that organic beings became more and more perfect from the commencement of life on the earth to the time of man's appearance." — M. Rozet.

See also Buckland, chap. 12. Says Kirby (Bridgewater Treatise, chap. 4): "The first plants and the first animals are scarcely more than animated molecules and appear analogues of each other; and those above them in each kingdom represent jointed fibrils. It is singular and worthy of notice that the Creator after the creation of inanimate matter probably first imparted the living principle to bodies of the same form with the molecules and fibrils, into which that matter is resolvable, thus uniting by common characters things essentially distinct, and preserving unbroken that wonderful chain which links together all created things."

["So completely is nature imbued with this plan, — with the thought of successive gradations — that even in those walls built up by corals in the depths of the sea, we read the mind of the Creator, as well as in those higher developments which characterize the structure of animals and assign to each class its respective standing, and also in the order in which they have been introduced upon earth from the earliest periods to the present time." "In the lowest fossiliferous strata we find fishes, subsequently we find reptiles, then birds, then mammals, and lastly man. So here in the order of succession we have a coincidence with their gradation according to structure." — Agassiz, Graham Lectures, pp. 71, 107.]

[2] ["Coming to the noble form of man, we find the brain so organized that the anterior portion covers and protects all the rest so completely that nothing is seen outside, and the brain stands vertically poised on the summit of the backbone. Beyond this there is no further progress, showing that man has reached the highest development of the plan upon which his structure was laid. The brain of man occupies not merely the foremost but the uppermost position. It is not merely forward but upward: forward in the direction of all progress in intellectual culture; upward in the direction of all moral excellence; forward and upward towards that mind according to whose image man is made." — Agassiz, Graham Lectures, pp. 109, 110.]

in the providential development of nature's resources to the knowledge and use of man. Look back upon the history of our own country and you see a condensed but faithful epitome of the world's history in this respect.

Little more than two centuries ago the savage roamed undisturbed over the whole continent, beheld with superstitious amazement or stupid indifference all the energies and operations of nature, and suffered the pangs of want and starvation amid all the exuberance of fertile prairies and teeming forests, mighty rivers and grassy meadows, tropical suns and fertilizing showers.

But the forest has been gradually felled, and the prairie subdued; boundless fields of grain and fruit drink in the rain and the sunshine; the produce of every clime is borne on the mighty rivers, wafted by the wind that whistled idly along their channels, or propelled by steam that has been elicited from their own waters by fuel which once stood embowering them above, or lay imbedded beneath and by their side, and where thousands starved, millions now live in plenty and luxury, and hundreds of millions might live upon the new and vast resources which are in a process of daily development. Throughout the world society on the whole has been on the advance, government has been gradually improved in theory and in practice, the arts and sciences have multiplied and advanced, and the means of subsistence and happiness have greatly increased. There seems to be in society a capacity and a tendency to progress unto perfection, which it is not unreasonable to suppose it may attain in another and a better world.

Religion has also been progressive. Universal idolatry was followed successively by the patriarchal, the Mosaic, and the Christian dispensations, each of which was a great advance upon the era that preceded. The true religion was confined at first to a single family, then to a single nation. Under the last dispensation it is enjoined as a sacred duty to propagate it among all mankind, and the church feels more and more every year her obligation and ability to set up in all the earth that kingdom which "consists in righteousness, and peace, and joy in the Holy Ghost."

Divine revelation was at first only a faint streak of light glimmering in the East; like the natural sun it rose gradually into view till it became full orbed; it has ever since been rising higher and higher above the obscurity of the horizon, and breaking more and more through the mists and clouds of earth; in its meridian splendor it will enlighten every land; and it will never decline from the zenith, but fade away in the brighter glories of the Lord God and the Lamb in their upper kingdom. Such then is the law of God's universal government:

> "From seeming evil still educing good,
> And better thence again, and better still,
> In infinite progression."

There have been exceptions to the law of progression in religion. There were sad relapses among the Jews, and Christianity has had its dark ages. But even here the analogy holds. There have been exceptions to the progress of society. Society has had its relapses and its dark ages.

And there were exceptions to the law of progression in the successive creative acts which geology discloses.[1]

[1] Buckland, Chap. 12. p. 115 (London, 1836). "[It is a geological fact, that it is fish of the higher order that appear first on the stage, and that they are found to occupy exactly the same level during the vast period

There was a general advance from lower to higher grades of existence. But occasionally more perfect organizations, both animal and vegetable, are found to prevail with, or even before, the less perfect. As if the Creator, while he usually proceeds according to established rules, intended to show, by occasionally departing from them, that he is not necessitated to abide by those rules.

It is worthy of a passing remark here, that in the development of nature, providence, and grace to the view and for the benefit of man, there is usually a progress or a relapse together. Witness the dark ages when the three kingdoms seemed to be all shrouded in darkness — when the light of natural science, of social knowledge and virtue, and of spiritual wisdom seemed at once to have been extinguished. Look again at the Reformation when the eclipse passed off simultaneously from nature, providence, and grace, and they all shone out with unprecedented lustre. In our own day, it were difficult to say whether discoveries in nature, improvements in society, or advances in the propagation and application of Christianity are progressing with the most rapid strides.

10. The types and prophecies of revelation are not without analogy in nature and providence. That is, there is something in the constitution and course of nature so analogous to the typical and prophetic parts of the Bible as to remove all *a priori* objections against them, and even create a presumption in their favor, yet not so nearly resembling them as to invalidate their

represented by five succeeding formations. There is no progression." Hugh Miller, Old Red Sandstone, Chap. iii. This fact, and others of a similar nature, which are stated with great frequency in the works of Miller and Agassiz, effectually dispose of the Development Theory, which is a perversion of the doctrine of gradation.]

special sacredness — their peculiar claims to an immediate divine origin.

As the former dispensation in religion was typical of the latter, so in the earlier stages of nature there seems to be something like types of the later stages. The organs of the earlier species of animals were comparatively rude and imperfect, yet they were similar organs to those of the later species, and performed similar offices — offices as similar as their situation and circumstances would allow. The common mind would not condemn it as a misnomer to call the forms and features of the monkey types of human forms and features. The naturalist finds such types[1] far down the scale, and far back in the history of animal life. It was this correspondence of parts throughout the animal kingdom which led Lamarck to broach the theory that all animals, including man, are but the same species, having the same essential organs but developing them more fully and perfectly as time advances and circumstances become more favorable. Though clearly false, the theory was founded on indubitable and interesting facts. It is now settled[2] that the animal species are radically and incommunicably distinct; and the resemblances in gen-

[1] Type is the very word which naturalists have chosen to express the analogy between the earlier and ruder organizations on the one hand, and the later and more perfect organizations on the other. ["The plan of man's organization begins with the fish, and we can trace it through the successive geological formations. . . . . . Is it then too much to say, that when the first vertebrate was called into existence in the shape of a fish, it was part of the plan of that framework into which its life was moulded, that it should end with man, the last and highest in the order of succession." — Agassiz, Graham Lectures, pp. 107, 138.]

[2] [So it was considered by naturalists generally when this was written. There has since been a revival of Lamarck's theory in a new form, or rather under a variety of forms, but only to meet a more triumphant refutation from such men as Agassiz. See references in the next note.]

eral organization between the earlier and ruder animals and the later and more perfect species result not from natural propagation and favoring circumstances,[1] but from creative power exerted at successive periods and according to such a law as to constitute the first ages, "shadows of better things to come."

Moreover as the rites and institutions of the former dispensation were not less wisely adapted to the character of the Israelites and the then state of the world than those of the latter dispensation are to the present character and condition of mankind; so the organization of the earlier animals was no less wisely adapted to the then state of the earth's surface than the organization of the later animals is to its present state. Buckland discovers in the entombed remains of the old world as clear and beautiful marks of design and adaptation as Paley finds in the living world. Each religious dispensation was perfect in its time; each grade of animal organization perfect in its place.

In the developments of nature and providence to the eye of man, the past often contains something typical and almost prophetic of the present, and the present of the future. "Coming events cast their shadows before," and seers of nature and providence are raised up, who, though they "know not precisely what, or what manner of time is signified," are yet enabled to discern and predict in some measure what is to come. Such seers were Burke and Adams,[2] who foretold the issue of the French and American revolutions; and Newton and Leibnitz, who had a glimpse, and threw out hints, of

[1] See this demonstrated in Graham Lectures, Lect. iv. and v.

[2] The allusion is to a youthful letter of the elder Adams, which paints the revolution and its issue with much truth and beauty.

many subsequent discoveries in natural science. Seneca foretold the discovery of a new world,[1] and Socrates and Plato anticipated the advent of a divine teacher, advising to forego the usual sacrifices till such a teacher should come, and "representing with prophetic sagacity and precision that he must be poor and void of all qualifications but those of virtue alone, that a wicked world would not hear his instructions and reproofs, and therefore in three or four years after he began to preach, he would be persecuted, imprisoned, scourged, and at last put to death."[2] It cannot be denied that great men have occasionally been endowed with a peculiar gift of descrying future events and forewarning their less gifted contemporaries of what they may hope or fear. Why, then, should prophetic inspiration in the manner and degree in which it is claimed by some of the sacred writers, be thought a thing so incredible, *a priori*, that no amount of evidence can entitle it to credence? The same God who endowed Newton and Leibnitz, Adams and Burke, Seneca, Socrates, and Plato, with sagacity and foresight so much above the mass of their contemporaries, may have given, nay, *has* given, to Isaiah and Jeremiah, Daniel and John, a prophetic vision so much surpassing the ken of these gifted minds that every candid reader of their predictions must acknowledge them to be divine.[3]

[1] Venient annis saecula seris,
Quibus Oceanus vincula rerum
Laxet, et ingens pateat tellus,
Tethysque novos detegat orbes.
Senecae Medea, 374–377.

[2] See Harris's Great Teacher, p. 50, where it is suggested, that Socrates and Plato enjoyed a degree of inspiration.

[3] I am aware that this analogy has been more frequently used (and therefore at first view may rather appear) as an infidel objection than as a con-

11. In the universal law of progression of which I have spoken, the earlier stages are preparatory to the later stages, and the latter reap most of the advantages of the former, together with many peculiar to themselves. This is obviously true in the kingdom of grace. The patriarchal dispensation was introductory to the Mosaic, and the Mosaic preparatory to the Christian; while the Christian, with all the benefits of former dispensations, combines many advantages peculiar to itself. The Israelites lived not for themselves, but to be examples unto us; and their history was written "for our admonition, on whom the ends of the world are come." We have the accumulated wisdom and experience of the church in all past ages to guide us in the management of ecclesiastical affairs and in the discharge of our religious duties.

firmative argument to inspiration. One reason for presenting it here, is a desire to exhibit it in a different aspect and relation. It should be remembered that an analogy is "an agreement or likeness between things in some circumstances or effects when the things are otherwise entirely different." (Webster). Prophetic sagacity and prophetic inspiration "agree" in so far that God bestows peculiar gifts of foresight upon the possessors of both, yet differ so much in the manifestation and measure of the gifts, that they can be confounded only by a very stupid mind or a very corrupt heart. They come under one very broad general principle of the divine administration, so that the one serves to illustrate and confirm the other, but the mode of the divine agency is so different in the two cases as not to invalidate the peculiar claim and the sacred authority of inspiration.

It has been the belief of every nation, in every age, that their great men were inspired, and pagan nations have entertained views of the nature and manner of inspiration strikingly analogous to those which the Bible authorizes. Infidels have urged this fact as a proof that there is no such thing as real inspiration. But it proves the contrary, just as the shadow proves the existence of the substance, and the counterfeit shows the existence and the value of the genuine. It shows that God has laid a foundation for inspiration in the constitution of the human mind upon which we should expect him to set up a corresponding superstructure. If he intended to impart inspiration, it would be wise to implant in man a preparation and an expectation to receive it; and having implanted such an expectation, it were strange indeed if he should never meet it.

So it is in society. The progress of society is owing in no small degree to the wisdom derived directly or indirectly from past ages. The Grecian and Roman republics were constituted and administered not for themselves only, but for the instruction and benefit of all subsequent republics. All the despotisms and limited governments of the Old World have risen or fallen, maintained their institutions or modified their policy, for the benefit of the New, whither light from every quarter and every age has converged. All that have lived before us have lived for our admonition, on whom the ends of the social and political world are come.

It is so in nature also. Ever since man was placed on the earth its surface has been undergoing changes, all preparatory to the present state of things, all conducive to the support and comfort of its present increased and increasing population. Our alluvial meadows and extending deltas, our beds of peat and bog iron, our collections of vegetable mould, and indeed all our existing soils are the gradually accumulated resources of successive generations. And if the conclusions of geology are not to be set aside, a similar process of preparation and accumulation for the benefit of man was going on for ages previous to his existence. The whole of the earth's surface[1] is a spacious storehouse of relics and treasures which have been collecting in all past times to supply and enrich mankind in time of need, just as society and the church at the present time are built upon the ruins of other churches and societies,

[1] "No small part of the present surface of the earth is derived from the remains of animals, that constituted the population of ancient seas." — Buckland.

instructed by their experience, and enriched by their remains. We draw our fuel and our food, our comforts and our delicacies, from the remains of vegetable and animal life[1] in former ages; and as the matter which constitutes the bodies of the present generation once entered into the constitution of other bodies, so the opinions and feelings of our minds are the opinions and feelings of other minds modified by constitutional idiosyncrasies, improved by experience, and enlarged by the accumulations of time and the favor of circumstances. It seems to be a law of the natural and the moral world that man shall grow only by living upon the relics of his predecessors; rise only by standing upon the tombs of his fathers; extend his vision only by looking from the monuments of the mighty dead. Dissolution is going on everywhere in our world, but it is everywhere preparatory to another and a better organization. One race of animals is destroyed, and a more perfect race succeeds them. One generation of men goeth, and a a wiser and better generation cometh in their stead. Society and the church are perpetuated and improved by the very processes of disruption which seem to threaten their annihilation. Death bears a most important and wonderful part in the whole economy of vegetable, animal, social, and spiritual life. The plant decays in the autumn and lies down in a wintry grave, only to revive in all the freshness and gaiety of spring. The insect becomes its own winding-sheet, and then unconscious awaits a resurrection to a higher order of existence. The nation declines and falls, to rise again

[1] "At the sight of a spectacle so imposing, so terrible, as that of the wreck of animal life, forming almost the entire soil on which we tread, it is difficult to restrain the imagination from hazarding some conjectures as to the causes by which such great effects have been produced." — Cuvier.

under a better form and happier auspices, and to attain to a higher degree of social perfection. The human body " is sown in corruption, to be raised in incorruption; it is sown in dishonor to be raised in glory."[1] The soul, like the butterfly (which in the Greek language — the language alike of nature, of philosophy, and of revelation — has the same name[2]), drops its clayey chrysalis to spread its pinions in a purer atmosphere, and bask in the brighter sunshine of a celestial day. The natural world, like the fabled phenix, its allegorical representative, will one day rise from its own ashes, and wear a new drapery of beauty and glory.[3] And the church, the city of the living God on earth, will be dissolved only to be built again into the New Jerusalem, the capital city of the new heavens and new earth, whose walls will be precious stones, its gates pearls, its streets pure gold, and the Lord God and the Lamb the temple and the light thereof.

12. After our Saviour had manifested his creative power by feeding a great multitude with a few loaves and fishes, he showed his economical wisdom by saying, " Gather up the fragments which remain, that nothing be lost." The same blending of these apparently incongruous attributes is conspicuous in all the works of God. Nothing can transcend his power when he sees fit to exert it, and nothing can exceed his economy when the exercise of power is unnecessary. He creates

[1] In view of the analogies to the resurrection, with which nature is so replete, no wonder that Clement, the apostolic father, exclaimed: " Consider, my beloved, how the Lord shows us our future resurrection perpetually."

[2] Ψυχή, the name at once of the soul and of the butterfly, its image.

[3] 2 Pet. iii. 12, 13. This doctrine of revelation is confirmed by natural science; by the philosophy of cause and effect no less than the philosophy of analogy.

nothing to be lost, provides nothing to be wasted, gives nothing that need not be given. He might have created fertile soils at once, and provided fuel as it was needed; but he chose by a natural and gradual process to collect them when they were not wanted for immediate use, and preserve them till they were. He might have made a plentiful deposit of useful minerals and precious ores on every farm; but he has chosen to scatter them in veins or beds beneath the surface of the earth, and employ our skill and energy to discover and procure them. He might have revealed the natural history of the primeval earth to us in his word; but he chose not to reveal what we might better discover for ourselves, and he has left us to gather that history from the organic remains of primitive ages.

In his providence God might have led every age and country to make its own inventions and discoveries and improvements, but he has chosen the more economical course of transmitting them from one age and country to another. And he has suffered nothing truly valuable[1] to be lost. We often think and regret that important knowledge has perished forever, but in process of time it proves to have been unimportant, or it is revived just at the time when it is most needed, and in just such a way as to render it most curious, interesting, and valuable.[2]

In like manner God might have communicated a

[1] Perhaps I should have said nothing essential — nothing whose place cannot be otherwise supplied.

[2] [Witness the exhuming of the Nineveh slabs in these days of philological research, when they can be deciphered, and the deciphering of the Egyptian and Assyrian monuments in these days of unbelief, when their testimony to the truth of the Scriptures is needed to antidote the scepticism of the age.]

distinct revelation to every people of every generation. But what it was man's power and privilege to do he has left him to do, and made it his duty to collect the scattered portions of revealed truth, promulgate them to all nations, and transmit them to the end of the world. He has communicated barely what it was needful for man to know, and what he could not learn from reason and experience; and of all that has been revealed there is no evidence that anything has been lost.

Thus in all his works God does all that is necessary, however much it may cost, and nothing that is superfluous, however easy it might be — gives nothing that is not valuable, and suffers nothing that is truly valuable to be irrecoverably lost.

13. Another analogy which forces itself upon our attention as pervading the divine works, is an obvious disregard of human distinctions, that is, such distinctions of time, space, rank, etc. as men are wont to deem important.

We who are of yesterday and die to-morrow, and are subject to incessant changes and vicissitudes from the day of our birth to the day of our death, attach great importance to the distinction of time. But in the sight of him who is the same yesterday to-day and forever, "a thousand years are as one day, and one day as a thousand years." Accordingly men are hurried and fretful in their proceedings, impatient of delay, and ever hastening to the issue. But the divine plan of operations is calm, gradual, and deliberate; and though in some of its stages it may appear imperfect or unwise, it will ultimately prove to have originated and advanced in perfect wisdom.

The divine, untaught in science, looks upon the geological theory of the earth's existence for indefinitely long periods before the creation of man, and exclaims: "How absurd! What! the earth tens of thousands of years in a fluid state—a state of ignition even, devoid of living beings, or inhabited only by salamanders! And hundreds of thousands of years more entirely or chiefly covered with water, devoted to the formation of limestone and coral beds, and inhabited only by polypes and lizards and alligators, et id omne genus. For ages without any inhabitants, and for myriads of ages inhabited only by irrational and hateful animals without any intelligent lord. Who can believe that the Creator was guilty of such weakness and folly![1]"

On the other hand, the infidel geologist looks upon the theological doctrine of the slowly successive periods of revelation, and the protracted delay of the work of redemption with like incredulity and amazement. "What!" he exclaims, "hundreds of generations of immortal beings suffered to live and die in ignorance of God and a future state, and that God revealed to them for the first time in flaming fire, and that future state disclosed only to their agonized sensibilities, and their hopeless, endless despair! The only possible scheme of human salvation delayed in its execution for four thousand years, and for two thousand years longer promulgated only to a small minority of the human family! Who dare utter or believe such a libel on the wisdom and goodness of God?"

Now both these objections spring from ignorance and

[1] Is it any less difficult to believe that the universe was a blank for eternal ages before a single creature existed? Yet so it must have been, unless creatures have existed from eternity. Capt. Symmes argued that the earth is hollow, because it was absurd to suppose God would occupy so much space with mere inert matter

narrow views. The divine untaught in science, and the geologist ignorant of revelation, both see that in some of his works God disregards those distinctions of time to which we attach so much importance, while they both deny that he acts on the same principle in his other works. But the principle is universal. Revelation lays it down as a general principle, that in his sight "one day is as a thousand years, and a thousand years as one day"; and reason would lead us to expect that the infinite and eternal God would not view time as it appears to us.[1]

So also the distinctions of space and rank are disregarded by him who pervadeth alike the atom and the universe, and to whom the loftiest and the lowest of his creatures are alike less than nothing and vanity. The sceptical philosopher declares it to be unreasonable and incredible that the God who makes and sustains and governs an infinitude of worlds should so concern himself with our little world as to give his Son to die for its redemption; and still more improbable that he would condescend to such a concern for obscure individuals as is implied in the doctrines of a particular providence, personal election, and the indwelling of the Spirit.

The illiterate Christian, on the other hand, cannot believe that there are many hundreds of shells, once enshrining living animals, in a grain of limestone,[2] and

[1] The man who is neither a divine nor a naturalist (shall I add neither a Christian nor a scholar) is the only man who can consistently urge either of the objections specified in the text. He must give up all claim to consistency who professes to be either, and yet does not admit that the same objection which he urges against his antagonist is equally valid against himself.

[2] "Soldani collected from less than an ounce and a half of stone found in the hills of Casciana, in Tuscany, ten thousand four hundred and fifty-four microscopic chambered shells. Of one species of these shells he cal-

myriads of animalcules in a single drop of water.[1] And many an educated Christian thinks it beneath the Almighty to people a world with polypes, and muscles, and snails, and lizards, etc.

But he has given up two thirds of the earth's surface to the fishes and monsters of the deep, and peopled a large portion of the land with lizards and serpents and vermin; and may he not have left the whole earth for a time without an intelligent lord, to be overrun with inferior animals—animals, which we in our reasoning, yet erring pride, are prone to despise? He has created infinitely more animalcules than larger animals, and may not he who creates them, redeem man? He does form and feed sumptuously every day the snail and lizard and serpent, so loathsome and odious to us, though not to him; and may he not elect and dwell with and provide for the humble Christian, number the very hairs of his head, and cause all things to work together for his good?

These things are all true, and all spring from the same general principle in the divine government—such a disregard for the distinctions of space and rank as leads him to lavish his bounty and his grace on places and creatures which seem too minute to deserve the attention of the great Sovereign of the universe. "If there be one thing" says an eminent naturalist, "more surprising than another in the investigation of natural phenomena, it is perhaps the infinite extent and vast importance of things apparently little and insignifi-

culates that a thousand individuals would scarcely weigh one grain."—Buckland, p. 117.

[1] "Hundreds of thousands [of the infusoria] may be seen in a single drop of water."—Kirby's Bridgewater Treatise.

cant."[1] What intelligent reader of the Bible and of the history of the church can avoid seeing that the same characteristic feature pervades the spiritual world, from the fall of man in Eden to his complete restoration and final confirmation in the celestial Paradise!

14. The same end is sought in each of the three kingdoms, viz. the highest happiness of the creature and the glory of the Creator.

The God of the Bible appeals to his chosen people of old to say what more he could have done for them than he had done; and in the gift of his Son he makes the same appeal to Christians in the melting eloquence of that love which language cannot express.

The God of nature manifests a like intention, an effort, so to speak, to secure the utmost amount of happiness. Every element teems with animal life; every spot is replete with happy existence. The desert air swarms with insects; the wilderness and the solitary place are full of inhabitants suited to the locality.

"So is this great and wide sea wherein are things creeping innumerable, both great and small beasts." The sea is as amply furnished with vegetables[2] and the larger animals as the land; while the drops of the former, like the particles of the latter, are densely peopled with animalcules.[3] To multiply happy existence still

[1] So also Pliny: In his tam parvis, atque tam nullis, quae ratio, quanta vis, quam inextricabilis perfectio.

[2] Marine, like land, animals depend upon the vegetable kingdom for subsistence; and Brongniart has shown that the existing submarine vegetation seems to admit of those great divisions which characterize to a certain degree the plants of the frigid, temperate, and torrid zones. — See Buckland, p. 451.

[3] The powers of reproduction in the infusoria are such, that from one individual a million were produced in ten days; on the eleventh day four millions, and on the twelfth sixteen millions. — Buckland, on the authority of Ehrenberg.

more, thousands of animals, beyond the number which the vegetable world is capable of sustaining, subsist by preying upon others ; and the very carcasses of animals that die a natural death furnish food for a numerous army of scavengers, which, in providing a suitable diet for themselves, remove what would otherwise prove a source of annoyance and disease to other animals.[1]

And the modes and forms of animal existence are not more multiplied and varied than are the contrivances to render life happy. Natural history is little else than an enumeration of manifest proofs that the character of the Deity is wisdom and goodness, and the end at which he aims is the happiness of his creatures.

And the history of God's dealings with man teaches, as a whole, the same lesson. Every organ of his frame, every element in his constitution, every event in his life, is designed and adapted to promote his happiness. If he abused no part of his original constitution and perverted no bounty of providence or gift of grace he

[1] "No sooner is the signal given, on the death of any large animal, than multitudes of every class hasten to the spot, eager to partake of the repast which nature has prepared. If the carcass be not rapidly devoured by rapacious birds or carnivorous quadrupeds, it never fails to be soon attacked by swarms of insects, which speedily consume its softer textures, leaving only the bones. So strongly was Linnaeus impressed with the immensity of the scale on which these works of demolition by insects are carried on in nature, that he used to maintain that the carcass of a dead horse would not be devoured with the same celerity by a lion as it would by these flesh flies (*Musca vomitoria*) and their immediate progeny; for it is known that one female will give birth to at least twenty thousand young larvae, each of which will, in the course of one day, devour so much food and grow so rapidly as to require an increase of two hundred times its weight; and a few days are sufficient to the production of a third generation. The very bones are the favorite food of the hyena, whose powerful jaws are peculiarly formed for grinding them into powder, and whose stomach can extract from them an abundant portion of nutriment. No less speedy is the work of demolition among the inhabitants of the waters, etc." — See Rodget's Bridgewater Treatise, Vol. ii. p. 49.

would be entirely happy; and the miseries he suffers are intended to secure his ultimate highest happiness, by reclaiming him from past and deterring him from future abuses and perversions. Moral beings can be happy only by being virtuous and holy, and all the provisions of providence and of grace are directed towards the great object of making them happy in that way. For this object God inflicts natural and providential evils. For this object he subjected his beloved Son to untold agonies. For this object, in part at least, he will punish forever the incorrigible sinner. And I know not how a being of infinite benevolence could exhibit more convincing and affecting proofs of his regard for the highest happiness of the universe, than in the very pains which he inflicts so unwillingly upon the children of men, and the agonies which he laid upon his beloved Son, for the sake of securing a higher degree of happiness on a larger scale.

The highest possible amount of happiness is also the aim and tendency of that universal law of progression which we have already considered. An infinite progression of goodness and happiness will produce a greater sum total than any changeless state, however exalted; just as the sum of any progressive infinite series in mathematics, however small the first term, is greater than the sum of any unchanging infinite series, however large the fixed term may be. How delightful it is to the enlarged and benevolent mind to contemplate the onward and upward progress of a holy and happy universe through infinity. Who can sum up that progression? Who can grasp, even in imagination, such an aggregate of excellence and bliss? Oh, they know little of God, who deny his benevolence, little of his universe, who think it not made to be a happy universe.

With the happiness of the creature the glory of the Creator is associated as the end of all his works. That glory consists in the display of his glorious attributes, and the exhibition of those attributes is manifestly a chief end of nature, providence, and grace.

Is the natural creation a display of his power? So is the new spiritual creation.[1] Does the system of nature illustrate his wisdom? The plan of redemption illustrates it more.[2] Is the goodness of God conspicuous in his works of creation? It is not less conspicuous in his works of providence and grace. Is his terrible and resistless justice set forth in his providential dispensations? These exhibitions of his displeasure at sin are premonitions of that great day revealed in the Scriptures, when he will judge the world in righteousness. Is the uniformity of nature's laws and operations a standing monument of his truth and fidelity to his promises? The prophecies fulfilled and fulfilling, the promises and threatenings of his word executed, likewise show his veracity.[3] He is at once the author, the subject, and the object or end of the book of nature, the book of providence, and the book of grace. All his works are dedicated to himself — to what other being could they with propriety have been dedicated? They treat of himself, the greatest and best subject. They speak of him consistently and harmoniously. One book may speak more of his natural, and another more of his moral attributes. One may treat of some particular

[1] Eph. i. 19; Ps. cx. 3.
[2] Eph. iii. 10.
[3] This analogy is often adverted to in the Scriptures. Ps. cxix. 8, 90; Matt. v. 18.

topics which are omitted in another, or may discourse of the same topics more clearly and fully; but God is the sum and substance of them all, his character their subject, and his glory their end: "All his works praise him, and all his saints bless him." In nature, the heavens declare his glory, and the firmament showeth his handi-work. In providence, day unto day uttereth speech, and night unto night showeth knowledge of him. And the great end for which the church is established, is to show forth the praises of him who called its members out of darkness into his marvellous light. Everything, animate and inanimate, voluntarily and involuntarily, responds to the call of the "sweet singer of Israel": "praise ye the Lord"; and the student of nature and the observer of providence may unite with the Apocalyptic seer, and say: "Every creature which is in heaven, and on the earth, and under the earth, and such as are in the sea, and all that are in them, heard I saying, Blessing and honor and glory and power be unto him that sitteth upon the throne, and unto the Lamb, forever and ever."

I might specify other analogies. I might adduce the intimate analogy between the doctrine of social liabilities in this life, with which nobody thinks of finding any fault, and the proper doctrine of the imputation of Adam's sin and of Christ's righteousness, of which multitudes complain; in other words, the analogy between what we actually suffer and enjoy in consequence of our involuntary connection with others in this life, and what we are alleged in the Scriptures to suffer and enjoy in consequence of the constituted connection between us and the first and second Adam. I might speak of that uniformity amid variety which forms so characteristic and interesting a feature both in the constitution and course of nature, and in the composition and operation of the Bible — which pervades the vegetable, animal, and spiritual kingdoms, the forms and features of mankind, their languages and social institutions, and their moral and religious characters. I might advert to that happy blending of beauty with utility, which constitutes a striking analogy between the divine works and the divine word; in the former of which natural religion joins hands with the music and poetry of nature, while, in the latter, revealed religion is "wedded to immortal verse." I might mention that simplicity of means which exalts the divine wisdom so far above all human skill, and which is so well expressed in those oft-cited lines:

> "In human works, though labored on with pain,
> A thousand movements scarce one object gain;
> In God's, one single can its end produce,
> Yet seems to second, too, some other use."

But why should I specify. The whole natural world, in its constitution and laws, its particular and aggregate, is a counterpart of the spiritual world.[1] Every object in the former is a kind of image or type of something in the latter. Nature is a preliminary dispensation, like the Mosaic, true and holy so far as it goes, insufficient by itself, imperfectly understood without a further revelation, but, when thus understood, illustrating and confirming the Christian dispensation. The temple of nature, like Solomon's temple, is full of types and

[1] The writer does not mean to countenance the mysticism of the Hutchinsonians, or the subtile speculations of the Platonists, but simply to present the external world in that intimate relation to the spiritual world which it sustained in the mind of the sacred writers, who certainly saw everywhere marks of the divine presence and emblems of heavenly things.

shadows of heavenly things, though the "candlestick" of Christianity must be lighted up in it before they become distinctly visible. Have not the flowers a language, and the brutes a voice, to teach us the domestic, the social, the Christian virtues?[1] Read Pollok's description of nature's preaching:

> "The seasons came and went, and went and came,
> To teach men gratitude, and, as they passed,
> Gave warning of the lapse of time, that else
> Had stolen unheeded by. The gentle flowers
> Retired, and stooping o'er the wilderness,
> Talked of humility and peace and love.
> The dews came down unseen at eventide,
> And silently their bounty shed, to teach
> Mankind unostentatious charity."

Read this, and much more of the like nature in the context, and say whether it is all poetry, or whether the objects of nature and the events of providence do in truth teach us lessons of spiritual wisdom. Follow, above all, in the train of our Saviour, and as he utters his parables and delivers his sermons, see all nature a picture-gallery filled with likenesses and sketches of heavenly things. Indeed it is a striking characteristic of all the sacred writers, that they find memorials and types of God and heaven in every natural object and event; and the allegories, the similes, all the figurative language of the Bible, is a standing illustration of the analogies that pervade the realms of nature, providence, and grace.

Now I need not spend time in establishing the inference from these numerous and striking analogies, that the realms in which they prevail have the same head.

[1] Matt. vi. 26–30; Prov. vi. 6–8; xxx. 24–28; Isa. i. 3.

When we see similar laws administered in a similar manner in different provinces, and the same characteristic features prevailing, with only those differences which diverse circumstances require, we infer that they are under the same government. The same striking and characteristic peculiarities of sentiment, style, and imagery, prove the books in which they are found to have the same author. When I apply these principles to the present subject of discussion, I am constrained to believe that nature, providence, and grace are provinces governed by the same head, books written by the same great author. I would as soon believe that man administers the providential government of the world as that he devised and established the church; and when I come to the conclusion that man made the heavens and the earth, then I may be ready to believe that unaided man was the author of the Bible.

A few remarks which are suggested by the foregoing argument, but could not conveniently find a place in it, will close this discussion.

1. Analogy affords us the best means of answering objections both against science and religion. The scientific man has few objections to urge against religion which do not lie with equal force against nature and providence; and the religious man has few objections to urge against science which, if valid at all, would not be equally valid against religion. Press home upon both the analogy, and if you do not convince, you will silence. Does the man of science or the business man object to the theological doctrine of divine sovereignty? Show him that the same doctrine is written on every page of nature and providence. Does the theologian charge with absurdity the prolonged pro-

cesses and protracted periods of geology? Point him to the fact that his own science and his own sacred books disclose similar processes and periods. Does the sceptic scout the idea that eternal life is suspended on so pusillanimous a trait as humility, and so involuntary a principle as faith? Show him that the requirement of these virtues, so far from being arbitrary, accords with the nature of things, and that the knowledge and happiness of this life are suspended on the exercise of the same virtues. Does the Christian doubt whether God would condescend to create myriads of infusoria in a drop of water, or people a world with successive generations of irrational creatures? Remind him that God has condescended to provide for, and redeem a world of sinners, whose "foundation is in the dust," who are "crushed before the moth," and who are "accounted to him as less than nothing and vanity." Does the fatalist pretend that his exertions for salvation are rendered fruitless by the immutable purposes and laws of God? Tell him that he would not for a moment stake any temporal good on the principle of that objection, though all temporal good is equally dependent on immutable laws and purposes. In like manner we may answer almost every objection of the scholar against the Christian, of the Christian against the scholar, and of the man that shows any common sense about anything against both the scholar and the Christian. If ministers would employ analogical reasoning more, and abstract reasoning less, they would be more successful in combatting practical and hurtful error. On the other hand, why need they forget that analogy is not more truly a "powerful engine" than an impartial one, which if not applied by themselves to the correction of their own errors, will be wielded against them by others to their no small discredit, if not their utter discomfiture.

2. It is very important that the teacher of religion, and quite desirable that the private Christian, should be a student of nature and an observer of providence. Besides silencing objectors and confirming his own faith, he would thus find fresh light and beauty shed upon the truths of religion. Nature and revelation are parallel columns in God's universal harmony, and providence is a divine commentary upon them both. Should they not be studied together?

Coleridge somewhere remarks[1] that he admired Shakespeare's wisdom and power on a first perusal in his youth, and on reading him a second time, after years of study and improvement, Shakespeare's wisdom and power appeared to have increased quite as much as his own. This remark is far more applicable to God's works than to those of any mortal. The more wisdom and power we bring to the study of them, the more we discover in them. Each increase of the magnifying power of the telescope is attended with a corresponding accession to the extent, beauty, and grandeur of the visible universe. Every improvement of the microscope discloses new beings, new wonders, new and more delicate strokes of a divine artist. The observer's mental vision too is improved, not to reach the full height, nor penetrate the whole depth, nor range all the compass of nature's mysteries, but while he solves one of these mysteries to discover more than one which he leaves unsolved. So that the philosopher who now looks out upon the divine works from the highest vantage ground, with the most acute and profound mind and the most

[1] I give only the substance of the remark from memory.

perfect helps to his ocular and mental vision, may well feel, as did the immortal Newton, that he has scarcely glanced along the shore and discovered a few beautiful shells, while before him spreads the unexplored and illimitable ocean of truth.

The Bible is also boundless in the compass of its truths, exhaustless in its treasures and beauties. Its contents seem to enlarge in extent, and magnify in importance, and increase in variety and interest in precise proportion to the progress of society and the improvement of the individual reader. So that the Christian who knows the most, not only sees the most to admire in what he has read, but expects to find the most that is new and admirable in his future study of the sacred volume; and so far from ever feeling that he has comprehended its whole scope, or exhausted all its riches, he will be ready to exclaim, "it is high as heaven, what canst thou do; it is deeper than hell, what canst thou know: the measure thereof is longer than the earth and broader than the sea."

Now if knowledge of every sort is a help to the acquisition of further knowledge (and it is, for every truth stands more or less related to every other truth), a portion of the knowledge of one class of God's works will help us to acquire a knowledge of another class. Familiarity with one of Shakespeare's dramas leads to a better understanding and a higher appreciation of another. The student who has mastered one production of a classic author will master another production of the same author more easily and more perfectly. Why should not this principle apply to the different productions of the divine mind? Has it not been so in the past study of the divine works? It was the knowledge and influence of the Bible that gave the first impulse and the first clue to discoveries in natural science; and fresh discoveries in natural science are ever impelling and guiding in the study of the Bible, explaining many particular passages, and correcting in general wrong modes of inquiry.

What new grandeur and glory pervade the universe when viewed in the light of the Bible, as created, pervaded, and controlled by one omnipotent, omniscient, almighty, and all-wise Spirit. The classics contain exquisite poetry, but the Bible surpasses them in exquisite poetry, I had almost said as much as in pure morality and sound philosophy. Nature is grand and beautiful and instinct with life, as portrayed on the classic page. But the universe, as seen in the light of revelation, is more beautiful and grand, animated by a purer and loftier spirit, and lighted up with a brighter, diviner radiance.

On the other hand, how has science shed light upon the Bible? With what new interest have modern discoveries invested such passages of Scripture as the first chapter of Genesis, the fortieth of Isaiah, and the eighth Psalm. The modern astronomer, any enlightened Christian of these days, sees a beauty and sublimity beyond the conceptions, may I not say, of David and Isaiah themselves in such descriptions as these: "When I consider thy heavens, the work of thy fingers, the moon and the stars which thou hast ordained; what is man that thou art mindful of him, or the son of man, that thou visitest him." "Who hath measured the waters in the hollow of his hand, and meted out heaven with the span, and comprehended the dust of the earth in a measure. All nations before him are as nothing, and are counted to him less than nothing and vanity." All such descriptions, all the illustrations of the divine wisdom and goodness in the Bible, will be enhanced in beauty and sublimity and impressiveness, in exact proportion to our increasing knowledge of the divine works. A perfect system of mental science, should such a system ever be discovered, would probably add to the clearness with which we understand and the power with which we realize divine truths, no less than the discoveries in natural science have already done. So far, then, from being alarmed at the progressive influence of science upon religion, it is with emotions of delight too big for utterance that I look down the tract of time, and see, with the eye of faith, science and religion pouring a flood of light upon each other; seal after seal broken, and page after page of surpassing beauty and glory opened to view simultaneously in nature and revelation; doubts removed, and mysteries explained; the elements conquered, and the passions subdued; man reclaimed, and God honored; and the world at length irradiated with the blended beams of a sanctified literature and an enlightened Christianity. To the men of that happy day, "heaven above will indeed be but a reward for heaven enjoyed below." To behold the dawning of that day, and pray and labor for its approaching consummation, is a privilege which prophets and kings of former times never enjoyed.

3. It is the duty and the interest of every man to fall in with the analogies — the harmonious arrangements — of nature, providence, and grace. Take an illustration of my meaning. It has been already observed that nature, providence, and grace in their development to man usually advance together, and that all are making

simultaneous and gigantic strides in our own day. It becomes us, then, to notice the point towards which they converge, the end to which they are advancing. Do I mistake in saying it is the conversion of the world? See in heathen lands walls of prejudice and caste and despotic power, high as heaven and hard as adamant, prostrated to make way for the gospel; see at the same time in Christian lands resources accumulated in the hands of benevolent men, associations formed on the broad scale and in the enlarged spirit of universal Christian philanthropy, means of conveyance improved, languages mastered, rags converted into Bibles, sailors into missionaries, and the elements into winged messengers — all united to convey the gospel to the ends of the earth; and even if you did not see the church awakened to an unprecedented interest in this specific object, could you doubt that the era for the world's conversion is approaching? And is it safe for you to oppose, is it wise for you to neglect, are you willing to stand aloof from an enterprise which nature, providence, and grace are co-operating to achieve?

The same questions, or similar questions, may be asked respecting most of the analogies and divine arrangements which we have been considering.

Humility and faith sustain the same important relation to the kingdom of nature, the kingdom of providence, and the kingdom of grace — they are necessary and profitable for all things, having the promise of the life that now is, and also of that which is to come. Is it then consistent with your duty and interest to denounce the one as a mark of meanness, and the other as an arbitrary requirement?

To co-operate with God is the highest honor to which

man can aspire ; to resemble God, the highest perfection to which he can attain. Instead of finding fault, then, with that arrangement which requires a union of divine and human agency in every important concern, we should humbly and gratefully acknowledge the condescension and love of God in permitting us to co-operate with him in his benevolent designs, and be equally ready to avail ourselves of his gracious aid, and render to him our poor but faithful and devoted service.

While we fall in with the divine plan, we should endeavor to act ever on general principles, to be guided by general laws, and to render to them as uniform and complete obedience as if they were self-executing.

Though we have no right to do evil that good may come, we may strive to resemble God, and rejoice that we live in a world where we can resemble him, and co-operate with him in bringing good out of evil, order out of confusion, and light out of darkness.

So long as we do our duty we should not allow our faith to be shaken or our feelings to be greatly disturbed by the slow process of human amelioration on the one hand, or the sudden and violent revolutions that may occur on the other, but should be " steadfast, immovable, always abounding in the work of the Lord," following the leadings of providence, promoting in God's wise manner God's holy and benevolent end — the progress of ourselves and others in knowledge and virtue, the highest happiness of the creature, and the greatest glory of the Creator.

To return from these particular illustrations to the general principle of this head. The laws of nature, providence, and grace, are all laws of God, all alike obligatory, and all clothed with the same sacred authority. "He that offendeth in one point is guilty of all." He that wittingly violates one of the codes, arrays them all against him. But he who obeys them all, will find that they conspire most happily to aid each other and to bestow a great reward. It is not enough to obey only the natural, or the providential, or the moral laws. Duty is fulfilled, happiness is secured, by universal and perfect obedience. He only is an educated man who has been trained to the utmost of his ability to "discover, apply, and obey all the laws by which God governs the universe." He who has been thus trained in the school of nature, the school of providence, and the school of grace, he is an educated man; educated for time and for eternity, educated for earth and educated for heaven. Whether he is engaged in temporal or spiritual concerns, whether he undertakes to reform, men in this world, or prepare them for the next, he will not go against wind, tide, and current, but he will do it in the way of divine appointment, in accordance with all the divine laws, and with the harmonious co-operation of all the divine attributes.

II.

THE HOMERIC QUESTION.[1]

THE books whose titles we have placed below[2] mark a new era in classical scholarship; an era signalized by the union of German learning with English common sense and practical wisdom. Germany is the land of scholars, but it is also the land of sceptics, theorizers, and dreamers. If German learning has passed into a proverb, German want of faith and ignorance of affairs have become a byword. German scholars are the world's teachers in philology; but they need, themselves, to be taught the first principles of theology and anthropolgy. Prodigies in the knowledge of books, they are no less prodigies in that ignorance of themselves and of things around them which necessarily involves a practical misunderstanding of past ages, and in that unbelief which is often connected with the excess of credulity. They have almost revived the dead languages. They have almost reproduced the private life of the old Greeks and Romans. But they cannot understand the civil and political institutions of antiquity, because they have little or nothing to do with the government of their

[1] [Reprinted from the Bibliotheca Sacra, Vol. xiv. No. 57, Oct. 1857].

[2] History of Greece. By George Grote, Esq. Vol. ii. London : John Murray, Albemarle Street. 1846. Part i. Legendary Greece.

A Critical History of the Language and Literature of Ancient Greece. By William Mure, of Caldwell. Second edition. Vol. i. London : Longman, Brown, Green, and Longmans. 1854.

own country. And they have spread the mists and fogs of the dream-land in which they live over the ancient world, superseding its myths by more incredible fables of their own, substituting for its possible facts their own impossible fictions, turning history into poetry, and reducing poets to nonentities, and thus virtually annihilating both.

English scholars, on the other hand, have eschewed the wild speculations of their German cousins, but have been equally innocent of their comprehensive and profound scholarship. They have either confined their studies to mere words and metres, or, if they have launched out into the real life of antiquity, they have set out with too little capital to bring back a very valuable return cargo — too often have gone out and returned with those strong social and political prejudices, which could not but mislead their explorations and blind their eyes to the true character of the people and their institutions.

But German scholarship is at length beginning to pervade the English mind — the minds of English merchants, gentlemen, and statesmen, as well as clergymen and scholars by profession. And the legitimate offspring of a union so auspicious is seen in such works as those of Bishop Thirlwall, Dr. Arnold, Mr. Grote, and Colonel Mure.

Grote's History of Greece, though not entirely free from paradoxes, and perhaps prejudices, of its own, has exploded the monstrous misconceptions and misrepresentations of Mitford; and rescuing the constitution and history of the Athenian Commonwealth at once from the darkness of ignorance and the grosser darkness of prejudice, has brought it out into the twofold light of the philology of the Teutonic and the commerce and freedom of the Anglo-Saxon race. The English tory and the German recluse are alike incapable of understanding Athens; it was reserved for an English merchant and gentleman, saturated with the learning of Germany, to write her history. Not the politics only, but the literature of Greece, has been cast into the crucible of the English merchant-scholar; and the result, though we are sorry to say it is not wholly purified of the dross of German scepticism, is rich with the gold of true learning, and transparent as the crystal of good common sense. Recently completed, in twelve large octavo volumes, and reprinted in a compact and neat American edition, the History of Greece will gradually permeate the American mind with its juster ideas of the Athenian polity, and with its invaluable lessons of Grecian culture.

Mure's Critical History of the Language and Literature of Greece is a more recent work, still unfinished, and comparatively little known in this country; though we trust, when it is completed,[1] it will be republished and as extensively read as the History of Mr Grote. Possessing the same familiar acquaintance with the results of German philology and the same sterling good sense which distinguish the great historian, and confining his attention to the language and literature of the Greeks, he has given us a more thorough and exhausting analysis of that literature; while, with a sturdy faith, which it is refreshing to see combined with such entire candor, such profound research, and so perfect a mastery of the subject, he resists and puts to rout the whole army of

[1] [The hopes of scholars were disappointed by the too early death of the author.]

German literary sceptics, from Wolf to Nitzsch. The first four volumes, which have already appeared, bring the history down only so far as to include Herodotus. The first two volumes are taken up with the criticism of the language and the epic poetry of the Greeks; the third, with lyric poetry and the early history of writing; and the fourth, with Herodotus and the earlier Greek prose compositions.

We do not propose to review both, or either, of these works; but rather to avail ourselves of them as an occasion, and also as helps, to review a subject which they have discussed at much length, namely, the Homeric Question.

The present seems to be a fit time for such a review. Literary scepticism, in one of its forms at least, seems to have run its round even in Germany, and the cycle is coming to an end. The Wolfs and Heynes, that contended for the equivocal honor of having originated it, have passed away, and there is no one to take up their mantle. The Hermanns and Lachmanns, who would recognize no man as a scholar who had not laid ruthless hands on some part of the poems of Homer, or dissected some other sacred relic of antiquity—just as, among our American Indians, he is not counted a man, who cannot show his scalps—have, at length scalped each other; and the land is no longer vexed with their unscrupulous and sacrilegious warfare. Nitzsch, "the last of the Mohicans," formerly the most strenuous advocate of the Separatist theory, is now no less zealous in maintaining the one-authorship of the Iliad and the Odyssey.

So in sacred literature. Aforetime, in Germany, "a man was famous according as he had lifted up axes upon the thick trees," even the sacred cedars of Lebanon.

Moses and Isaiah, like Homer and Hesiod, were robbed of their "lively oracles," and of all but a dim, shadowy, and pitiable existence. But not a few of these famous robbers repented of their sacrilege in their more advanced years; and a generation is now rising up which scarcely knows them. At the present moment, perhaps, the German mind is swinging from the extreme of scepticism towards the extreme of submission to authority.

There is a certain period in the life, as of an individual so of a nation, when there is a tendency to scepticism. Childhood believes implicitly. Youth doubts, disbelieves, *mis*-believes, runs into all sorts of wild vagaries. Mature manhood, in well constituted minds, tends to that faith which is grounded partly in a believing disposition, and partly in knowledge and experience. The age of infidelity—of infidel writers and scholars—in England, came and passed away with the eighteenth century. It was not till the present century that the same spirit, though in another form, reappeared in Germany; and there are not wanting indications that she may be exorcised of the evil spirit, in no small measure, before the nineteenth century comes to a close. Such a period forms, if not an attractive, yet an instructive, chapter in the history of the human mind; and though our attention will be directed to a single phase of it, and that a literary one, still it is inseparably connected with a corresponding theological tendency, and therefore is doubly worthy of a candid and careful investigation.

In few words, the Homeric Question is simply this: Were the Iliad and Odyssey, in substantially their present form, the production of a single author? The question resolves itself into two parts: Was each of the poems, separately considered, the work of a single poet? And, allowing this to be the fact, were both the work of one and the same poet?

To the first question antiquity returned but one answer. Without a dissenting voice, all who spoke the Greek, and all who spoke the Latin tongue, recognized unity of design and unity of authorship in each of these great poems. Homer wrote the Iliad, the whole Iliad, and the Iliad as a whole. Homer, the same Homer or another, wrote the Odyssey also, as a single, connected poem. On this point, no Greek or Roman ever whispered a doubt.

At the earliest period in Grecian history, of which we have any record, both these poems, together with several others which have not come down to us, but which we know from contemporary notices related to the same subject, and were often rehearsed in connection with them, passed unquestioned under the common name of Homeric poems. In the golden age of prose composition, however (and the fact is worthy of notice as showing that Herodotus and Thucydides, Plato and Aristotle, were not so utterly devoid of critical discernment as they are sometimes represented), the inferiority of these secondary poems to the great primaries about which they revolved was so clearly seen, that they felt under the necessity of referring them to different authors, while they appropriated to the Iliad and Odyssey alone the illustrious name of Homer. It was not till the time of the Alexandrian grammarians that the first doubt was ever raised, so far as we know, whether the Iliad and Odyssey both proceeded from the same mind. Only two names (Xenon and Hellanicus) are mentioned as advocates of the new heresy, and those two rescued from oblivion only by the answers to thei: novel opinions. With the solitary exception of these two men and their few and unknown followers (called the Chorizontes, or Separatists), the whole succession of the Alexandrian grammarians, with Zenodotus, Aristophanes, and Aristarchus at their head, to whom we are indebted for the standard ancient edition of Homer, agreed with the unanimous voice of the long line of poets, historians, orators, and philosophers, that the Iliad and the Odyssey were not only each the work of a single author; but both the production of one and the same great poet.

This unanimous sentiment of Grecian antiquity was as unanimously received by Roman authors, by Byzantine grammarians, by scholars in the Middle Ages and after the revival of letters; until, towards the close of the seventeenth century, "certain novelties of opinion began to transpire," and several writers in several countries, Perrault and Hedelin in France, Bentley in England, and Vico in Italy, expressed, at different times and in different degrees, their doubts as to the truth of the received doctrine. Perrault (Parallele des Anciennes et des Moderns: 1688) suggested that the poems of Homer are but a collection of many little poems of different authors. Hedelin (Dissertation sur l'Iliad: 1715) went so far as to deny the personal existence of Homer. Bentley (Reply to Collins's Discourse on Free Thinking: 1713) says: "Homer wrote a sequel of songs and rhapsodies. These loose songs were not collected together, into the form of an epic poem, until five hundred years later." Vico (Principii di Una Scienza Nuova: 1725) says: "Homer left none of his compositions in writing, as we are told by Flavius Josephus, in his Tract against Apion; but the rhapsodists went about singing the works separately, some one, some another, at the feasts and public solemnities of the Greek cities. The Pisistratidae first divided and arranged, or caused to be so arranged, the poems of Homer into the Iliad and Odyssey, whence we may judge what a confused collection of materials they must previously have been." In 1770, Robert Wood, in that "Essay on the Original Genius of Homer," which set the example of studying the Iliad itself on the ground where the scene was laid in order to a determination of the vexed questions touching the time and place of the poet's birth, argued more at length the position that he could not have committed his poems to writing, because the art of writing was of subsequent invention. But these suggestions were little heeded by their countrymen and contemporaries; and the current of opinion flowed on, undisturbed, in its old channel.

They were destined, however, to find a more fortunate, if not a more able, advocate in an age and country more favorable to the propagation of novel opinions. That country was Germany; that age was the close of the eighteenth century; and that advocate was F. A. Wolf. Combining the suggestions of Bentley, Vico, and Wood, and expanding them into an elaborate argument, he brought out, in 1795, his famous Prolegomena ad Homerum, which, borne on the wings of the controversy between himself and Heyne, who disputed not the truth of the theory, but the honor of having originated it, soon wafted it to every corner of Germany. Self-consistent only in always denying the proper unity of the poems, Wolf usually maintains the theory of separate and independent lays, first compiled into one epopee by

7*

Pisistratus, who was also the first to commit them to writing; but he sometimes seems to admit the existence of a primitive nucleus, which, by successive accretions, grew at length, in the days of the same Pisistratus, into the form and size of the present Iliad and Odyssey; and sometimes he argues the question whether the two poems are by the same Homer or by different Homers; thus apparently conceding a real existence and a real author to each. In like manner, his followers, agreeing only in the negative part of his theory, have held the most opposite opinions as to the actual constitution and history of the poems; nearly all, however, witholding their assent to the extravagant part which he assigned to Pisistratus in their composition; and the general tendency of his earlier followers being towards the disintegration, and that of the later towards the reintegration, of the poems; in other words, the former generally tending to depart more widely from the received doctrine, and the latter inclining more towards a return to the established faith. The extreme of the former tendency is reached by Lachmann (Betrachtungen über die Ilias), who has resolved the Iliad into fifteen originally distinct and, as he thinks, clearly defined lays. Heyne, Hermann, Thiersch, W. Müller, and F. Schlegel lean in the same direction. The opposite tendency is seen, in different degrees in K. O. Müller, Ulrici, Welcker, Lange, and Nitzsch. The same individual who was at first swept away by the tide of innovation, has, in some instances, come back on the returning wave. The change of Göthe's opinions, in this direction, is recorded in one of his latest works (Homer noch einmal);[1] and Nitzsch has battled against "the extreme left" of the

[1] See Grote's History of Greece, Part i. chap. xxi.

followers of Wolf, till, from being the zealous advocate of the Separatist theory, he has become the no less strenuous and able champion of the one-authorship of the Iliad and Odyssey, though he still maintains that there have been large interpolations and additions to the primitive poems.

Out of Germany the hypothesis of separate and independent lays has met with little favor. English scholars, with scarcely an exception, hold to the unity of the Odyssey substantially in its present form. They maintain, also, the unity of the Iliad, though some of them do it with less confidence, and only with important modifications. Grote thinks the latter poem an Achilleid, subsequently enlarged into an Iliad by additions, amounting in all to nearly half of the entire poem. The Odyssey he holds to be a later production and by another author; in which view he was preceded by Richard Payne Knight (Prolegomena ad Homerum) and Henry Nelson Coleridge (Study of the Greek Classics). Clinton (Fasti Hellenici, Vol. i.) and Mure defend strenuously the old doctrine of the one-authorship of both the poems, though the latter was originally, "like most young scholars, a zealous disciple of the Wolfian school, till he was led, by a twenty years' diligent scrutiny of its doctrines, to a thorough conviction of their fallacy."

The historical evidence which Wolf adduces in support of his hypothesis of a chaotic Iliad and Odyssey, reduced to order and committed to writing, for the first time, under the Pisistratidae, so far from sustaining it, implies a pre-existing unity, which was only restored and enforced by Pisistratus and his successors;[1] and

[1] See Grote's History of Greece, Part i. chap. xxi.

this hypothesis is so improbable in itself, as well as so contradictory to the best authorities, that, in its primary Wolfian form, it now numbers few if any supporters. "Xenophanes of Colophon and Theagenes of Rhegium, both cotemporary with Pisistratus, wrote commentaries on Homer. But a written commentary on a work itself unwritten, is surely a thing unheard of."[1] If authorities are to be consulted, there is none better than Aristotle; and he represents Lycurgus, the Spartan lawgiver, as "having, in the course of his travels, received the poems as written documents from Creophilus of Samos, and brought them to Lacedaemon, centuries prior to the time of Pisistratus."[2]

The followers of Wolf, while they, for the most part, abandon the Pisistratian part of his hypothesis, and refer to an earlier period and to a succession of bards, the reduction, or rather the gradual growth, of the Homeric poems into their present form, still avail themselves of his arguments, together with others of their own, against the original unity and the proper Homeric authorship of the Iliad and Odyssey. These arguments have a wide bearing on sacred as well as classical literature and antiquities; and, in this point of view, as well as because they belong to the history of the Homeric Question, they must here be briefly stated and canvassed.

The grand historical argument on which they rely is, first, the alleged fact that the Iliad and Odyssey were not originally committed to writing, since writing was not in common use at so early a period; and then the inference that they were not originally composed in their present form and compass, since poems so long could not be composed without the aid of writing.

[1] Mure, Vol. i. p. 207. [2] Ibid.

In proof of the alleged fact, the evidence brought forward is, concisely, as follows:

1. No inscription is known to exist of a date prior to the fortieth Olympiad, B.C. 620.

2. Papyrus, the only suitable material which the Greeks had for writing long poems upon, was not easily accessible to them till the reign of Psammetichus, king of Egypt, B.C. 650, and not plenty, as some maintain, till a century later, in the reign of Amasis.

3. Prose composition was not practised in Greece till the time of the Seven Sages, B.C. 600.

4. The Homeric poems themselves make but a single allusion to writing, even in its rudest form; and that single passage is of doubtful import.

5. The flexibility and freedom of the Homeric language, its license of metrical usage, particularly in contracting and resolving vowels, proves that it was as yet unwritten.

6. The Aeolic digamma existed as a consonant sound at the time of the composition of the poems, but does not appear in the written copies, and therefore must have vanished from the language in the interval between their composition and their reduction to a written form.[1]

7. The authors of epic verse, in the Homeric age, are not called writers, or even poets, but singers (*ἀοιδοί*). They invoke the aid of the Muses, "daughters of memory"; and blindness, so far from being a disqualification for the functions of a bard, seems rather to have been commonly associated with the popular idea of the office.

This sevenfold array of arguments wears a somewhat

[1] The fifth and sixth arguments have been insisted on chiefly by critics later than Wolf, especially by Richard Payne Knight. The first four were brought forward by Wolf himself. The seventh is urged with considerable force by Grote.

formidable appearance. Some concede the point that the Homeric poems were not originally written, who still maintain their original unity. Grote comes to the conclusion that they were probably not committed to writing till about the middle of the seventh century B.C. (660–630).

Before proceeding to examine the validity of these arguments, it should be distinctly understood what is the point in dispute. We freely admit, and fully believe, that the Homeric poems were usually recited, and not read, for some time after their original composition; and whenever they were for the first time committed to writing, it was probably not so much for the sake of finding readers as for the convenience of reciters. Thus much is now generally conceded by intelligent advocates of the one-authorship of the Iliad and Odyssey. We even confess to a spontaneous conviction, a sort of instinctive feeling, whenever we read the poems, that they were not only composed for hearers, instead of readers, but that they were originally composed in the mind of the poet without the constraint and hinderance of writing as he composed. But that they were not committed to writing, and could not have been, by the author, or any one else in his age — this we are far from admitting. It is essential to the validity of these arguments against the received doctrine, that they not only show the improbability, but the impossibility, of a written Iliad and Odyssey in the Homeric age. This is the real issue now before us; and this the arguments above enumerated are by no means sufficient to demonstrate.

1. Inscriptions. Not one in a thousand of the inscriptions which existed in historical times have come

down to us through the wreck of conquests and the wear of ages that have passed over Greece. Is it then incredible that there may have been hundreds in ante-historical times, and yet not one of them be now extant? That inscriptions were common in the age of Solon (B.C. 600) we know from his law prohibiting the erasure of them. And we have the best authority that can be found among Greek authors — the authority of Herodotus, Aristotle, Plutarch, and Pausanias, for inscriptions reaching back as far as the first Olympiad (B.C. 776), and even as early as the age of Iphitus and Lycurgus (B.C. 850–825).[1] But were this claim admitted in its fullest extent, it would by no means follow that there were not written books at an earlier date. "Niebuhr has shown that written books existed in Rome under the Tarquins; but the date of the oldest extant Latin inscription is later by several centuries than the expulsion of the kings;"[2] and the oldest extant specimens of Hebrew epigraphy are later, by five hundred years, than the Psalms of David, and nearly a thousand years later than the books of Moses.

2. Writing materials. The commercial factories of the Greeks established at the mouth of the Nile, in the reign of Psammetichus, introduced into Greece a more copious supply of papyrus; but it was known, though "scarce,"[3] at a still earlier period; and, prior to the introduction of papyrus, parchment was in so common

[1] A full citation of authorities in an argument so comprehensive and so condensed as this, would occupy almost as much space as the argument itself, and would be of little interest to our readers. See, on this subject of early alphabetic writing, Hug, Erfindung der Buchstabenschrift, Kreuser, Vorfragen über Homeros, and especially Mure, Vol. iii. pp. 397 sqq.

[2] Rom. Geschich., Vol. i. p. 526. See Mure, Vol. iii. p. 441.

[3] Herod. iv. 58.

use for written books, that books were still called parchments (διφθέραι) by the Ionians[1] two centuries after parchment had been superseded by the cheaper and more convenient Egyptian material. Moreover, the Hebrews, Phoenicians, and other Aramaean nations, from whom the Greeks derived the use of parchment, together with alphabetic writing itself, had written books — had quite a body of poetical and even historical literature, while they had no better supply of writing materials than the Greeks.

3. Prose composition. The preference of poetical or prose composition depends on the taste of the people, not on the extent to which writing and writing materials prevail ; as is shown by the comparison just adverted to between the Greeks, whose early literary productions were all epic poems, and the Hebrews and other neighboring nations in the East, whose early literature, though they were no better provided with writing materials, was for the most part historical prose. At the same time there can be no reasonable doubt that " epistolary or diplomatic correspondence, oracular edicts, public records, codes of laws, and other strictly useful documents in Greece were written in prose, from a very remote period" — long prior to that of the Seven Wise Men.[2]

4. Homeric allusions to writing. Suppose there were not a single allusion to writing in the entire poems (a question which we waive for the present), would this suffice to disprove its existence ? The argument from

[1] Herod. Ibid. So the Latin *libri* proves the existence of books written on *bark*, before the βίβλος of the Egyptians and the Greeks was introduced among the Romans.

[2] Plut. Pyth. Orac. See Mure, Vol. iii. p. 458; and below, p. 91.

silence, if it proves anything, proves the poet's entire ignorance of any such thing as writing. But who can credit such entire ignorance of a bard who had wandered over all the shores and islands of the Aegean, and "seen the cities and manners of many men," in an age when the arts were so far advanced, when the kindred arts of casting, carving, tapestry-weaving, and embroidery, were so well understood! The argument from silence would prove the entire abstinence of Homer's heroes, at their common meals and at their festivals, from those universal articles of good cheer, boiled flesh, fish, game, poultry, and not a few other things, to which he happens to make no allusion, but which are common in every age. The argument from silence would prove the poet's ignorance of painting, and its entire absence in that age, even from the palaces of kings — an art of far more poetical interest than writing, more likely to attract the attention and excite the interest of the personages, especially of the Odyssey, and less likely to be passed over in silence by the the poet. "If Helen, in spite of the poet's silence as to painting, could embroider on a large piece of tapestry the adventures of the Trojan war, Homer, in spite of his silence as to writing, might record them on a few large sheets of diphthera." [1]

5. Homeric license. "The text of Chaucer, between whom and Homer there are various other features of analogy, presents a mass of poetical and grammatical licenses, rivalling, or even surpassing, those of the Iliad and Odyssey." [2] Does this prove an unwritten "Canterbury Tales?"

6. The Aeolic digamma. "The digamma never, at

[1] See Mure, Vol. iii. p. 481. [2] Mure, Appendix, Vol. iii. p. 519.

any period, either in Ionia, Boeotia, or Aeolia, in the epic poetry of Homer or Hesiod, or in the lyric odes of Alcaeus or Sappho, formed a necessary ingredient of manuscript orthography. The reason, also, is apparent. Being not a proper consonant, but a mere liquid element, the powers of which could be sustained, or dispensed with, at the discretion of the poet, it seemed more elegant as well as convenient to omit it constantly than to insert it constantly, where its effects were so inconstant." Such is the conclusion at which Mure arrives, at the end of a very elaborate discussion of the subject, in his Appendix; and though we have been accustomed to concede not a little weight to this argument of Payne, Knight, and others, we do not see how Mure's arguments and conclusions can well be invalidated.

7. Blind bards, and Memory, the mother of the Muses. It is not denied that the early epic poets were singers nor that they sung their poems from memory, and therefore invoked the aid of Mnemosyne and the Muses. But this would not of itself demonstrate, even in regard to the earliest, that they never committed their productions to writing. Still less would the same usage, when adopted by their successors, authorize any such inference. It became a fixed usage of epic and lyric verse to invoke the aid of the Muses; a practice which lasted not only through all periods of Greek and Roman literature, but has been perpetuated in modern poetry, and has not become obsolete even in these days of printing by steam. Why does no one argue an unwritten Aeneid from the "Arma virumque *cano*" of Virgil; or an unwritten Paradise Lost, from the blindness of Milton and his repeated invocations of the Muses? The

History of Herodotus was rehearsed at the Olympic games, and his nine books have come down to us bearing the names of the nine Muses. At the same time we know they were also written. As for those who can believe that Homer himself was always blind, we can only say, with Paterculus, that they must themselves be blind in all their senses.

In opposition to these arguments, thus susceptible of explanation, and in proof of the actual existence of writing in the Homeric age, we have the following facts and authorities:

1. The unquestionable existence and common practice of writing at a still earlier period among the Egyptians, the Assyrians, the Hebrews, and the Phoenicians, as is proved by the extant literature, or by the ancient monuments of those nations; and the acknowledged existence of written books among the Romans in the earliest periods of their history, under the government of the kings.[1] It is quite incredible that the quick-witted and early cultivated Greeks were behind the warlike and barbarous Romans, were behind all their neighbors in the West and in the East, in the use of letters; so far behind those with whom they were connected, commercially and politically (to say nothing of a common origin and common alphabet), that they were ignorant of all literary use, if not of the very existence of letters, for centuries after those neighbors had them in constant use in literary composition and in the transaction of business.

2. The tradition that alphabetic writing was introduced into Greece from Phoenicia several centuries prior to the Trojan war, which is confirmed; which, in

[1] Cf. p. 83.

all but the definite fixing of the time, is demonstrated to be a fact by the manifest identity in name and form of most of the letters of the Greek alphabet with the Phoenician and the Hebrew. And, though the time of the introduction of letters from the East [1] is indefinite, there can be no doubt that it was at a very early period; since, in the earliest period at which we find any mention of alphabetic writing (in the seventh century before Christ), its introduction was referred back to a remote and immemorial antiquity. Moreover, the universal opinion in Greece — whatever difference there might be in regard to names and dates — the unanimous opinion ascribed the invention or the introduction of letters to the ante-Homeric age.

3. The letter or letters of Bellerophon (Iliad, vi. 168 seq.). The facts in this much-disputed matter are simply these: Bellerophon was falsely accused by Antea, wife of Proetus, king of Argos, precisely as Joseph was accused by Potiphar's wife — one of those innumerable incidents and illustrations of a primitive state of society by which the reader of the poems of Homer is perpetually reminded of the books of Moses. The king, wishing to dispose of him, and yet scrupling, himself, to lay violent hands on him, sends Bellerophon to his ally Iobates, king of Lycia, with a letter, directing that the bearer should be put to death. Was this a real letter, written in alphabetic characters, or were the characters mere cypher, hieroglyphics, or picture-writing? This is the point in dispute. In either case, it

[1] Mure interprets Cadmus as etymologically equivalent to East-Man, and so in itself expressive of the Eastern origin of those Cadmean colonies and influences of which s(many Greek writers have so much to say. Cf. Herod. iv. 147; Pausan iii. 1, 7; Diod. v. 58.

clearly answered all the purposes of a letter. On either supposition, it was a communication by signs, written or scratched[1] on a tablet, and sent to a person at a distance; and even if the signs were hieroglyphics or cypher, a people like the Greeks, who had advanced so far in the art, would not be long without alphabetic writing.

But the presumption is, that it was a real letter. It answered, as we have said, every purpose of a letter. The whole process of transmission and delivery is described just as if it were a letter. The Greek word by which it is designated (σῆμα), though ambiguous in itself, yet being employed by the poet both in the singular and the plural (the singular, σῆμα, to denote the whole, and the plural, σήματα, to denote the parts which make up the whole), precisely as γράμμα and γράμματα were employed in the later Greek, *litera* and *literae* in the Latin, and letter and letters in English, — this fact, especially when taken in connection with the evidence already given that alphabetic writing was already known in Greece, creates a strong presumption that it was a real letter.

And this presumption is strengthened into an almost certainty by two things, which are placed beyond dispute by the nature of the case, or by the express declaration of the poet: 1. It was a sealed despatch, whose purport was concealed from the bearer, and that not by unintelligible signs, but by the folding of the material, (ἐν πίνακι πτυκτῷ, *in a folded tablet*). This certainly looks more like ordinary letter writing than cipher or hieroglyphics. 2. The contents of the despatch were

[1] The original word (γράψας) will bear either of these meanings, and in the connection must mean one or the other.

various, copious, and intended to provoke Iobates to the execution of the order. The writer is expressly said to have "written in the folded tablet many soul-harassing things" (θυμοφθόρα πολλά);[1] that is, doubtless, a detailed account of the alleged crimes of Bellerophon, and the reasons why he should be put to death. How utterly inconsistent such copious detail is with the supposition of hieroglyphics or any form of picture-writing need not be remarked. We have then, as we can scarcely doubt, an actual instance of alphabetic writing in the Iliad itself. For other less conspicuous allusions to written documents in the Homeric poems we must refer the reader to Mure.[2]

4. The law and practice of ostracism at Athens, implies the ability of the citizens generally to read and write, whenever it was introduced. At the latest, this cannot have been later than the revision of the Athenian Constitution by Clisthenes[3] (B.C. 510). According to the more commonly received opinion, it was a provision in the laws of Solon. And this general ability to write, thus implied as existing or expected to exist, in the age of Solon, or at the latest in that of Clisthenes, could not have sprung up at once, like a mushroom from the earth. It must have been the growth of several generations, not to say several centuries.

The scytale (σκυτάλη), or parchment staff,[4] by which

[1] This rendering of θυμοφθόρα, though different from that often given, is demanded by the etymology of the word, and by habitual Homeric usage. See Liddell and Scott, and places there cited. The plural form of πολλά implies variety as well as copiousness.

[2] See Vol. iii. p. 487 sqq.

[3] See Grote's History.

[4] So called from σκῦτος, a skin. It was a staff, about which a long narrow strip of parchment was rolled spirally, and then the despatch was written on its surface; so that when unrolled, it would of course, be illegible.

the Spartan magistrates sent despatches to the public servants abroad, implies the same ability on the part of those who were eligible to the Spartan ephorship, that is, of all the citizens of that most illiterate of the Grecian States.[1] And this is alluded to as well known (so well known that σκυτάλη had become another name for message) by Archilochus,[2] at the close of the eighth or the beginning of the seventh century before Christ. If such was the state of education in Sparta in the time of Archilochus, we may well believe they might have had a written Homer in Athens and in Asiatic Greece in the age of Lycurgus and of the poet himself.

The same state of general education is implied by the written and posted laws of Solon, Draco, Lycurgus, and perhaps earlier lawgivers; by written oracles, treaties, records, and registers in the temples and public archives, for which we have the testimony of the best Grecian authors;[3] by legal provisions for public education, and incidental allusions to schools[4] and public libraries; by the advanced state of the arts and sciences as far back even as Homer himself; by the tacit understanding as well as the explicit declarations of the whole succession of poets, historians, and philosophers, from Pindar and Hesiod[5] (not to say Homer) downwards. Add to all

Commanders and other public agents abroad had a precisely similar staff, about which they rolled the parchment, and thus the despatch became legible again.

[1] The Spartans did eschew literary culture, but were most carefully educated in all that was needful to qualify them for the duties of war and the state.

[2] Quoted by the Scholiast on Pindar Ol. vi. 154.

[3] See p. 693, and Mure, Vol. iii. p. 416 sqq.

[4] Herod. vi. 26; Aelian, Var. Hist. vii. 15; Athen. i. 4; Aul. Gell. vi. 17; Herod. v. 90.

[5] In Hesiod's Maxims of Chiron, a work of acknowledged high antiquity, and quoted and paraphrased by Pindar, it was enjoined that children

this the direct authority of Aristotle, for a written Homer brought from Samos by Lycurgus,[1] and the universal belief in a written Homer by Greek authors; and, though the authority and the belief might, of themselves, be insufficient to convince us, yet, when supported by such a variety and force of circumstantial evidence, does it not command our assent? Can we, at least, deny the possibility of a written Iliad and Odyssey?

5. The Homeric poems themselves, so far forth as they bear evidence of an original unity and extent too great to be secured, either in their composition or in their preservation, without the aid of writing; so far forth these poems themselves go to prove the existence of writing in the Homeric age. This argument will have more or less weight with different individuals. In the estimation of some, it amounts almost to demonstration. Thus Hug, in his excellent treatise on Alphabetic Writing, reverses the reasoning of Wolf, and instead of disproving the integrity of the Iliad by denying the existence of writing, he infers the necessary existence of writing from the palpable unity of the Iliad. "Aristotle," he says, "has not erred, when he praised the perfect unity of the Iliad. It is incredible that a poem at once so unique and so complete, so admirable in its construction, so perfect in its minutest details, should have been produced without any aid from writing. It would be a miracle. To this art, then, is Homer indebted for his superiority over all his predecessors." And if we had to choose between the reason-

should not be instructed in letters until seven years old. See Mure, Vol. iii. p. 451.

[1] See p. 80 above

ing of Hug and that of Wolf, we should, by all means, adopt the former alternative. But we cannot think, that the unity of the Iliad is so indissolubly connected with alphabetic writing that they must of necessity stand or fall together. Our reasons for this opinion we will give presently. We only say here, that so far forth and so early as we find proof of the existence of a poetical literature whose unity or whose aggregate amount forbids the supposition of their being composed or transmitted without the aid of writing, so far and so early we have a demonstration of the existence of writing. And when we take into consideration, not only the composition but the preservation of the Homeric poems, and not only the Homeric poems, but the half a dozen other poems,[1] of nearly equal length, which we know very early clustered around them, and also the rival school of Hesiodic poetry, all belonging to the same general and mythical age, we have an aggregate amount of literary productions, aside from the length and unity of each particular poem, whose preservation, to say nothing of their original composition, without the aid of writing, would, in our estimation, be little short of a miracle.

In view of all these considerations, we cannot doubt the possibility, indeed we cannot but maintain the probability, of a written Iliad and Odyssey in the Homeric age; if not written by the poet himself in the process of composition, yet committed to writing by his contemporaries for the sake of a more perfect preservation of the poems.

[1] For a full account of these poems, the Thebais, Epigoni, Cypria, Little Iliad, Ilii Persis, Nosti, etc., etc., see Mure, Vol. ii. p. 248 sqq. He makes out ten or twelve cyclic poems.

But were we obliged to admit the improbability, or even the impossibility, of a written Iliad and Odyssey, we should not feel constrained to concede the impossibility of the composition of one or both of them by one author. Were the alleged fact of Wolf proved beyond a doubt, the inference which he drew from it would by no means follow.

Even in these days of devices to aid, and thus to impair, the memory, there are not wanting instances of a power to remember little, if at all, inferior to that ascribed to Homer. It is said of the late queen of Spain, that she had only to read or hear hundreds of verses of a poem she never heard of before, and she could repeat them word for word immediately, or weeks and months afterwards. And what is "to our purpose quite," Scaliger committed Homer entire to memory in twelve days, and all the Greek poets in three months. But not to instance persons of extraordinary capacity, clergymen who are in the habit of preaching from memory, with or without writing, require little or no direct effort beyond that of composition to commit their discourses to memory; and by frequent delivery a large number of discourses become so fixed in the memory, so incorporated, as it were, with their mental and physical constitution, that they know them, as the saying now is, by heart; or, as the Greeks say, ἀπὸ στόματος. The prodigious number of songs which the rhapsodists of Modern Greece treasure up in their memories, and sing to the lyre, at the *paneghyris* in the country villages, is an illustration still more in point. And it is an interesting analogy between Modern and Ancient Greece, that there are still two classes of rhapsodists — those who sing their own productions, and those who sing the verses of others; and that not a few of those who follow this profession are blind.[1] Of two hundred and fifty specimens in the collection named below, one is supposed to date back as far as the middle of the sixteenth century, since which time it has been preserved in writing. The rest are unwritten, and the most ancient is said to be a century and a half old.

Instead of being neglected and despised, as it is by too many young men of genius in our day, the memory was honored and cultivated by the great men of Greece and Rome as the foundation of their greatness. Great commanders, like Cyrus, Themistocles, and Lucullus, knew every soldier in their armies. Great civil as well as military officers, like Scipio and Adrian, knew all the people of Rome. Great orators, like Carneades, could rehearse the contents of almost any book to be found in the libraries, as if they were reading. Great philosophers, like Seneca, by the mere force of unaided memory, were able to repeat two thousand words upon once hearing them, each in its order, though they had no natural connection with each other. It was no strange thing for educated men at Athens to know the Iliad and Odyssey by heart.[2] And this in an age of books, written records, and all sorts of substitutes for the memory, and by practical men, with whom the cultivation of the memory was a secondary thing.

Who, then, can set bounds to this faculty in an age when the memory of the bard is not only the library, but the archives of the nation; when recitation is a profession, and memory the chief study; when Mnemosyne is honored by rehearsers and hearers as the

[1] Fauriel's Introduction to his Chants Populaires de la Grèce Moderne.
[2] Xen. Symp. iii. 5.

mother of the Muses; and the singer of his own verses, or those of others, is the pride of the people, the favorite of kings and princes, the ornament and glory of the festivals of the gods? If Scaliger could learn the poems of Homer by heart in twelve days, could not Homer himself compose and preserve them in his own memory? Composition is not a hinderance, but a help to remembrance. To compose, with many preachers and public speakers, is to remember; and their memory is the storehouse of all their oft-repeated productions. How much more may this be true; how much more must it have been true of the composer and public rehearser of verse in a primitive age? Of course we are not to suppose that Homer threw off the Iliad at a single heat, perhaps not in a single year. It grew as he rehearsed it, and he rehearsed it as it grew, till it became, as it were, a part of himself; and he could no more forget it than his right hand could forget her cunning. At the same time, if we could suppose he needed any help in remembering the successive parts as he composed, or the entire poem when it was finished, a whole tribe of rhapsodists — the Phemii and the Demodoci of the age — stood ready to aid him. Indeed, willing or unwilling, they could not be restrained from catching his inspired utterances as they fell from his lips, and rehearsing them for the entertainment of the circles in which they respectively moved.

There is, then, no impossibility, or violent improbability, in either of the alternatives, which Wolf so stoutly denies. The Homeric poems might have been committed to writing in the Homeric age, and they might have been composed without the aid of writing. We have dwelt on these points at considerable length, partly because of the great importance which has been attached to them as the main arguments against the integrity of the Iliad and Odyssey; but partly, also, because they are in themselves questions of great interest, whose influence, according as they are seen in a true or a false light, must extend over the entire field of ancient literature, and affect the authority of the Hebrew scriptures not less than the credit of Greek poetry.

The way is now clear for us to interrogate the poems themselves, and examine impartially the internal evidence of unity or diversity of authorship which they present in their own structure. And here several facts require to be noted as preliminary to this inquiry, or rather as indirect testimony.

1. The Iliad and Odyssey have been recognized, ever since the days of Aristotle,[1] as not only each the production of a single author, but as the standard of epic unity for all time. That this is a fact, none will deny. It seems to us also to be a fact of some significance, entitled to some consideration even in this age of profound critical erudition, and more profound critical self-complacency. The prince of Greek philosophers had some acquaintance with the language and literature of the Greeks. The father of ancient and modern science, the classifier and systematizer of all knowledge, the most analytic and comprehensive mind of ancient times, not to say of all ages, had some idea of epic unity. The masters of the Alexandrian school had some critical acumen. The sacramental host of Greek authors and scholars knew something of the contents and spirit of the Greek Bible. Athens, Alexandria, Rome, Constantinople, Modern Europe, were not entirely blind to the

[1] See Aris. Poetic, passim.

true character of the Homeric poems before the dawn of the eighteenth century. The superiority of our age in critical acumen and philological learning is not denied. But it may be doubted whether the minute critics of the day are not as blind to the soul of ancient poetry as the minute philosophers are to the spirit of true religion. The eye may be so trained to the discernment of microscopic objects as to become incapable of wide views, to say nothing of telescopic vision. The ear may be so filled with gross earthly sounds as to be deaf to the music of the spheres.

2. The rank which literary men, in all ages, have agreed in assigning to the Homeric poems is irreconcilable with the theory of several authors. The age or the country has usually been deemed singularly fortunate which has produced one Homer. That any one country or any one age should have produced twenty Homers, or twenty poets (call them by what name you will) of the very same, and that the very highest, order of poetical excellence is utterly incredible. That all these poets, of the very first order of original genius, should have confined their lays to one war, and to a very small portion of that war, is still more incredible. And that Pisistratus, or some nameless bard or scribe of his day, could have brought twenty different lays of twenty different Homers into an epic, to which all men of taste and learning for twenty-five centuries should ascribe the palm of genius and poetical excellence, is most incredible of all. As well might the Parthenon have been constructed from materials planned by twenty different architects for twenty different edifices. We cannot conceive of a perfect work of art being produced in any such manner. It were too much like

supposing the world we live in to have been put together by a creature, from twenty little worlds made by twenty different creators. The creature who could do such a work were more wonderful than all the original creators. And if we believed that Pisistratus, or any man of his day, rendered such a service as some suppose to the Iliad and Odyssey, we should think him the most remarkable man that ever lived. We should honor him as our Homer. Nay, we should worship him as the " Magnus Apollo " of the literary pantheon.

No more can we conceive of a masterpiece of poetical genius and art *growing*, as the Iliad and Odyssey are represented in the more recent and more popular form of that theory to have grown out of some greater or smaller lay, under the hand of successive bards, through successive generations. As well might we conceive the Parthenon as having grown by successive additions or enlargements of the primitive plan, under the direction of successive architects, till what was a small temple or a rude hut in the days of Solon stood forth in the age of Pericles, as it has stood ever since, the admiration and study of the world.

The two ideas — such a work and such workmen, such a production and such a process — are incompatible. Accordingly we find, as might be expected, that just in proportion to the amount of patchwork which each man's particular form of the theory presupposes in the Iliad and Odyssey, in just the same proportion the advocates of the new theory are disposed to depreciate the perfection of the poems.

3. The authority which has always been conceded to the Homeric poems, as correct representations, if not of the geography and history, yet of the manners and

customs, of Greece in the heroic age, is inconsistent with the hypothesis of diverse and successive authors. As early as the time of Solon a line of Homer was sufficient to settle a disputed territory or a contested succession. Solon himself is charged with having interpolated a verse "for the sake of gaining a disputed point against the Megarians, who, on their side, set forth another version."[1] The Greek historians habitually refer to Homer as the standard authority in Grecian antiquities;[2] and Strabo, the father of Greek geography, reposes more confidence in Homer than in Herodotus, Ctesias, and Hellanicus. Modern critics, Wolf and his followers not excepted, not only see in the Homeric poems a faithful mirror of life and manners in the heroic age, but appeal to his speech or his silence as the standard authority in reference to the dialects, races, names, and migrations of the ancient Greeks. How this accords with the idea that they are the mere patchwork of a dozen or twenty different authors, belonging to as many different times and places, or that they were the growth of successive ages, down to that of Solon or Pisistratus, it is difficult to see.

But so far forth as the authority of the poems in such matters is relied on, so far forth their substantial unity is, *ipso facto*, acknowledged. For example: the absence from either poem of the names Hellas for Greece, of Hellene for its inhabitants, and of Peloponnesus for its southern peninsula, proves the non-application of those names then, and then only, when the poems were written; in other words, proves the usage in question

[1] Plutarch's Solon. See Grote, Part i. chap. 21. Interpolated into what according to the Wolfian hypothesis?

[2] E.g. Thucyd. i. 3.

just as far, and no farther, than it proves the substantial integrity of the poems.

In proportion as the testimony of the poems is one, the presumption is that they proceeded from the same age and the same author; and in proportion to the intrinsic improbability of the facts in which the poems agree throughout, the improbability increases that they could have proceeded from different authors in different ages. The omission, whether owing to ignorance or to whatever cause, of all reference to the use of cavalry in war; and the exclusion of boiled meat, game, and other articles of good cheer from the table of the heroes; these, and the like negative peculiarities, in the poet's account of manners and institutions, singular enough in one Homer, become quite inexplicable and incredible when extended to a combination of a dozen or a score of authors, and those scattered along through several successive generations.[1]

4. The manner in which the Iliad and Odyssey were treated by the poets of the epic cycle, proves their existence in substantially their present form in the time of those poets; that is, as early as the First Olympiad. "Those poems, unfortunately, no longer exist in their integrity. Several of them, however, as may be collected from their remains, or the notices concerning them, contained in the choice of their subject and mode of treatment proofs of a systematic imitation of the Iliad and Odyssey, and, by consequence, of a familiarity with their text, as already extant in the form in which we now possess it. While a veneration for the great master induced the disciples or imitators to select subjects connected with those on which he had shed

[1] See these and other similar points well presented in Mure, Vol. i. p. 224.

lustre, a similar feeling, or the fear of entering into competition with him, also led them to avoid encroaching on the ground he had occupied. Arctinus, the next most celebrated poet of the school, took up, in his Aethiopis, the series of adventures before Troy, precisely at the stage in which the Iliad ceases, and carried them on to the death of Ajax. The Lesser Iliad continued the interrupted tale to the fall of the city, which catastrophe was also treated by Arctinus, in a work entitled The Destruction of Troy.[1] The author of The Cypria treated the previous subject from the birth of Helen, and brought it down to the exact epoch at which the Iliad commences. The Nosti filled up the interval between the Iliad and the Odyssey. Each of these works, while vastly inferior, both in design and execution, to their two prototypes, emulated at least the comprehensive scope of their action, borrowing also much of their own epic machinery, such as catalogues of warriors, quarrels among the chiefs, funeral games, and other similar details."[2]

5. Those who deny the one-authorship of the Iliad and Odyssey, do not allege that there is any marked discrepancy of matter or manner, of style or spirit, between the two poems, still less between the different parts of the same poem. On the contrary, they acknowledge a remarkable uniformity and consistency in the pictures of society, in the portraiture of character, in the very genius and spirit, as well as the style and sen-

[1] Ilii Persis. The Lesser or Little Iliad was probably by Lesches of Lesbos. These inferior poets were very far from treating each other with the same deference with which they all treated the Iliad and Odyssey. They did not scruple to handle the same subject which had already been handled by their brethren.

[2] Mure, Vol. i. p. 212.

timent, of the poems; while, at the same time, they recognize a broad line of separation in these respects, between the Homeric poems and the other Greek poets. "Immo," says Wolf, in his Prolegomena, "congruunt in iis omnia ferme in idem ingenium, in eosdem mores, in eandem formam sentiendi et loquendi."[1]

Now who would ever think of imputing such similarity, nay such identity, to the productions of Shakespeare and those of the other dramatic writers of his day; to the writings of Milton and those of his contemporaries; to the works of any great poetical genius of modern times, and those of any, even the best, authors of the same age? We have not been accustomed to think so lightly of the difference between genius and mediocrity, or between the highest poetical excellence and the nearest approaches to it. It is not so easy a thing to rival Shakespeare in delineation of character, Milton in sublimity of thought and language, or even Pope in sweetness of versification; still less to vie with Homer in the combination of all these excellences. As well might fowls of every feather flock around the bird of Jove, and soar with him to the sun! Let the opponents of the integrity of the Iliad and Odyssey undertake to manufacture, out of the whole compass of English or German poetry, two epics of fifteen thousand lines, that should wear throughout the air of consistency and uniformity which they themselves concede to these poems, "idem ingenium, eosdem mores, eandem formam sentiendi et loquendi!"

> Sudet multum frustraque laboret,
> Ausus idem.

And the argument for the integrity of each poem is

[1] To the same purport is the language of Hermann, Opusc. Vol. vi. p. 72.

strengthened rather than weakened by the distinction which these critics sometimes labor to establish between the two poems. This twofold separation of the Homeric poems, first from all other Greek poetry, and secondly from each other, must rest, if it has any basis, on a twofold unity: the one of a more general nature, and the other of a more specific kind; and what can these be, but the former identity of authorship, and the latter identity of plan?

Genius may be unequal to, and even inconsistent with, itself; but mediocrity never can be equal to genius. Hence, as Mure well argues, similarity of genius, style, and spirit affords much stronger proof of identity of authorship than dissimilarity does of diversity. The discrepancies which are so much insisted on in the Iliad and Odyssey, are chiefly those petty anachronisms and self-contradictions, and those slight diversities of style or sentiment, which are incident to human imperfection on the one hand, or which, on the other, genius overlooks, and even exults in as the very element of freedom, and the proof of superiority to those minute accuracies which shackle ordinary mortals.

For example, the Teicho-scopia in the Third Book of the Iliad, represents Helen on the wall, pointing out the Grecian heroes to Priam and his counsellors, as if they had hitherto been strangers to each other, and were now brought face to face for the first time. Yet we learn from the complaints of the desponding commander-in-chief of the Grecian army, in the Second Book, that they had already been encamped before Troy for nine long years. And this accords with the plan of the poem, the turning-point in which is the slaying of Hector as the immediate consequence of the reconciliation of the chiefs, and thus (in the fall of its chief defender) a preparation for the speedy downfall of the city. The inconsistency is not perhaps so great in reality, as at first view it appears to be, since we know that after the first conflicts in the open field, finding themselves unable to cope with their adversaries in pitched battle, the Trojans retired within the walls, and the most enterprising of the Greeks, with Achilles at their head, gave themselves up to the conquest and sacking of the neighboring towns that were less strongly fortified.[1] It is not therefore impossible or improbable, that in the tenth year of the war, the forms and features of the Grecian chiefs should be far from familiar to the king and counsellors of Troy. Still we do not believe that Homer felt the necessity of any such justification of the Teicho-scopia; and we do not regard this as the true explanation of the apparent inconsistency. It was fitting that at an early stage in the poem, and especially on the eve of a single combat between the rival claimants to the hand of Helen, Helen herself, the object of the strife, should be introduced. A bird's-eye view of the scene of conflict, and the principal actors in it, was also appropriate to the same stage of the grand epic. The poet, with characteristic skill, seizes on the period of inaction, while Hector is sending to Troy and making arrangements for the single combat between Paris and Menelaus, and introduces the scene on the wall, at the west gate, to fill up the interval. In short, the Teicho-scopia fills its place in the book and in the poem as perfectly as the grand gateway formed the entrance to the cella of the Parthenon. And this was all the poet thought of or cared for. It was poetically true, proper, and probable; and he never raised the question

[1] Iliad, ix. 352 sqq.; 328 sqq. et passim.

whether it was historically accurate. At the same time, he does not entirely forget himself. That the Teichoscopia belongs to the same advanced stage of the war with the rest of the poem is implied in the πολὺν χρόνον (v. 157) during which the Greeks and Trojans had been struggling for the possession of such a prize, and in the changes and deaths which had taken place since Helen left her native land (v. 243). And that it belongs, like all the other books between the first and the eighteenth, to the period of Achilles's non-participation in the strife, appears from the fact that he, the son of a goddess, and the universally acknowledged champion of the Greeks, is not seen among the heroes on the plain.

The same remarks apply to the detailed and admirable story of old Nestor as he is seen by Agamemnon, marshalling and haranguing his troops, as if it were the first time he had ever drawn them out in order of battle on the plain of Troy; a story, historically speaking, out of place in the tenth year of the war, and yet poetically true to the character of the Pylian sage and perfectly appropriate to its place in the plan of the poem.[1]

The chronological discrepancies between the different parts of the Odyssey — such for instance, as the want of synchronism between the voyage of Telemachus and the return of Ulysses — may, with strong probability, be referred to mere inadvertence. It is at least doubtful whether the poet was conscious of any discrepancy. No simple reader and admirer of the poem would be likely to notice it. And none but a critic who looked more at the arithmetic than at the poetry; none but an anatomical student, who has dissected the poem, instead of gazing on its living form and features, would deem it any blot on the fair proportions of the Odyssey.

[1] Iliad, iv. 292 sqq.

As to the differences in style, manners, and mythology between the Iliad and the Odyssey, they have been partly exaggerated, and in part they admit of a ready explanation. It has been said, for instance, that the language of the Odyssey is more cultivated and refined than that of the Iliad; the state of society more advanced; the morals and religion more elevated; the gods more human and less divine, less grossly corporeal and more spiritual and invisible in their presence and agency. These topics are too numerous and too extensive to be discussed at length in this Article. The reader who wishes to examine the subject in detail, will find the facts well summed up in Mure's chapter on the Doctrine of the Separatists.[1] And if he will look at all the facts in the case, we are sure that he will come to the conclusion that the gods of both poems are essentially the same ungodlike medley of virtues and vices, of grandeur and weakness, visible to mortal eyes in different forms and degrees, according to the ends to be answered by their appearance;[2] that as in the character and conduct of the leading heroes, so of the principal gods of the two poems, there is a striking analogy and consistency in so many particulars as to preclude the supposition of different authors;[3] that the tables may

[1] Vol. ii. p. 119.

[2] See the striking similarity of language as well as sentiment in two passages cited by Mure, Iliad, xx. 131: χαλεποὶ δὲ θεοὶ φαίνεσθαι ἐναργεῖς; and Odyssey, xvi. 161: Οὐ γάρ πω πάντεσσι θεοὶ φαίνονται ἐναργεῖς.

[3] For instance, in the absence of Jupiter in the Iliad, and of Poseidon in the Odyssey, at a festival of the Ethiopians, while important events are transpiring; in Jupiter's yielding to the entreaties of Thetis in the one, and giving place to the resentment of Poseidon in the other, on which so much of the action of the two poems turns; in the deception, by a god appearing in a dream, of Agamemnon in the one, and of Telemachus in the other; and even in the alleged discrepancy between the two poems as to the wife of Hephaestus, since the Odyssey indirectly explains why it is that Aphrodite

be turned, and it may be shown that in many respects the morals and religion of the Iliad are of a higher tone than those of the Odyssey, the arts and sciences more advanced,[1] society and language more refined; and that all these differences are not only explained but demanded by the different subjects and scenes of the two poems, together with a probable change in the poet's situation and period of life. Let it be granted that the Iliad was the work of his earlier life and the Odyssey of his more advanced years (a supposition not only suggested by tradition, but almost necessitated by the mutual relation of the two poems); that the same bard, equally familiar in his wanderings, with Asiatic Greece and the islands of the Aegean, on the one hand, and with European Greece and the Ionian isles on the other (as each poem proves its author to have been), might have chosen to make each familiar scene the centre of a separate poem; and that he chose, as the versatility of his genius not less than the fitness of things would naturally lead him to choose, subjects as different as the scenes — the one a warrior, youthful and brilliant, the very beau-ideal of heroism in the heroic age, and the other a wandering adventurer, experienced and versed in all arts, the pattern of wisdom and fortitude — let these postulates be granted, and every other difference follows from these as necessarily, almost, as a corollary from its proposition; let these germinant ideas be cast into a mind original and versatile as Homer's, and the Iliad and Odyssey, with all their manifest differences but more marked resemblances, spring up as naturally as different

has been divorced (namely for her amours with Ares), and thus opened the way for Charis, who appears as his wife in the Iliad.

[1] E.g. embroidery, Iliad, iii. 125 seq.; and the working of metals, as in the shield of Achilles, Iliad, xviii. 428 seq.

trees spring from different seeds in the same soil. Thus (to illustrate by a difference between the two poems, which attracted theattention of ancient as well as modern critics), the brilliant Iris is the befitting messenger of the gods in the splendid scenes of the Iliad, while the busy and dusty Hermes is equally appropriate to the humbler services which he performs in the Odyssey; and, as if to demonstrate that this is the true explanation of the difference, in the Iliad, when a similar service is to be performed — in conducting Priam to the presence of Achilles — Hermes is employed, and is brought upon the stage with the same seven verses of description (identical, word for word) with which he is introduced in the Odyssey.[1] A battle of the gods in the Odyssey were as clearly out of place as the prodigies of the far-off isles of the Mediterranean in the Iliad. We do not expect to find the wit of Falstaff in Hamlet, nor the soliloquies of Hamlet in the Merry Wives of Windsor. We should like to see Shakespeare or Milton subjected to the dissecting process according to the rules and methods by which Homer has been cut to pieces. We venture to affirm that, in proportion to their length, there are fewer self-contradictions, and far more marked resemblances in plan, style, and sentiment, between the Iliad and Odyssey than there are between Hamlet and the Merry Wives of Windsor, or between the Paradise Lost and Comus. If freedom from self-contradiction, direct or implied, be the test of integrity, the Aeneid, the Inferno, Don Quixote, must all be resolved into separate lays, and their authors reduced to myths and nonentities.[2] No great poem, that was ever written under

[1] Cf. Iliad, xxiv. 339 ; Odyssey, v. 43.

[2] See this point well illustrated in Mure's Appendixes to Vol. i. and ii.

the most auspicious circumstances, will bear the test of such criticism as has been unhesitatingly applied to these productions of an antiquity so remote and so rude as, in the opinion of these critics, to be destitute of the art of writing!

6. This suggests the further remark, that the utter disagreement of these critics among themselves deprives their criticism of all its force. They have only to be brought together, and, like acids and alkalies, they neutralize each other. Were the Iliad and Odyssey to be so divided as to meet the views of all (waiving the impossibility of the same part being in half a dozen different places at the same time), not only would they be dismembered limb from limb, but dissevered muscle from muscle, nay, disintegrated particle from particle; and not only the two great epics, but the half a dozen or dozen, half a score or score, of separate lays would be annihilated in the process. Let every lay be removed and every line be blotted which has at any time been pronounced an interpolation or an addition, and, like the picture which was hung in the market-place and every spectator invited to try his hand at amendment, not a feature would be left visible in the great epic painting of Greece in the Heroic Age. Add to this the fact that Wolf and his followers so contradict themselves,[1] as well as each other, that according to their own rules, scarcely any one of their own critiques can be the production of a single author, and the rest of the world may certainly be excused from attempting to follow them in such tortuous and diverging paths. And what does all this discordance of opinion indicate? Not their want of learning and acuteness, but the slippery

[1] See p. 77 above.

ground on which they stand; the shadowy nature of those differences of style and coloring on which they build their arguments. The ancients doubtless went to the extreme of faith and veneration in their famous challenge, which declared it alike impossible "to wrest the thunderbolt from Jove, the club from Hercules, or a line from the Iliad." But the moderns have gone to the extreme of absurdity and impiety in the utter dismemberment and annihilation of this divine poem. If the shade of Homer were asked which of all the lays and lines expunged from his works by the critics were spurious, he might not perhaps answer as Lucian makes him, — none; but it is quite certain he would not answer — all; since in that case the poor bard would have nothing left.

7. All the principal parts of the Iliad, even those that have been most suspected, and still more all the principal parts of the Odyssey are bound to all the other parts by a network of mutual reference and connection, which, like the nerves and veins of the human body, must be cut and tied before a limb can be amputated. Mure has done excellent service in illustrating this point; and the reader who will take the pains to examine in detail his copious summary of the contents of either poem, and to trace out the references backward and forward in the foot-notes, however familiar he may have been with the outlines of the story, will be surprised to see how numerous are the links, or rather how complete is the network which connects every book indissolubly to the books that precede and follow it; and however he may have been previously inclined to believe in the integrity of the Homeric poems, he can hardly fail to be established in a more steadfast as well as a more intelligent

conviction of that integrity. Then, with the summary or the poems themselves in hand, let him take some leading topic — the absence of Achilles, for instance, after the first book until the eighteenth; or the construction of the rampart, rendered necessary in the eighth book, by the disasters consequent on the accession of Achilles, and accordingly never mentioned in the battles previous to that book, but constituting a prominent feature in those of the following books; the promise of Jove to Thetis in secret at the commencement, and the gradual disclosure and execution of his plan to honor her son, yet through him to slay Hector, and thus prepare the way for the overthrow of Troy; Jove's interdict in the beginning of the eighth book, prohibiting the gods to participate in the strife, and the actual absence of the gods (with attempted exceptions, which only strengthen the argument) from that time till the interdict is withdrawn in the twentieth book — let him take any one of these topics, and following it through, see how often it is alluded to, and how consistently with it the whole course of the dialogue and the action proceeds, and he will find that any one of these series of allusions, with the corresponding course of action, is of itself sufficient to link the successive books together as with a chain of adamant. Let him especially apply these tests to the most suspected portions of the Iliad — the Catalogue, for instance, in the second book; the prowess of Diomed in the fifth and sixth; the embassy to Achilles in the ninth; the Dolonea in the tenth; the shield of Achilles in the eighteenth; or the burial rites in the twenty-third and twenty-fourth.

Perhaps there is no part of the Iliad which wears so

much the appearance of a disconnected episode, and which might be detached from the poem with so little violence to the connection as the Dolonea or night-watch. Yet on close examination this book is found to be connected with the foregoing and following books, not only by a chain of references, but as an essential link in the progress of the action. "The sleepless anxiety of Agamemnon during the night, owing to the gloomy prospects of his host after the disasters of the previous day; his allusion to the prowess of Hector as the immediate, and to his quarrel with Achilles as the remote, cause of his distress; to the bivouac of the Trojans on the plain, to the construction of the rampart and the posting of the guard, with his pointed mention of Rhesus of Thrace, unnoticed among the chiefs of that country in the Catalogue, as but recently arrived in the Trojan camp; all guarantee the previous existence of the first nine books of the poem in their substantial integrity. Nor, even were it not self-evident that this episode could only be intended as a continuation, not as a conclusion, of the foregoing narrative, are there wanting sufficiently plain, though not quite so specific allusions to a sequel."[1] Besides, "in the first nine books of the poem there is no allusion to any special military connection or comradeship between Ulysses and Diomed. The subject of the tenth book hinges essentially on the formation of that comradeship. In the ensuing battle, accordingly, of the eleventh book, those two heroes are found still, conjointly and in partnership, stemming the tide of war." And what is perhaps still more remarkable, the brilliant and cheering exploits of the tenth book are necessary "to account for the change of

[1] Mure, Vol. i. p. 265.

feeling in the army between the ninth and eleventh books, from despondency at the close of the one to cheerful hope and confidence at the commencement of the other."[1]

8. Besides this network of mutual reference, there is another chain running through the mechanical structure of the Iliad and Odyssey, which is still more distinctively Homeric — which forms such a connection between the several parts of each poem, and also between the two poems, as pervades no other poetical compositions of the same extent. We refer to those often repeated verses which mark the transitions in the dialogue; the familiar but not hackneyed lines by which each speaker is introduced and dismissed from the stage; the technical descriptions and illustrations of a feast or a battle which occur as often as a feast or a battle is described; the repetition of orders, messages, and proposals, at full length, perhaps two or three times, in the very same words; and all the other epic common-places as they are sometimes called, which not only impress the reader with a spontaneous conviction of the integrity of each poem, but assure him when he passes from one to the other that he is still travelling with the same guide, and that too a guide so intelligent as to see everything just as it is, and so faithful as to tell everything just as he sees or hears it. There are some two thousand verses of these several sorts, which are the same, word for word, in the Odyssey as in the Iliad. The naked fact, thus stated, is certainly no small evidence of identity of authorship. No other two poems, ancient or modern, bear this evidence so ample and palpable on their surface.

[1] Mure's Preface to his second edition of Vol. i., where, in a foot-note, he gives credit to Rev. Mr. Blake of Stobo for these last suggestions.

But this connection is not merely superficial. It enters into the substantial merits and the characteristic excellences of the Homeric poems. Common-place as (to the superficial reader) these repetitions appear to be, they exhibit the same master-strokes, the same marvellous power of individualizing men and things, and portraying them to the life, which, as manifested in the whole of his works, signalize Homer as the greatest of all painters from nature and from real life. Thus Diomed seldom speaks in council. Directly the opposite of what Agamemnon hastily accuses him of being, and partly perhaps in intentional refutation of that groundless charge, he is more valiant in deeds than in words.[1] But when all the other chiefs in the absence of Achilles are reduced to the silence of despair, then in repeated instances he comes forward with a brief harangue, full of hope and courage; in every instance it meets the instantaneous approval of all, restores their confidence, and rouses them to vigorous action. This distinctive trait in the character of Diomed, and in the style of his eloquence, together with its unfailing influence on the other leaders and the Grecian host is set forth again and again in successive books (among the rest, in the much suspected and greatly wronged tenth book) in those apparently common-place, but really most characteristic and significant repetitions:

ὣς ἔφαθ᾽ · οἱ δ᾽ ἄρα πάντες ἀκὴν ἐγένοντο σιωπῇ ·
δὴν δ᾽ ἀνέῳ ἦσαν τετιηότες υἷες Ἀχαιῶν ·
ὀψὲ δὲ δὴ μετέειπε βοὴν ἀγαθὸς[2] Διομήδης ·
Ἀτρεΐδη, σοὶ πρῶτα μαχήσομαι ἀφραδέοντι, ...

[1] Iliad, iv. 400.

[2] The reader scarcely need be reminded how appropriate this epithet, "good at the rescue" is to the trait of character we are illustrating.

ὣς ἔφαθ᾽· οἱ δ᾽ ἄρα πάντες ἐπίαχον υἷες Ἀχαιῶν,
μῦθον ἀγασσάμενοι Διομήδεος ἱπποδάμοιο.[1]

In like manner, Achilles has his own characteristic common-place: ἀλλὰ τὰ μὲν προτετύχθαι ἐάσομεν . . .[2] never used by any other speaker but repeatedly by him, falling in with the abruptness and sententiousness which distinguish all his speeches, and even that of the shade of Achilles in the Odyssey,[3] and picturing to the life his impetuous and impatient spirit. Old Nestor brings out in the repetitions which mark his eloquence, not only the general characteristics of old age, but some of the most distinctive features of his individual character; not only wishing that he were young again, as when he slew Ereuthalion[4] but showing his lively sense of shame at the degeneracy of the times, and his peculiar sensitiveness to the good opinion of men.[5] How characteristic of the self-condemned and conscience-stricken Paris is his repeated

Ἕκτορ᾽ ἐπεί με κατ᾽ αἶσαν ἐνείκεσας, οὐδ᾽ ὑπὲρ αἶσαν.[6]

These parallel passages, which have ever been regarded as among the best proofs of identity of authorship, sometimes take the form of kindred ideas and images with more or less of similarity, but not exact identity, of language; as in the wish of the two leading female

[1] Iliad, ix. 29 sqq.; cf. ix. 693; x. 218; vii. 398; xiv. 103 sqq.

[2] Iliad, xvi. 60; xviii. 112; xix. 65; xxiv. 523, 524. προτετύχθαι occurs only in the Iliad, and in the Iliad proceeds only from the mouth of Achilles. Mure was the first to call attention to this characteristic of Achilles's speeches so appropriate to his character. The frequent recurrence of the transitional and adversative particles ἀτάρ, αὐτάρ, ἀλλά, ἀλλ᾽ ἄγε, ἀλλά . . . ἐῤῥέτω, etc., is highly characteristic of the speeches of Achilles.

[3] Odyssey, xi. 492; cf. Iliad, xx. 351.

[4] Iliad, iv. 319; vii. 149 sqq., etc.

[5] Iliad, i. 254; vii. 124; xv. 691, etc.

[6] Iliad, iii. 59; vi. 333.

characters of the two poems: Helen (Iliad, vi. 345) that she had been, and Penelope (Odyssey, xx. 63) that she might be, swept away by the tempest or engulfed in the waves; the care taken in regard to the hero of each poem[1] that he may not suffer present evil, coupled with the declaration that hereafter he will suffer "what the Fates had spun for him at his birth"; the hatred of deception expressed by Achilles in the Iliad (ix. 312) and by Eumaeus in the Odyssey (xiv. 156), and enforced by the same strong comparison, "hateful as the gates of Hades"—an image of hatefulness which the poet applies only to this hateful vice. In these and many similar passages the parallelism lies not in the exact form of words, but in the general cast of conception and expression, thus indicating not a repetition from the memory of the bard, but a like action of the same original and creative powers of mind under similar circumstances, and showing the same marvellous faculty to individualize and characterize things in these passages, as in the others above cited he has shown to distinguish and portray persons. More commonly, however, where Homer has occasion to repeat the same ideas he does it in the same words, and with good reason; for those words are so exactly the living image of the ideas, that to vary them were to mar the image.

The same principles—the same power of discrimination on the part of the author, and the same inference that the author is one and the same—are involved in those descriptive and distinctive epithets which Homer applies to persons and things with the uniformity of

[1] In regard to Achilles by the goddess Hera (Iliad, xx. 126 sqq.) and in regard to Ulysses by the god-like Alcinous, king of the Phaeacians (Odyssey, vii. 195 sqq).

common-place, but with the discrimination of a master in painting. These epithets are in fact pictures in miniature of the persons and things to which they are applied. It is as if the poet when he was about to introduce an actor on the stage, first held up before the audience a picture of the man, so drawn to the life, that you not only recognize the actor at once whenever he appears, though amid a multitude of other actors, but you know beforehand, more or less perfectly, how he will speak and act. Thus the epithets by which the two protagonists are distinguished from other men and those by which they are distinguished from each other, exhibit these two heroes not only in their most characteristic features, as unitedly "the destroyers of cities," and as severally "the lion-hearted," and "the versatile," "the crusher of heroes," and "the man of many expedients,"[1] but also in a variety of other proper and interesting attitudes; while those by which the inferior heroes and even the contending nations are characterized, constitute a whole gallery of portraits and groups, in which individual and national character stands out almost visibly before the eye. And not only the science of human nature, but the profoundest philosophy of the material and spiritual universe is not unfrequently shadowed forth in Homeric epithets, as "the cope of heaven is imaged in a dewdrop."

The dramatic structure of the Homeric poems is one of their most characteristic features. The mere extent to which dialogue prevails over direct narration were

[1] It is worthy of notice how the many-sidedness of Ulysses is set forth in his epithets, most of which contain πόλυ in their composition. Mure has gone into particulars on this subject of Homeric epithets (Vol. ii. p. 75 sqq.) and given numerically their application to different persons, and their distribution between the Iliad and the Odyssey.

sufficient of itself to distinguish these from any other epic poems in existence. But when we further observe with what masterly skill and power the dialogue is made to develop character and history, it becomes distinctive not only as an outward form, but as a spiritual element; it becomes, like the epithets and the common-place, and pre-eminently above even them, a proof of that insight into human nature, of that creative or rather representative faculty, in a word, of that original genius, which never was, and probably never will be, found in such perfection in more than one man of the same age.

9. The perfection of the plot affords a strong argument for the integrity of each poem; and this, together with the striking similarity of the plot in the two poems, affords evidence scarcely less convincing that they both proceeded from one and the same author.

The plan of the Iliad and the Odyssey has been the admiration of men of taste in all ages. Aristotle held them up as the ideal of the epic, and for two thousand years they remained the undisputed standard. Horace[1] praises the simplicity and modesty of Homer's introductions; his skill in the choice of his subject, and the selection of his materials; the rapidity with which he ushers his hearers into the midst of the matter, and hurries them on to the issue; the consistency of the parts and the completeness of the whole; in a word, the faultless excellence of the plan: "qui nil molitur inepte," while at the same time he grieves that he sometimes falls below himself in the execution: "quandoque bonus dormitat Homerus." How diametrically opposite all this is to the notions of the Wolfian school need not be remarked. Nor is it difficult to show that Horace is

[1] Ars Poetica, 136 sqq.

the more correct in his judgment; that he has, in fact, set forth in these few lines of his Epistle to the Pisos the characteristic merits of the Homeric poems.

The general object of the Iliad was, as its name imports, to illustrate the war of Troy. But the author does not, like a tasteless and common-place poet, begin with the birth of Helen, the cause of the war, "nec gemino bellum Trojanum orditur ab ovo," and trace the whole series of events in historical order. He seizes upon the crisis of the war, nay, the hinge of that crisis, and groups all persons and things, agencies and events, about that central point. The crisis of the war was in the tenth year just before its close, when an unforeseen and most unlikely concurrence of circumstances brought about a sudden change in the course of events, and resulted in the death of Hector, the sole bulwark of the Trojan city. The hinge of that crisis was the quarrel between Agamemnon and Achilles, the commander-in-chief and the foremost warrior of the Grecian army, and the withdrawal of the latter — in anger at the commander's insult, and in disgust at the acquiescence of the troops — from the Grecian cause.

Since the first encounters on the plain of Troy, the Trojans, worsted in the conflict, had retired within the walls of the city; and the Greeks, despairing of a siege, or direct assault, had occupied themselves mainly with capturing the neighboring towns and ravaging the country,[1] in the hope of thus compelling an ultimate surrender. But no sooner were the Trojans apprised of the quarrel of the chiefs, and the consequent withdrawal of Achilles,[2] than they took courage, sallied from the gates, and with the aid of Jove, who had

[1] Iliad, vi. 415; i. 163; ix. 328, etc. [2] Iliad, ix. 352 sqq., et. passim.

promised to avenge Achilles, so triumphed over their adversaries, that at length they encamped over night on the plain, and threatened ere long to burn the Grecian ships and drive the Greeks themselves into the sea. Under these circumstances, Achilles is so wrought upon by the entreaties of his friend Patroclus, as to consent that he shall go forth, clad in Achilles's armor, and turn back the tide of war. Patroclus goes forth, repels the Trojans, but in the end is slain by Hector. Achilles now renounces his resentment against Agamemnon, concentrates all his wrath on Hector, slays him, and thus ensures the speedy downfall of Troy. That downfall is not narrated; but it has been foreshadowed from the beginning, and now it is clearly seen to be near at hand. But Troy was destined to fall by meaner hands than those of Achilles,[1] and by more ignoble means than this last great battle in the open field, in which the champion of the Greeks slays the champion of the Trojans. No subsequent event could compare in poetical interest, nor even in real importance, with this battle. No other moment in the whole war so brings out the heroes on both sides, so enlists the sympathies of men and gods, is so pregnant with the final issue. This, then, is the crisis; and it all turns palpably, from first to last, on the anger of Achilles. The poet accordingly seizes upon this turning-point, and announces the wrath of Achilles, in connection with that plan and purpose of Jove of which it was the instrument,[2] as the subject of the Iliad. And there is not a little truth in

[1] Iliad, xx. 30; Odyssey, viii. 502.

[2] Iliad, i. 5: Διὸς δ' ἐτελείετο βουλή. See Granville Penn's Primary Argument of the Iliad for a masterly analysis of the poem in this theological point of view.

the strong language of Hug: "The very proposition of the poet is a head of Medusa, which turns to stone every audacious hand that would rob him of a single book."[1] At least, we cannot but subscribe to the more sober conclusion of Mure, that "the anger of Achilles, with its consequences, really includes all that the Iliad relates, and excludes all that it omits."

His subject thus announced, the poet begins, with many incidents but few ornaments, as if he were not finishing a lay, but laying the foundations of an epopee. The first book contains not a single simile, but shifts the scene and consumes more time than all the subsequent books together. The earlier books are all clearly introductory, being designed to set before the reader, in successive pictures, the principal actors in the grand drama; the causes, authors, and leaders of the strife; the forces on both sides; and the state of feeling in the Grecian army and at the homes of Troy. It is only in the eighth book that Jove enters in earnest upon his purpose to avenge Achilles, and sends such disasters on the Greeks that they are fain to entreat and purchase, at any price, his return to the Grecian ranks. But he is implacable, inexorable. The tide of Trojan success rolls on, though not without an occasional ebb. Agamemnon, Menelaus, Ulysses, Diomed, Ajax, Antilochus, all perform prodigies of valor; but all are insufficient to stem the advancing flood. Patroclus comes forth in Achilles's armor; and while he is mistaken for that hero himself, drives the Trojans before him. But they discover their mistake, rally, slay Patroclus, and the flying Greeks with difficulty bear off his dead body. The flood swells higher, goes over the ramparts which the

[1] Erfind. der Buchstab.

Greeks have lately built around their ships, reaches the ships themselves, and threatens to sweep the soil clear of its invaders. Nothing checks its progress till Achilles himself, unarmed, but clothed by Athena with more than his wonted grandeur of form and voice, shows himself on the rampart, and by his terrible shout sends every Trojan warrior flying to the gates of Troy. A lull succeeds, in which the hero vents his grief over the body of his friend, and Thetis brings a new suit of armor, forged by Hephaestus, for her son. Then the storm of Achillean wrath bursts upon the Trojan host. He slaughters or drives before him every living thing on the plain of Troy. The gods enter the field with him, and somewhat equalize the strife, else he had entered the city with the fugitives, and, contrary to fate, levelled it with the dust."[1] He encounters Hector, slays him, and drags his lifeless body, trailing in the dust, behind his chariot to his own tent. The funeral rites are then performed over the body, first of Patroclus, and, at length, of Hector; and the poem dies away on the ear as naturally, as sweetly, as it began; ending in the simple, touching words: "Such burial the illustrious Hector found."

We have neither time nor patience to discuss the tasteless, soulless objections that have been urged against these concluding books, as not coming within the scope of the subject. They are essential to the development of Achilles's character — as intense in his love as he is in his hatred, and as superior to all other heroes in knightly courtesy and generosity as he is in military prowess. Moreover, the poem could not have ended till the rites of burial were first performed over the body of

[1] Iliad, xx. 23 sqq.

Patroclus and the mangled corse of Hector; because, according to Aristotle's definition of an end, there would still have been indispensable duties which, as the Greeks viewed it, must needs have succeeded, and in reference to which, in this case, the previous conduct of Achilles could not but have excited painful anxiety. Two, at least, of the tragedies of Sophocles,[1] that perfect master of tragic unity, are prolonged to considerable length beyond the catastrophe, for the same reason as the Iliad — to put the mind of the Greeks (who had a religious horror of remaining unburied, of which we can scarcely conceive) at rest as to the due burial of the heroes of the tale.

We hasten to show, in few words, how very similar, and yet not tamely like, is the plan of the Odyssey. The Odyssey is intended as a sort of sequel to the Iliad, to acquaint us with the subsequent fortunes of those who were engaged in the war of Troy. Achilles, Ajax, Agamemnon, Menelaus, Nestor, Ulysses, Paris, Helen; what became of them afterwards? Did they ever reach home? In what state did they find things after their long absence; and what reception did they meet with from their wives and children and people? With a view to satisfy this natural curiosity the poet selects the hero who was the last to reach home, seizes on the last and that the tenth year of his wanderings, and the last month of that year, when his long frustrated desire was at length to be accomplished, and groups all other persons and events about that most eventful epoch of that most adventurous hero's life. He announces his subject, in few words, at the outset; and that, as in the Iliad, in the form of an invocation to the Muse. The

[1] Ajax and Antigone.

earlier books are introductory, and more than usually simple. They show us the principal scene of action in Ithaca, the homes of Nestor and Menelaus, and the island-prison of Ulysses; and we hear from the lips of those heroes, in succession, the wondrous story of their adventures, involving also more or less of the fortunes of their compeers and the fate of Troy, but never encroaching on the field of the Iliad; and giving peculiar prominence to that master-piece of story-telling and half-epic, half-romantic song—the adventures of Ulysses. As in the Iliad, so in the Odyssey, through more than half of the entire poem the principal hero is absent from the principal scene of action, though we never for a moment lose sight of him in the background, as the real centre of every movement, whether of gods or men. Meanwhile, the young sprigs of nobility from Ithaca and the neighboring islands sue for the hand of the faithful Penelope, insult his youthful son, and prey upon his dilapitated estate as if it were their own. Things wax worse and worse, the suitors and servants grow more and more reckless of duty and fearless of punishment; they even threaten to take the life of the young prince, and to lay violent hands on his mother; till the *πολύμητις Ὀδυσσεύς* appears on the stage. And when he comes to the palace, and his affectionate old dog dies for joy at his return, and his faithful nurse recognizes him in the bath, but all other eyes are blinded, and most hearts are hardened against the master of the house, who enters it in the guise of a beggar; when the suitors, in the face of portentous signs, load him with insults, such as in those good old times it was deemed impious to heap on the meanest stranger; when Penelope listens with a strange fascination to the unknown beggar's feigned history of himself, and is visited with unaccountable dreams of the return of her lord; when that despised beggar draws the bow which no suitor could bend, and sends the arrow whizzing through the mark, of which the prize was the hand of Penelope; in a word, when the plan of the inventful Ulysses is ripe for execution, and, with the aid of Athena, he throws off his disguise, stands forth in more than the force and fire of his early youth, and rains his deadly shafts among the guilty and trembling crew who had so long triumphed in the vain assurance of his death, — the plot is brought to a conclusion of such moral grandeur as no other poet has reached. It finds its parallel in the *περιπέτεια* of the Iliad, and nowhere else.[1]

This sublime crisis is followed by more tranquil scenes; scenes of touching interest and tender pathos, like, and yet not like, those which we have characterized as a lull after the first outburst of Achilles in the Iliad — the recognition of Ulysses by Penelope, the interview between the long-absent son and his aged father, the conducting of the souls of the suitors down to Hades. Another battle ensues in which Athena gives her favorite hero an easy victory over the rebellious portion of his subjects; and then the poem ends more abruptly, but not less simply, than the Iliad. In short, the two plots are exceedingly alike in principle and general impression, and yet not a little unlike in details; too much alike to have proceeded from different authors, yet too unlike to be chargeable with sameness or repetition; just as similar and just as dissimilar as an origi-

[1] This parallel is suggested in the Quarterly Review, No. 89, and has always struck us as an argument of great force.

nal genius like Homer would naturally plan an Odyssey and an Iliad.

Is it possible that a plot so perfect as either of these was the production of an ordinary mind; nay, of an indefinite number of such minds, living and working at unknown intervals of time and place? Is it possible that the perfection and the similarity of the plots should both be the result of mere accident?

10. The power of delineating character which is shown in both poems, and the consistency which is preserved in the greater and the minor characters, demonstrate the same master-hand throughout the Iliad and Odyssey.

It will not be necessary to dwell on this argument. The power of reproducing real characters, or creating ideal ones, with perfect truth and consistency, is confessedly one of the rarest endowments which God has bestowed on the most gifted of the sons of earth. It is the prerogative of genius only to see just how all sorts of men will act in all circumstances, for the very obvious reason that genius only combines in itself, and in large measure too, all those various talents and susceptibilities proper to humanity which exist singly or in smaller measures in ordinary mortals. In the Homeric poems the difficulty is greatly enhanced by the infinite variety of characters of different grades and orders of being, real or imaginary, — gods and demigods, heroes and common men, sirens and sorceresses, monsters and prodigies, horses and dogs, that appear upon the stage; by the equal diversity of scene and element in which they act their respective parts — on Mount Olympus, at the bottom of the sea, in Hades, at the summit of Ida, on the plains of Troy, in the city, in the camp, in the homes of Troy, Ithaca, Pylus, and Sparta, in the islands of the then far-off and fabulous Mediterranean, in Europe, Asia, and Africa, on the land, on the water, in the water, in the air; and by the dramatic structure of the poems in which character is not drawn out in narrative and description, but developed in dialogue and action before the eyes of the spectators. And yet it is universally acknowledged that with the exception of Shakespeare no poet has ever exhibited this rare power, beset in his case with these peculiar difficulties, with such unconscious ease and in such faultless perfection, as the author of the Iliad and Odyssey. He has turned these very difficulties into more splendid successes and triumphed in fields which other men have not dared to enter.

Follow the Homeric gods, as a class or as individuals, through all the scenes of love and hate, joy and sorrow, doing and suffering, feasting and fighting; from the councils round the throne of Jupiter to the series of single combats on the plains of Troy; from Jove sitting apart on Mount Ida, and balancing the destinies of nations, to Ares sprawling over seven acres at the feet of Athena in the Iliad, or fast bound in the toils of Hephaestus in the Odyssey — scenes so strangely mingling the tragic with the comic, and so constantly in both poems passing by a single step from the sublime to the ridiculous, that you know not whether to laugh or weep over them — follow the Homeric gods through all these various yet analogous scenes, and, whatever you may think of the gods, you can scarcely fail to be impressed with the oneness and the exalted genius of the poet. The Calypso and Circe, the Cyclops and Sirens, and other monsters of the Odyssey, are unlike in kind to anything in the

Iliad, else they would not be in keeping with the strange and fabulous regions into which Ulysses wanders; but they gather about the man of many wiles as naturally as the pantheon of the Iliad hovers around the son of Thetis; and they excite pretty much the same mingled emotions of laughter and compassion, of fear and disgust; they are manifestly the offspring of the same fruitful yet unerring imagination; just as Shakespeare's fairies, hobgoblins, and witches show the same fertile and self-consistent genius which appears in his divinest creations.

We will not delay on the wonderful variety and distinctness of the principal human personages in the Iliad, nor on the equally wonderful consistency with which each speaker acts his part, the speeches beautifully harmonizing with each other and with the actions, and the actions perfectly according with each other and with the speeches; a uniformity amid variety, like that of nature herself; for no one has had the hardihood to deny it. We hasten to seek out the same persons in the Odyssey, and we recognize them at once as old acquaintances, with the same familiar forms and features, the same peculiar manner of speaking, and the same characteristic modes of action. The Ulysses of the Odyssey is the Ulysses of the Iliad placed in different circumstances, but displaying the same essential traits of character — artful, inventful, deeming discretion the better part of valor, and stratagem the noblest art in war; patient, self-possessed, self-relying, all-enduring, never at a loss for a word or an expedient, always equal to himself and to every emergency. Calling himself the father of Telemachus in the Iliad; the Odyssey is the history of his superhuman trials and struggles to see again his beloved Telemachus, Penelope, and Ithaca. Nestor is still the orator and the sage of Pylus, only more than ever garrulous of himself and the good old times, rejoicing in the admiration of others, rich in the treasures of experience, and yet richer in the flow of his honeyed eloquence. Menelaus is still in nature, as also in name, "the sandy-haired," ardent, affectionate, self-sacrificing. He mourns his brother dead as he loved and honored him living, and would gladly forego all the honors and advantages of the war if Agamemnon might be restored to his fraternal embrace. Helen is still the fair penitent, and though restored to the favor of her rightful husband, still calls herself the shameless dog, in remembrance of her unfaithfulness.

The very shades of departed heroes show "the ruling passion strong *after* death." Agamemnon is a great weeper in Hades, even as on earth his tears flowed like the streaming of a "dark-watered fountain from the goat-left rock,"[1] and woman is still the root of all his troubles. At sight of his successful rival for the armor of Achilles the ghost of Ajax stalks away in gloomy silence, the perfect picture of Ajax himself on the plain of Troy, as he strode from the battle-field, half-indignant, half contemptuous, with his shield slung over his lusty shoulders, stuck full with Trojan spears.[2] The shade of Achilles, with all the intensity of his fiery and impassioned nature, mourns over his short-lived though brilliant destiny, and declares that he would rather be the meanest slave on earth than rule over the spirits of all the mighty dead.[3] And Patroclus is still his silent and deferential companion.

[1] Iliad, ix. 14; cf. Odyssey, xi. 391.

[2] Iliad, xi. 556 sqq.; cf. Odyssey, xi. 543.

[3] Odyssey, xi. 489.

The minor personages, the suitors and servants, the heralds and squires, the bards and goatherds, Thersites the buffoon, the archer Pandarus, the beggar Irus, the nurse Euryclea, and last, not least, the old hunting-dog Argus, all have their own characters and parts, which are as distinct from each other as their faces, and as well sustained as the jesters and grave-diggers, sentinels and executioners, Pistols and Quicklys, of Shakespeare's fancy.

National character is generalized and distinguished. The Trojans are generally false and fair, greater in speech than in action,[1] godlike in form, but deficient in moral principle. The Phaeacians are the celestials of the heroic age, vain and boastful of their fancied superiority, looking with pity or contempt on outside barbarians, but listening with wonder to the shipwrecked mariner's strange adventures, and beholding with astonishment his manifest superiority to themselves in all manly exercises.

Now this matchless power of conceiving and representing human nature in all its various phases, so rare in any poem, so universal in these; this were, of itself, sufficient to demonstrate the absurdity of the hypothesis which refers the Iliad and Odyssey to a number of different authors. But when we further observe the consistency with which each character is sustained, from the beginning of the Iliad to the end of the Odyssey, we see the most convincing demonstration that both poems must have proceeded from one and the same author. That consistent and complete idea of Ulysses, for instance, could not have been the offspring of more than

1 Aeneas, Iliad, xx. 199 sqq. and Hector, passim. Hence the English use of the word "hector."

one mind. As well might Ulysses himself have been the son of more than one father. That portrait of Helen begun in the Iliad and finished in the Odyssey is no patchwork of several authors. As well might Guido's Magdalen have been painted by half a dozen different masters. Each one of the characters, of either or both of the poems, is as palpably and necessarily the work of one hand as the Venus de Medici or the Apollo Belvidere.

III.

THE HOMERIC DOCTRINE OF THE GODS.[1]

NAEGELSBACH'S Homeric Theology[2] has been a standard work ever since it was given to the public in 1840, and it still remains the most systematic and complete treatise on that subject with which we are acquainted. It is only necessary to look over his copious index of seven sections, divided and subdivided, classified and arranged, with the help of all the letters of the Greek and Latin alphabet, as well as the Arabic numerals, to see the exhaustive German fulness and methodicalness with which he has treated the Homeric Olympus. And when we pass from the index to the work itself, we are pleased to find that this large promise is amply fulfilled; that while the classification of topics exhausts the subject, the copious illustrations constitute a complete *resumé* of passages pertaining to the religion of the Greeks in the heroic age.

Mr. Gladstone's Studies on Homer and the Homeric Age is a more voluminous work, more suggestive, and

[1] [Reprinted from the American Theological Review. Vol. iii. No. xii. Oct. 1861.]

[2] Die Homerische Theologie in ihren Zusammenhange dargestellt von Carl Friedrich Naegelsbach, Professor am K. B. Gymnasium zu Nurnberg. Nurnberg 1840.

Studies on Homer and the Homeric Age. By the Right Honorable W. E. Gladstone, D.C.L., M.P. for the University of Oxford. In three volumes. Oxford: at the University Press. 1858. Vol. ii. Olympus: or, the Religion of the Homeric Age.

more practical, but less scientific and complete. Borrowing freely from the German scholar, and readily acknowledging his obligations, the English statesman adds little to the materials, and omits many of the facts with their illustrations, but inquires with more eager curiosity into the origin of the religious ideas and usages of the early Greeks, and with the faith and reverence, as well as the practical wisdom, befitting a leader of the government in the leading state of Protestant Christendom, looks at every topic in its relations to Christianity and the Bible. Of course the minute accuracy of the German professor is not to be expected in the Chancellor of the English Exchequer. Still the work of Mr. Gladstone adds another to the many enduring monuments which perpetuate the fame of that country whose greatest statesmen have always been, at the same time, her best classical scholars.

Passing from these authors to the subject of which they treat, it is our purpose to confine our remarks, at present, to the Homeric Doctrine of the Gods.

When we speak of the Homeric theology, or the Homeric doctrine of the gods, we do not mean to imply that Homer had any such doctrine or theology clearly defined and systematically arranged in his own mind, still less that his poems were intended to be a catechism or a creed for the instruction of coming generations. Homer never preaches or delivers lectures. As his life and character can only be gathered from his works, so his religious sentiments are nowhere stated in form or didactically inculcated, but are everywhere presupposed in the plot, implied in the incidents, uttered and acted by his heroes and minor personages. Indeed it is not his own theology or his own opinions on any subject that he has given us; but, wholly objective, living only in his characters, he has perpetuated the living image of their religious ideas and usages. And these ideas and usages he has re-presented to us under all the varieties of individual opinion and experience, with all the self-contradictions that belong to false systems of religion, and with all the contrast between theory and practice, creed and conduct, which imperfect men always exhibit in real life, sometimes further exaggerated by a palpable but not readily measurable difference between the imagination of the poet and the people, and the traditions which they have received from a purer and more primitive age.

To discriminate between these differences, and to reconcile these contradictions, is sometimes not a little difficult. Still, beneath them all there is an underlying system of religious doctrine, which characterizes, and more or less controls, the men of the Homeric age; and Homer, with all his contradictions, was the Bible of the Greeks for many generations. An eye-witness to events contemporaneous with the earliest prophets and kings of Israel, a faithful voucher[1] for manners and customs and a state of society strikingly similar to those which existed among the Hebrew patriarchs, the primeval, and in their estimation inspired, bard, teacher, and historian of a people second only to the Jews in their influence on the education and development of mankind, Homer, and especially the theology of Homer, cannot but be a study of deep interest to the Christian who, with no narrow or one-sided view, sees one and the same hand,

[1] Such F. Schlegel takes to be the meaning of the word Ὅμηρος, a *voucher* for heroic life and times; though with the inborn scepticism of a German, he still doubts whether any such man as Homer ever lived.

the hand of God, in the history of the whole human race.

1. NUMBER AND CLASSIFICATION OF THE GODS.

The reader of the Iliad and the Odyssey will discover at once that the doctrine of the Divine unity, which, according to the Scriptures, and according to the most reliable history and soundest philosophy also, was once universal, has already disappeared from the Homeric world, and given place to the polytheistic conception of "gods many and lords many." Instead of one omnipresent and infinite spirit, alike present and alike powerful in all places and all ages, which is to us essential to the very idea of God, the divine essence, as conceived by these early Greeks, is already divided into as many classes of so-called divine beings — all, of course, more or less limited and degraded, as there are departments of divine agency, and some of these classes comprehend an indefinite number of individuals answering to the number and variety of existences in the department. At the same time there are not wanting evident vestiges of a primitive monotheism in the supremacy of Jupiter, the father of gods and men, whose will is accomplished in all the changeful and apparently conflicting course of events (Il. i. 5), who sits enthroned on Mount Olympus, weighing the destinies of the combatants, while the inferior deities all engage in the strife of battle (Il. xx. 21 sqq.; xxii. 209 sqq.); and who, though gods and men should combine against him, with perfect ease could lift them all and the earth itself up to heaven, or hurl them down to Tartarus at his sovereign pleasure (Il. viii. 5–27). There is also a kind of trinity, or triad, in the manifest and vast superiority of Zeus, Athena, and Apollo — the all-father, the wisdom that is born of him, and the son who is his voice or word. These three are seldom (never long) at direct variance with each other. In the Odyssey, Athena and Apollo are entirely at one with Zeus. In the Iliad, there is a temporary and partial alienation between Zeus and Athena, while he is avenging the wrongs of Achilles on the Grecians. With this exception, the son and daughter both act not only in harmony with their father, but in joyful subordination to his will. And the three are addressed together by mortals, as of one mind — almost as if they were one being — in that oft-repeated prayer, "Would that father Zeus, Athena, and Apollo, etc.," which the heroes of the Trojan war offer whenever they would fain see some work accomplished which is nearly or quite too great or too good to be hoped for (Il. ii. 371; iv. 288; vii. 132; Od. vii. 311; xxiv. 376, et al.). From the marked peculiarity, as well as the manifest superiority, of these gods, and from the anomalies in the functions ascribed to them — which are inexplicable on any theory of natural and homogeneous developement — Mr. Gladstone argues at great length and with much force,[1] that they are not strictly mythological, but traditional divinities, derived in the main features of their character and office, from some earlier and purer religion, and ultimately from a direct revelation, though these primitive features are obscured and disfigured by the superstitions of the vulgar and the inventions of the poet.

Besides these first three, there are six other divinities of unquestionably Olympian rank and residence, for whom Hephaestus has built palaces on Mount Olympus (Il. i.

[1] Vol. ii. sec. 2. The Traditive Element of the Homeric Theo-Mythology.

607), and who convene in the court of Zeus, as occasion requires, for a council or a feast. These are, Hera, sister and wife of Zeus; Ares, Hephaestus, and Hermes, his sons; and Artemis and Aphrodite, his daughters. Poseidon and Hades, brothers of Zeus, also clearly belong to the same rank, though, from the necessity of their office and province, the one has his ordinary dwelling in the sea (Il. xiii. 21; xx. 13), and the fixed abode of the other is in the invisible world under the earth (Il. xx. 61 sqq.). Hades comes to Olympus when he is wounded by Hercules (Il. v. 398). His wife, Persephone, is never seen there; but her rank, in her own right as well as in that of her husband, would entitle her to no inferior place among the Olympic deities. Dione and Latona, though inferior wives of Zeus, are of course among those who "occupy Olympian abodes" (Il. v. 383; xxi. 499). Dionysus (Bacchus) and Demeter (Ceres) are deities of high rank and power; but they seem to have their dwelling, not so much in heaven as on earth, among the sons of men. By adding to these sixteen principal deities three or four others of doubtful Olympian residence, or of a manifestly inferior grade, Mr. Gladstone contrives to make up twenty, answering to the number of tripods which Hephaestus was forging to stand around the wall in the well-built hall, where the gods were wont to assemble (Il. xviii. 373). But this is rather too trivial and incidental a circumstance to support the inference that Homer reckoned just twenty members of the Olympic council. Still less can any authority be found in Homer for the twelve greater gods as distinguished from the less — the Dii Majores as distinguished from the Dii Minores of the Romans.

About these principal deities cluster several who may

be called serving divinities, whose office it is to attend on their superiors. Thus Zeus, as the guardian of civil and political justice, is assisted by Themis, who convenes assemblies, whether of gods or men, and keeps order in them (Il. xx. 4; Od. ii. 68); Hera, as goddess of marriage by the Eileithyiae, her daughters (Il. xi. 271.); Apollo, by the Muses (Il. i. 603); Aphrodite, by the Graces. The Hours are the gate-keepers of heaven (Il. v. 749; viii. 393); Hebe is the cup-bearer of the gods (Il. iv. 2), and Asclepius and Paieon are their physicians. Iris, though originally an impersonation of the rainbow, as the name imports (Il. xi. 27), appears in Homer only as the messenger of the Olympian gods, particularly of Zeus (Il. xv. 144, et passim).

A second class of quasi-divinities are the allegorical deities, or impersonations of ideas, which are not mere poetical personifications on the one hand, nor on the other wholly mythological beings, but fill up at various intervals all the space between personality and allegory, though none of them possess such an established divine personality as to have their fixed times and places of worship. These are, for the most part, either military or moral. Among the impersonations of military ideas are Discord (*Ἔρις*), Din (*Ἐνυώ*), Uproar (*Κυδοιμός*), Rout (*Φόβος*), Terror (*Δεῖμος*), Panic (*Φύζα*), Rumor (*Ὄσσα*), etc., of which the first two have quite a fixed personality, while the others approach nearer to allegory, or hover between them. They are all, except Rumor, kindred or companions of Ares (cf. Il. iv. 440; v. 592; xiii. 299; xv. 119; ix. 2). Among the impersonations of moral ideas, or moral powers, are Destiny (*Αἶσα, Μοῖρα*) and the Fates (*Κῆρες, Κατακλῶθες*, cf. Il. xx. 127; xix. 410; Od. vii. 197); Death, and his brother,

Sleep (*Θάνατος*, *Ὕπνος*, Il. xiv. 231); the Dream-god also (*Ὄνειρος*, Il. ii. 6); the goddess of moral blindness (*Ἄτη*) daughter of Zeus, yet cast out from heaven, and the source of universal mischief on earth (Il. xix. 91, 126); the entreating and reconciling goddesses (*Λιταί*) who follow after Ate and repair the mischief she has done (Il. ix. 502); and the Furies (*Ἐρινύες*), who avenge all violations of natural and moral order (Il. xv. 204; xix. 260, 418; Od. ii. 135). These divinities are the subordinate agents of the superior gods, the military being mainly satellites of Ares, and the moral serving as the executioners of Zeus and of Hades (Il. xix. 87; iii. 279, compared with xix. 260).

A third class of subordinate divinities, allied to these last, but having their sphere in the material instead of the moral world, are the impersonations of the elements and powers of nature. Such are the wind-gods, the river-gods, the gods of the sea, and the nymphs of the fountains, the groves, and the meadows (Il. xx. 7; xxi. 135 sqq.; xxiii. 195–200). Occasionally a nymph is specified by name as the mother of some hero (Il. vi. 22, etc.); but generally they are spoken of as an indefinite and undistinguishable number (Il. xx. 7). Of the wind-gods, Boreas and Zephyrus are especially prominent. The nymphs of the sea, among whom Thetis, mother of Achilles, is prominent, are daughters of the old sea-gods, Nereus and Phorkys (Il. xviii. 141; Od. i. 72); Amphitrite is goddess of the waves and monsters of the deep (Od. iii. 91; xii. 97); and Poseidon presides over the whole realm of the sea, as his brothers Zeus and Hades do over the air and under the earth. There is also a sun-god (Helius) and an earth-goddess (Gaea) who are honored by sacrifices, especially as witnesses to contracts

(Il. iii. 103, 276). Eos (East), the goddess of the morning, has a distinct divine personality (Od. v. 1), but no worship. The river-gods are invested by Homer with great powers and prerogatives (Il. xxi. 194; xxiii. 142); and as Oceanus is the source of all the rivers and fountains, so is he the origin or genesis of all the gods (Il. xxi. 195; xiv. 244).[1] He, however, comes not to the councils on Olympus (Il. xx. 7), and seems to belong to the gods of olden time. With him is associated Tethys, the all-mother, as he is the all-father (Il. xiv. 201). Kronus and Rhea are still more emphatically gods of the olden time. Kronus is not only dethroned, but, with his Titan children, is imprisoned in Tartarus (Il. xiv. 274–279), whither they were sent down by Zeus, when he took possession of the government (Ibid. 204). Kronus, as the name imports, must have been originally a kind of impersonation of time. Oceanus, the all-surrounding, suggests in like manner the idea of all-encompassing space, while his epithets (the deep-flowing, swift-flowing, etc., Il. xxi. 194), and his name perhaps, denote the ceaseless flow of existence in and around that broad and deep channel. But while the conception of this whole class of divinities doubtless arose from the elemental ideas and powers of nature as represented in the Homeric poems, they are no longer identified with those powers and ideas, nor absolutely confined to an agency within their appropriate spheres. As a general fact, they preside over those elements, rather than are identical with them or personifications of them. They convene

[1] Compare the speculations of the Ionian philosophers, so many of whom make water the first principle. According to the genesis of the Scriptures, the Spirit of God moved upon the face of the waters in the beginning, when God created the heavens and the earth. The analogy is interesting; but the contrast is also striking.

with the other gods in the full assembly of Olympus, and exercise, with more or less freedom, the prerogatives characteristic of Homeric deities. The gods of the early Greeks are far from being mere deifications of the powers of nature. Even the class that approach most nearly to such a system are more or less free and independent of the elements over which they preside; and these same elements are also, at the same time, controlled by the superior gods, especially by the above-mentioned trinity, or triad (Od. ix. 67; ii. 420; Il. i. 479; xii. 17–25).

Our enumeration of the Homeric divinities would not be complete without an allusion to Proteus, Atlas, Circe, Calypso, the Sirens, the Cyclopses, and the other prodigies with whom Ulysses meets in his wanderings over the remote parts of the Mediterranean, and in whose names, relations, and functions, Nägelsbach and Gladstone agree in finding traces of an Egyptian and Phenician origin. Gladstone finds evidences of Phenician (and so perhaps Eastern) origin and ideas in Poseidon, Hermes, Demeter, Aphrodite, Hephaestus, and Dionysus.[1] The only Olympic deities whose names are common to the Greek and Latin languages are Jupiter, Apollo, Vesta, Latona, Proserpina, and Mars. These gods, so far as they take part in the war, espouse the side of the Trojans; and Gladstone regards them as peculiarly Pelasgian deities.[2] The others he supposes to have come into Greece later, with the Hellenic, or Hellic, element of the population. He classifies four, namely, Athena, Apollo, Latona, and Iris, as deities having their basis and the general outline of their attributes and character from tradition; five, namely, Jupiter, Neptune,

[1] Vol. ii. sec. 3. [2] Vol. i. sec. 7.

Pluto, Diana, and Persephone as deities of traditional basis, but with development principally mythological or inventive; and the remaining Olympians as deities of invention or mythology proper.

2. RELATIONS OF THE GODS TO EACH OTHER.

The Olympus of Homer is not conceived, in the main, according to any system of physical or metaphysical ideas, but is modelled according to the analogies of human life. These analogies are partly domestic and partly political; partly those of the family, and partly those of the state.

The principal dwellers on Olympus are the family of Jupiter, consisting of himself, his three wives, his four sons, and his three daughters, who are settled down around him, some married and some in single blessedness; some virtuous and pure, others, like himself, unfaithful to their wedded companions and indulging in unrestrained illicit intercourse with the children of men. The reader is constantly reminded of the Oriental monarch and his harem, of the royal family with their loose morals and manners, and the court with its intrigues and strifes, jealousies, and festivities. There is but little difference between the court and royal family of Priam in Troy and those of Jupiter in heaven, and that difference is decidedly in favor of the earthly sovereign. "It may be laid down as a general rule, that the divine life of Olympus, wherever it reproduces the human, reproduces it in a degraded form. Enjoyment and indulgence, when carried from earth to heaven, lose that limit of honorable relation to labor which alone makes them respectable." [1]

[1] Gladstone, Vol. ii. p. 334.

But a life of ease and sensual pleasure must sometimes give place to the cares of government, even in the court of Jupiter. And then the court becomes a council, and the royal family the councillors. Still, however, they sit with their golden goblets in their hands, and the beautiful Hebe serves them with the delicious nectar, while they look down upon the Trojan city and deliberate on the destinies of the combatants (Il. iv. 1). This ordinary and comparatively informal sitting is called a session (*θῶκος*, Od. v. 3) or council (*βουλή*, Hes. Theog. 802), and bears a close analogy to the councils of the chieftains in the Grecian camp. But on special occasions Jupiter convenes in due form an assembly of all the gods (Il. viii. 1; xx. 4), which is called by the same name (*ἀγορά*), and answers in every respect to the agora of the assembled Greeks, when Agamemnon summons them to consider some question of unusual moment (Il. ii. 51). Themis convenes and dismisses alike the assembly of men and of gods (Od. ii. 69; Il. xx. 4), and by implication keeps order in the meeting. In both alike, a few of the aristocracy alone take part in the debate, as Agamemnon, Nestor, Achilles, Ulysses, Diomed, in the Grecian assembly, so Zeus, Hera, Poseidon, Athena, and Apollo, in the assembly of the gods (Il. viii. 1 sqq.; xx. 1 sqq.; xxiv. 32). And as Agamemnon on earth, so Zeus in heaven, not only presides over the boule and the agora, but holds the result at his sovereign disposal, and sometimes decides and acts in direct opposition to the wishes of his advisers (Il. xi. 78), but sometimes yields his own preferences to theirs, and generally executes and represents, not his own will merely, but the will of the body over whom he presides. Here again, however, the advantage is in favor of the earthly, rather than the heavenly convocation. Zeus swaggers and threatens in a style that would disgrace an Oriental despot (Il. viii. 5–27); the celestials fret and chafe under his tryanny (Il. iv. 20–30); and perchance they settle the difficulty somewhat as the triumvirate at Rome did, by mutually giving over to destruction their most devoted and faithful worshippers (Il. iv. 51 sq.). It would almost seem as if the assemblies and the battles of the gods were intended for a burlesque on those of mortals, so uniformly comical and ludicrous is the representation. Even the so-called Homeric hymns wear very much of this aspect of burlesque, so inconsistent are they with all our ideas of worship or even of veneration.

3. NATURE AND ESSENCE OF THE GODS.

Human analogy does not cease with the mutual relations of the gods. It is the basis of all the Homeric representations of their nature and form. Neither his heroes nor the poet himself seems to have any other conception of the gods than that they are essentially like men. The difference is not in kind, but only in measure and degree. And this anthropomorphous, or rather anthropophuous representation is not, as it manifestly is in the sacred scriptures, the language of figure and of accommodation to human weakness. Nor is it merely the offspring of the imagination, the invention of the poet. It seems rather to be the prevailing, popular, fundamental idea of the divine nature. Not only do the gods assume at pleasure the precise form of men and the likeness of particular men, but they converse face to face, in their own proper form, with their favorite heroes, and enable them to distinguish gods from men (Il. v. 124; xv. 243; xx. 130); they appear, in their own proper form (ἐναργεῖς, Od. vii. 201, cf. xvi. 161), and sit at the feasts of the Phaeacians (Od. vii. 203) and the Ethiopians (Od. i. 26; Il. i. 424); and in their intercourse with each other, whether in war or in peace, whether on earth or in heaven, they are always conceived of as having the form and all the organs of the human body. Thetis takes hold of the bearded chin of Jupiter on Mount Olympus (Il. i. 501); Athena smites Ares on the neck, and overthrows him, in the battle of the gods, on the field of Troy (xxi. 406); Hera seizes Artemis by the wrists, takes the bow and arrows from her back, and raps her smartly about the ears (xxi. 489). We have a full-length description of Hera at her toilet in heaven (xiv. 170), and of Hephaestus at his forge on Olympus (xviii. 411). The gods are of superhuman size, weight, and beauty. Ares prostrate on the field of battle covers seven acres (Il. xxi. 407); the axle groans beneath the weight of Athena, when she mounts the chariot by the side of Diomed (Il. v. 838); and, to say nothing of the epithets applied to the goddesses, and even to such a scapegrace as Ares (Od. viii. 310), Calypso, not exactly an impartial witness it is true, claims that mortals of her own sex cannot compare with immortals in beauty of person (Od. v. 212). But all this so far from disproving, only proves, or rather presupposes a human form. Their blood is called by another name (Il. v. 340); but it flows from their wounded bodies just like the blood of mortals (Il. v. 416). They do not eat bread nor drink wine (Il. v. 341), but they are just as dependent on their ambrosia and nectar for nourishment as men are on their daily food and drink (Od. v. 93, 196–199). The gods are characterized in words as blessed (μάκαρες, Il. i. 339), living a life of ease and pleasure (ῥεῖα ζώοντες, Il. vi. 138), free from care and sorrow (ἀκηδέες, Il. xxiv. 526). Yet they are subject to fatigue and exhaustion (Il. iv. 26; v. 886); they need rest and sleep, Zeus himself not excepted (Il. i. 609); and wounds and bruises and miseries of every kind are so general among them, that when Aphrodite is wounded, and flees to the bosom of her mother for relief, the mother comforts her heart, on the principle that "misery loves company," with a whole chapter of the woes that other and more powerful deities have suffered at the hands of mortals (Il. v. 380 sqq.). The three principal gods are ordinarily exempt from such casualties. Yet even Apollo is condemned to serve the king of Troy a year for wages, and when he would fain touch his heart, Poseidon reminds him of the evils which they two suffered in this long and ignominious service (Il. xxi. 441). And Zeus himself, assaulted by the other Olympians, is protected by the interposition of the hundred-handed Briareus (Il. i. 399). Immortality is the only characteristic distinction which is, with uniform and undeviating consistency, ascribed to the Homeric gods; and when we consider the perpetual sorrows, sufferings, and vexations to which they are subject, we cannot but agree with Longinus, that such an immortality is a doubtful blessing; that it is in fact but immortal misery. So far as we can gather from the Homeric poems, there is no evidence that the Greeks of that age ever conceived the idea taught by our Saviour to the woman of Samaria, as a first lesson in religious truth, and learned by our children in answer to the first question in the catechism, that God is a spirit infinite, self-existent, and unchangeable in his being and perfection. Practically, at any rate, their god was altogether such an one as themselves. And no better definition could be given of the divine nature, as it is habitually represented in the Iliad and Odyssey, than that it is human nature somewhat exalted and exempt from death. The Homeric god is essentially a celestial and immortal man. Accordingly, Immortals is their most frequent and characteristic designation.

4. THE ATTRIBUTES OF THE GODS.

The immortality which Homer imputes to his divinities is a very different attribute from the eternity which we ascribe to God. It is only existence without end.[1] Existence without beginning is an idea which the early Greeks and Trojans never express, and would seem never to have conceived of any of their gods. They trace them back through a series of generations — through Zeus and Kronus (or Old Time) to Oceanus and Tethys, whom they style the all-father and all-mother of the gods; and there they leave the chain unsupported, the mystery of existence as unexplained as if they had stopped with Zeus himself. Perhaps, in common with the earliest Ionian philosophers, the poet conceived of an eternally existing, ever-flowing chaos (which they call water and he calls Oceanus), as the source of all existence, celestial as well as terrestrial, divine as well as human.

In theory, the gods know all things (*πάντα ἴσασιν*, Od. iv. 379), and can do all things (*πάντα δύνανται* Od. x. 306). They know the future as well as the past and the present (Od. xx. 75; xii. 189), and they can act not only near at hand, but they can also help and save

[1] *Ἀειγενέται*, like *αἰὲν ἐόντες*, is simply equivalent to *ἀθάνατοι*.

with perfect ease even at a distance (Od. iii. 231). At the same time, even Zeus is practically ignorant of much that is going on, not only in his kingdom among men, but among the gods in his own court (Il. xviii. 185: *οὐδ' οἶδε Κρονίδης ὑψίζυγος οὐδέ τις ἄλλος ἀθανάτων*). The grossest deception is practised upon him by his ungoverned and unscrupulous consort; and while he is fast locked in sleep in her embrace, on Mount Olympus, his rebellious brother interferes with the execution of his plans and purposes on the field of battle (Il. xiv. 153–400). While he is absent at a feast among the Ethiopians he is no more capable of attending to the progress of the Trojan war or to the petitions of the inferior deities than an earthly sovereign can receive the petitions of his courtiers or regulate the affairs of his kingdom while he is travelling in a far country (Il. i. 423). The mockery which Elijah addresses to the worshippers of Baal, is applicable in every particular to the Homeric worshippers of Zeus: "Cry aloud, for he is a god: either he is talking, or he is pursuing, or he is in a journey, or peradventure he sleepeth, and must be awaked" (1 Kings xviii. 27). Zeus leaves Olympus and takes his station on Mount Ida, when he would watch the battle closely and guide its issues. The inferior gods can see farther and move more rapidly than mortals; but their powers differ only in degree, not in kind; it is not omnipresence or omniscience which they possess, but only human vision and locomotion magnified. They still see with their eyes, and move with their feet, and influence the battle only by their personal, bodily presence (Il. xiii. 10 sqq.).

The moral character of the gods is even more defective than their natural attributes. "In general, the chief note of deity with Homer is emancipation from the restraints of the moral law. Though the Homeric gods have not yet ceased to be the vindicators of morality upon earth, they have personally ceased to observe its rules either for or among themselves. As compared with men in conduct, they are generally characterized by superior force and intellect, but by inferior morality." Such is the language of Mr Gladstone. And the instances which he proceeds to adduce, fully justify this severe verdict. They manifest little love for one another.[1] In his domestic relations Zeus is now a fond and doting husband and father (Il. xiv. 314; v. 879), now a tyrannical one (Il. xv. 17; v. 890; viii. 360, 373). His children envy, hate, and torment each other in heaven (Il. v. pass.), and encounter each other in fierce conflict in the battles of men (Ibid. et Il. xx. pass.). "Force and terror on the one hand, and fraud and wheedling on the other," are the instruments of his family government, if that can be called family government in which the children govern the parents about as much as the parents govern the children (Il. i. 568, 500; xiv. 300). In all these respects however, it must be confessed, Mr. Gladstone to the contrary notwithstanding, that royal families on earth have not generally improved very much on the example of their illustrious predecessors.

The gods do not love mankind as a race. They envy human prosperity and glory as an encroachment on their own prerogatives (Il. vii. 460; xvii. 450; Od. v. 119), and they cherish almost implacable personal resentments against poor mortals who, whether intentionally or by accident, may fail to render to them due honor (Il. ix. 537).

[1] In two or three instances, Apollo and Athena (and they only) are addressed by Zeus with the epithet φίλε, *dear*. See Gladstone, Vol. ii. p. 70.

On the other hand, they have their earthly favorites, towards whom they cherish a blind attachment. Immortals are sometimes wedded to mortals (Il. ii. 820; xi. 1); and Zeus runs through a long catalogue of his mistresses on earth, that he may set forth his superior love, or rather his present passion, for Hera. Athena, Apollo, and Artemis are exceptions;[1] but, as a general fact, chastity is no virtue of Homer's celestials (Od. v. 119).

Holiness, which is the characteristic attribute of the God of the Bible, and which Aeschylus so often ascribes to Jupiter in his epithets (though the conduct of his Jupiter hardly answers to the ascription), is never even predicated of the Homeric gods, and there is nothing in their character or acts to deserve the name. The best of them manifest none of that stainless purity which turns away with unutterable loathing from all sin, and looks with impartial favor and unspeakable delight upon rectitude wherever it is found. Impartial love or hatred is a thing quite unknown in the Olympic circle; if it exists anywhere in the poems of Homer, it is in the hero of the Iliad, who hates falsehood as the gates of Hades (Il. ix. 310), and resents robbery and wrong in the commander of the host as keenly as in the lowest of the people (Il. i. 230, 231). For the sake of peace and quietness in his own family Zeus yields to Hera's insatiable anger against the Trojans, and sends Athena to move them to an unprovoked violation of the treaty of peace; moved by Athena, Pandarus lets fly a treacherous arrow, and wounds Menelaus; and then not only

[1] "The chastity of the traditive deities, Minerva, Diana, Latona, and probably Apollo, I take for one of the noblest and most significant proofs of the high origin of the materials which they respectively embody." Gladstone. ii. p. 356.

Pandarus, but the whole city and people of the Trojans must pay the penalty for the crimes of which, by their own acknowledgment as well as in the view of men, the gods were the authors (Il. iv. 64, etc.). Athena by deception lures on the patriotic and devoted Hector to destruction (Il. xxii. 223 sqq.). Thetis will not trust the word of Zeus, but insists on the confirmation of his irrevocable nod (Il. i. 514). So the sleep-god requires an oath of Hera (Il. xiv. 271); and when Hera finds herself in imminent peril of Jove's vengeance, she calls heaven, earth, and hell, and everything sacred, to witness to an equivocation, if not a downright falsehood (Il. xv. 36). The gods of the Iliad and Odyssey are anything but the unchanging standard of truth and rectitude on earth; in heaven they seem more like the impersonations of self-will and unrestrained license. In character, as well as in mutual relations, the Homeric Olympus is a depraved copy of high life in the Grecian camp and the court of Troy.

5. THE PROVIDENCE AND GOVERNMENT OF THE GODS.

According to Homeric representation, nature recognizes the gods not as creator, but as lord and master.[1] The inhabitants of the deep know their king, and pay him homage, gamboling about the chariot of Poseidon as he rides over the rejoicing sea (Il. xiii. 27). High Olympus trembles when Zeus gives his nod of confirmation (Il. i. 530). And when the gods enter the battle on the plains of Troy, the mountains shake, the earth quakes, and thunders reverberate through the skies (Il. xx. 54). Hera and Athena can not only command the thunder, but they can hasten or retard the rising and

[1] Cf. Nägelsbach, i. 8.

setting of the sun (Il. xviii. 239; Od. xxiii. 347). And all the gods seem to have the power to clothe themselves or to conceal other persons and things beneath a covering of cloud (Il. v. 23, 344; xx. 150; Od. xiii. 109, etc.). A preternatural darkness and a rain of blood signalize the fall of Jove's son (Il. xvi. 459, 567), while on the other hand, flowers of every kind spring up on the instant from the ground, and prepare a bed for Zeus and Hera on Mount Ida (Il. xiv. 347). "In short the supernatural becomes the natural," as Nägelsbach happily remarks, "when it is wrought by a god." It is, however, just these marvellous phenomena, signalizing special occasions, that are instanced by the poet, and that because they suit the poetic imagination, while we find few, if any allusions to the constant exercise of a wise and benignant divine providence over the elements and powers of nature. Poseidon in his unrelenting resentment for the blinding of the Cyclops, persecutes Ulysses with winds and waves and storms and tempests, despite the pity of all the other deities (Od. i. 20); and sometimes even the wind-gods dash in pieces a vessel against the will of their superiors (Od. xii. 290).

Nearly related to power over nature is the power which the gods possess to change and shape at will the human body. This power is exercised with especial frequency by Athena. When Achilles is to reappear for the first time on the battle-field, she invests the hero with superhuman grandeur and glory, which, with the accompanying voice of the goddess, drives all the Trojans, panic-stricken, from the field. And throughout the Odyssey the same goddess is continually fashioning the person of her favorite hero to suit the ever-shifting circumstances of his eventful life, now transforming him to the old and shrivelled beggar who, as his name (Irus) imports, was the messenger and representative of the god of the poor and the stranger, and now clothing him with a divine beauty, which his son intuitively refers to some god who, "coming upon him, easily makes him young or old as he chooses" (Od. xvi. 197); and the father himself explains the marvellous transformation by saying: "This is the work of Athena, who makes me just what she pleases (for she has the power), at one time like the poor beggar, at another like a young man in beautiful apparel; for it is easy for the gods who inhabit the spacious heaven either to glorify (beautify) a mortal man, or to harm (disfigure) him" (Ibid. 211).

The gods direct and control the minds of men also, at their sovereign pleasure. They are continually putting thoughts and plans into the minds of their favorite heroes (*ἐπί φρεσὶ θῆκε* Il. i. 55; Od. xviii. 158 et passim), courage and strength into their hearts (*ἐν σθένος ὦρσεν καρδίῃ*, Il. ii. 451; *μένος ἐν φρεσὶ θείω*, Od. i. 89, et passim), wisdom and eloquence into their mouths (Od. i. 384; xxiv. 260 et al.). In these cases the divine and the human agency are clearly distinguished from each other, and sometimes they are represented as co-ordinate, and the result is ascribed partly to the one and partly to the other (as in Od. iii. 26, Athena encourages Telemachus with the assurance that some thoughts will occur to his own mind, and the god will suggest others); though more frequently the human agency is conceived as subordinate to the divine, and produced, penetrated, pervaded by it (Il. ix. 703; Od. xix. 478, 485; xxiii. 260). Physical constitution, personal accomplishments, native talents and dispositions, intellectual attainments and moral virtues, all the qualities that distinguish or adorn the individual, are the gift of the gods. Prophecy is the gift of Apollo (Il. i. 72), hunting of Artemis (v. 51), skill in the arts of Athena (v. 61) and Hephaestus (Od. vi. 234), horsemanship of Zeus and Poseidon (Il. xxiii. 307), and Zeus allots all gifts to all men as he pleases (Il. xiii. 730). The gods gave manly beauty to Bellerophon (Il. vi. 156), seductive charms to Paris (Il. iii. 54), prodigious size and strength to Ajax (Il. vii. 288), to Ulysses wisdom and power of endurance (Od. xiv. 216), and to Achilles courage and irresistible might (Il. i. 178; ix. 254); but they have not given him self-control (ix. 255); and to Agamemnon Zeus has given the sceptre, but not valor, which is the greatest power (Il. ix. 39). And they not only give or withhold at pleasure, but they also take away at will what they have already given (Il. vi. 234; Od. xviii. 180, 251). Especially is wisdom and council the gift of the gods (Od. vi. 10), a peerless gift to a favored few for the safety of many (Il. xiii. 732); and it is the prerogative of the gods to take away the wisdom of the wisest as well as to impart wisdom to those who are destitute of it (Od. xxiii. 11 cf. Il. vi. 234).[1]

The gods have the absolute disposal of the destinies of men, order their circumstances, and allot to every individual good or evil as they will (*ὅπως ἐθέλῃσιν*, Od. vi. 188). It is in the exercise of this prerogative especially that all power is ascribed to them: "Zeus gives good and evil, now to one, now to another; for he can do all things" (Od. iv. 236; xiv. 444). This distributive providence is set forth under the image or symbol of two casks, which stand on Jove's threshold, the one containing evil and the other good, and from which he

[1] Cf. Prov. ii. 6; iv. 7; Eccl. ix. 15–18; 1 Cor. i. 19.

distributes to miserable mortals usually a chequered lot, to some unalloyed happiness, and to some nothing but sorrow and calamity.

A noble wife is from the gods (Od. xv. 26).[1] Children are their gift (Od. iv. 12; xvi. 117; Il. ix. 493).[2] Riches, honor, power, sovereignty, are suspended on their will (Od. i. 400; xi. 340; Il. ii. 670). The gods mete out all the dangers, difficulties, deliverances, changes of whatever kind in the changeful life of Ulysses (Od. i. 195; iii. 379; xxiv. 401, et passim). The will of Jove is accomplished in all the alternations of victory and defeat, as well as in all the final issues of the Trojan war (Il. i. 5). He spreads his protecting hand over individuals (Od. xiv. 184; Il. xxiv. 374); and he weighs in the balance the fate of contending armies and nations (Il. viii. 71.) Evil as well as good proceeds from the gods, as its original source (Il. vi. 282, 349, 357; Od. iii. 152, 160). Men carry the imputation to such an extreme as to transfer to them the responsibility of their own follies and crimes (Il. iii. 164, et al.). But Zeus repels the charge, and insists that they bring sorrow on themselves, beyond what is allotted to them, by their own folly and madness (Od. i. 33). Long life is by divine appointment (Od. xxiii. 286), and death comes to every individual just when and where Zeus and the other immortal gods bring it upon him (Il. xxii. 365). In short, the divine purpose and agency are as universal and all-controlling in the Iliad and Odyssey as they are in the Bible. Nothing can be more alien

[1] Cf. Prov. xix. 14. The sentiment in the text is uttered by Athena; and yet the wife is the main thing there, while in Proverbs it is the prudent wife and the virtuous woman.

[2] Ps. cxxvii. 3.

to the spirit of both than that atheistic philosophy which excludes God from any immediate concern with the government of this lower world. At the same time there is no trace in Homer of that all-wise paternal providence so universal in the Scriptures, which always watches over the good man, and makes all things infallibly work together for his good.

Life and death, good and evil, are represented by Homer as also the allotment of destiny (Il. xx. 127; xxiv. 49, 209; Od. xx. 76); but this destiny is so often, nay, so generally, spoken of as the destiny or allotment of the gods (*μοῖρα θεῶν*, Od. iii. 269) and the very words (*αἶσα, μοῖρα*) so naturally suggest the idea of a portion, lot, or allotment, that the presumption certainly is, that they mean the will or appointment of the gods, not without reference, however, it may be, to an eternal law of order and rectitude, which they can indeed transcend (*ὑπέρμορα*, Il. ii. 155; iv. 29; xvi. 441–443) and which men are sometimes represented as violating (Od. i. 35), but which the gods do not in fact contravene. There are passages which seem to conflict with this interpretation, yet it accords better than any other with the prevailing language and spirit of the Homeric poems.

6. MANIFESTATION OF THE GODS TO MEN.

In the early ages of the world, some generations previous to the war of Troy, the gods had frequent and familiar intercourse with men. Minos, king of Cnossus (four generations before the war), was the bosom companion and counsellor of great Jove (Od. xix. 179), and Peleus (only one generation previous to the war) was so dear to the heart of the immortals, that Hera gave him to wife the goddess Thetis, and the wedding-feast was graced by the presence of all the gods, and by the music of Apollo and his lyre (Il. xxiv. 60). In like manner, Tros and Laomedon, founders of the royal line of Troy, transacted business with the gods (Il. xxi. 444); Ganymedes, the son of the former, and Tithonus, the son of the latter, were taken up to heaven to dwell with the immortals (Il. xx. 234; xi. 1); and Anchises, the father of Aeneas, was (or ought to have been) the husband of the goddess Aphrodite (Il. ii. 820). Many sons of the immortals fought around the city of Troy, the offspring of frequent intercourse between the gods and the daughters of men in the preceding generation. But at the time of the war mortals are honored or dishonored by no such familiar intercourse. Only favored races and nations, themselves scarcely human, like the Ethiopians and the Phaeacians (the celestials of the heroic age), and a few heroes of rare excellence and special favorites of heaven (and these last only on special occasions), now see the gods face to face (Il. i. 423; Od. iii. 221; vii. 201–206; xvi. 161). And at the time of the poet this has already ceased, and mortals now know nothing of these high themes except what poets teach them under the inspiration of the all-knowing muses (Il. ii. 484.)[1]

Direct personal intervention in the affairs of men is confined to the inferior deities. Zeus sits on high, overseeing and presiding over all (Il. xx. 21); and if he would issue mandates to gods or men, Athena and Apollo are his representatives, and Iris and Hermes are his messengers.

Besides these personal appearances, which take place under a great variety of forms,[2] the gods (chiefly Zeus, Hera, Athena, and Apollo) manifest their presence or

[1] Cf. Nägelsbach, sec. iv. [2] Cf. Nägelsbach, sec. iv.

their will by signs (*σήματα*), wonders (*τέρατα*) auguries (*οἰωνοί*) and prophetic voices (*φῆμαι*); sometimes preternatural, like the bloody rain at the death of Jove's son (Il. xvi. 459), or the frightful appearances that foreboded the slaying of the suitors (Od. xx. 345), but more frequently they are ordinary phenomena, extraordinary only in the time and manner of their occurrence; sometimes of natural and obvious self-significance; sometimes requiring interpretation by the mouth of a prophet (Il. ii. 322), and sometimes ambiguous and intended to mislead (Il. xv. 377–379; xii. 200 sqq.). Omens are of frequent occurrence in Homer, and are generally trusted and highly prized; yet their practical value is not a little impaired by the possibility of deception, which always attends them; hence Hector thinks the one best omen is to fight for his country (Il. xii. 243); and he cares not which way the birds fly, right or left, east or west, so long as he acts in obedience to the direct command of Zeus, conveyed to him by the messenger Iris (Il. xii. 239, cf. xi. 186).

Dreams and visions are from Zeus (Il. ii. 63); yet they are sometimes merely natural or accidental, and sometimes deceptive (Il. ii. passim; xix. 547, 560; Od. xxiv. 12). Presentiments often foreshadow a coming reality, as, for instance, Hector's heart is saddened by prophetic forebodings of the approaching ruin of his country and his family (Il. vi. 447), and the head of Amphinomus is bowed down under gloomy anticipations of destruction to himself and the other suitors (Od. xviii. 153). Ideas and rumors of some great event sometimes so mysteriously pervade the minds of a whole people in advance of the reality, or, at least, of the intelligence, that they were referred to Ossa, as the voice or messenger of Jove (Il. ii. 93; Od. xxiv. 413). In the hour of death men often have a prophetic foresight of the future. Thus the dying Patroclus predicts the death of Hector by the hand of Achilles (Il. xvi. 851); and the dying Hector forecasts in detail the doom of Achilles at the hand of Paris and Apollo (Il. xxii. 358).[1] Prophets hear the voice of the gods, know their will (Il. vii. 45, 53), and thus are acquainted with the past, the present, and the future (Il. i. 70). Guided themselves by Zeus and Apollo (Il. i. 72; Od. xv. 244), they are competent to guide the affairs of men (Il. i. 71; vi. 438). The oracles at Dodona and Delphi already exist in the Homeric age (Od. vi. 327; xix. 296; Il. viii. 79; ix. 405), and individuals and nations go to them to learn the will of the gods. In short, the idea of revelation or manifestation of the gods to men, like the idea of providence, is a universal and all-pervading idea with the men and women of the heroic age.

7. WORSHIP OF THE GODS.

The worship of the gods is as universal among men as the feeling of dependence from which it springs. This philosophy of worship is expressly stated, though in a practical and incidental way, by the prudent and pious Pisistratus, son of the wise and aged Nestor (Od. iii. 46).

The gods claim, as their especial honor and prerogative, offerings at the hands of men, the food-offering and drink-offering, incense and the smoke of burnt sacrifices (Il. iv. 49). This is, as it were, a feast of fat things on their altar (ibid. 48). For this they hunger and thirst;

[1] Cf. Plat. Apol. Soc. cap. xxx. Compare also the prophetic blessings of the dying patriarchs (Gen. xlix. 1; l. 24; Deut. xxxiii. 1).

for this they have a keen appetite and a high relish (Il. xx. 405). Those cities and those individuals are most honored and beloved by the several deities, who offer to them, in particular, the most abundant gifts and sacrifices; if any person or place is saved from destruction, this is the motive for sparing it; if any one is reluctantly given up, this is specified as the ground of reluctance (Il. iv. 44; xx. 297; xxii. 170; xxiv. 69). If angry, their anger is to be turned away by offerings and sacrifices (Il. ix. 499). But wo to the individual who, intentionally or unintentionally, omits to offer the sacrifice which some god esteems to be his due; some dire calamity will soon befall him (Il. ix. 533).

As this interested, not to say selfish, view is often taken of the gods' delight in sacrifices, so from motives of self-interest, for the express purpose of propitiating the favor of the gods, public and private sacrifices are assiduously offered on every suitable occasion by the heroes of Homer's verse. Besides numerous temples, altars, and sacred groves, where offerings are continually made by the priests and priestesses (Il. ii. 549; vi. 88; ix. 405; viii. 48; Od. viii. 363, et passim), who seem to be designated as individuals to this office, and not set apart as a sacred caste (Il. vi. 300), the commander-in-chief offers sacrifices at the head of his army (Il. ii. 411; iii. 271), the king in the assembly of his people (Od. iii. 5), and the father on the altar of the hearth-protecting Jove in his private house (Od. xxii. 335). Offerings and sacrifices are accompanied with prayers (Il. iii. 296, et passim). Hence the priest is called a *prayer* (ἀρητήρ Il. i. 11) as well as an offerer of sacrifices. Prayers and sacrifices precede all battles, treaties, embassies, journeys, and all important public or private enterprises (Il.

ii. 402, 411; iii. 271, 275; ix. 174, 182; Od. ii. 431). Not only public festivals but private entertainments begin with libations and offerings of the choicest parts to the gods (Il. ix. 219). The hero must not even drink wine to refresh his thirst and weariness till he has first poured out a libation (Il. vi. 259; cf. Od. viii. 151). Indeed so universal was the custom of hallowing every employment and enjoyment with a previous libation, that beginning with the cup came to be a technical expression for this initiatory religious service (Il. i. 471). It was customary to begin and end the day itself, as well as every important enterprise of the day, with a religious service, usually a libation (Od. iii. 1–5, 334; Il. ix. 712).

As the sacrifices seem to be offered with a single eye, not to the glory of the gods, but to the attainment of some personal end, so the prayers, as Nägelsbach has remarked, consist for the most part of petitions for some specific object, with comparatively infrequent expressions of thanksgiving and praise, without any such thing as confession of ill-desert, but rather with claims to higher favor, and not unfrequently complaints of unmerited suffering or neglect (Il. i. 503–516; iii. 351, 365; viii. 236). Vows of future sacrifices, as well as catalogues of past services, are urged by the petitioners as motives for granting their requests (Il. i. 39; vi. 308). Obedience to the will of the gods is specified by Achilles as a condition of acceptable prayer, or rather (for even this hero looks at the prayer as a means to a personal object rather than as a duty or privilege) he openly proclaims the fact that the gods hear the prayers of those who obey them as his motive to obedience (Il. i. 216). Formulae of prayer, beginning with a reference to the attributes of the god, and continuing with an enumeration of the claims of the petitioner (εἴ ποτε, κ. τ. λ). are common (Il. i. 37; v. 115); and public prayers are repeated by the whole assembly (Il. iii. 297, 319). Prayer is offered in a standing posture, with uplifted hands (Il. iii. 275, 318), the hands having previously been washed, and the heralds having commanded a sacred silence (Il. iii. 270; ix. 171). The hero, stained with blood and gore, is especially forbidden to worship. When all these preliminaries have been religiously observed, still there is no certainty that the prayer will be heard; the god grants or refuses the request at his sovereign pleasure (Il. ii. 420; iii. 302).

8. INFLUENCE OF THE DOCTRINE OF THE GODS ON HUMAN CONDUCT.

It is the standing reproach of Christians, frankly and humbly confessed by themselves, as well as imputed to them by their enemies, that their life falls far below the standard of Christian doctrine. This, however, reflects no dishonor on Christianity, but rather sheds lustre on it, by showing how lofty that standard is which towers at such an unattainable height above the highest attainments of the best men that have ever lived. But the conduct of Homer's heroes is better than their creed—better, certainly, than we should have expected to result from such a creed. If, when we read the Christian Scriptures, we wonder that such a religion should not carry with it, wherever it goes, a higher individual and national life, the only wonder of the readers of Homer is, how any genuine religious faith and practice could survive the influence of such a doctrine and such an example of the gods. We should presume that such gods could inspire neither respect, confidence, nor affection. Themselves guilty of every vice and crime, it would be strange indeed if their worshippers were patterns of virtue and piety. And it is true that Homer's heroes do not manifest that sacred and awful reverence for their anthropophuous gods which Christians feel towards the infinite and holy One, whom they dare not think of as altogether such an one as themselves. It is true that they do not love their gods generally (even as we have seen the gods do not love mankind in general); they do not love them impartially, still less supremely, as Christians are required to love the Lord their God, with all their heart. Their love is not that reverential, complacential, admiring, and adoring affection which all intelligent creatures owe to their all-powerful and all-perfect Creator; but it is more likethe personal, partial, mutual, and not altogether unselfish, attachment which one human being feels towards another who is greater, but not perhaps better, and not of an essentially higher order of beings than himself. It is not *ἀγάπη*, but *φιλία*; it is not so much religious love and devotion, as it is personal friendship or loyalty towards an earthly superior.

This is especially true of the inferior deities, who have their clients and favorites among men, to whom they stand in a relation resembling not a little that of patrons and guardians. Towards these gods, in this relation, their favorite heroes manifest a loving, trusting, obedient spirit. There is much that is beautiful in the language and conduct of such heroes as Achilles, Diomed, and Ulysses towards Athena, among the Greeks, and such as Hector and Aeneas towards Apollo, among the Trojans (Il. i. 215; v. 815; xx. 86; Od. passim).

But it is the beauty of loyalty and chivalry, rather than that of piety and holiness.

The men and women of the Iliad and Odyssey are habitually religious. The language of religion is often on their tongues, as it is ever on the lips of everybody in the East at this day. The thought of the gods, and of their providence and government over the world, is a familiar thought. They seem to have an abiding conviction of their dependence on the gods. The result of all human action depends on the will of the gods; it *lies on their knees* (θεῶν ἐν γούνασι κεῖται, Od. i. 267 et passim), is the often repeated and significant expression of this feeling of dependence. Submission to their will is a duty, or rather an expediency growing out of necessity, because their power is supreme (ἐπειὴ πολὺ φέρτεροί εἰσιν, Od. xxii. 287 et passim). It is, accordingly, often confessed to be a submission against the will, and not a resignation of the human will itself to the divine (Od. vi. 190; xviii. 135). Hence the Grecian chiefs—Agamemnon, Ulysses, and others, usually devout men who fear the gods—do not hesitate to utter frequent complaints of the will and government of Zeus when he frustrates their plans and disappoints their expectations (Il. ii. 116; Od. xvii. 424).

The games at the funeral pyre of Patroclus, in the twenty-third book of the Iliad, are from beginning to end an illustration of a prevailing practical belief in the reality of providence and the efficacy of prayer. In the chariot race, Antilochus, though driving the slowest horses, enters the race relying on the favor of the gods, together with his skill in horsemanship and the wise counsels of his father, Nestor, and he wins the second prize; the first is borne off by Diomed, the favorite of Athena, through her direct interposition, while Eumelus, whose horses are by far the fleetest, breaks the pole of his chariot, and comes in last. In the foot-race, Ulysses is outstripped by Ajax the swift, till, as they draw near the goal, he lifts a silent prayer ("in his mind," ὃν κατὰ θυμόν, 769) to Athena, when Ajax slips and falls, and Ulysses, with his old limbs all made supple as youth by the goddess, wins the prize. And in the concluding contest with the bow and arrows, the famous archer, Teucer, in his proud self-reliance, without a vow or a prayer, lets fly an arrow and only severs the string that ties the bird, but Meriones waits to vow a hecatomb of first-born lambs to the far-shooting Apollo, though the bird the while is flying away at full speed, and he brings her down from an almost sightless elevation among the clouds (859–880). And all the people gazed and wondered, virtually saying, Amen. So in the race and conflict of life, they do not prosper who contend with the gods of heaven (Il. vi. 129; v. 406), while that man is a match for many who is dear to the heart of Jove (Il. ix. 116). Accordingly, the pious Nestor, Menelaus, and Ulysses triumph over all obstacles, and sooner or later reach home in safety, while the truce-breaker, Pandarus, falls in the battle which follows the breaking of the truce; the profane braggart Ajax, son of Oïleus, perishes by shipwreck on the way home; the proud and sullen Ajax, son of Telamon, goes down to Hades from the plains of Troy; the selfish and reckless Agamemnon is treacherously slain by his own wife and her paramour immediately on his return to his palace, and his murderer, Aegisthus, in turn, meets the just consequences of his crimes (Od. i. 42). As a general law, the characters of the Iliad and Odyssey prosper or suffer adversity according to their deserts. As in history, however, so in the Homeric poems, there are exceptions to this rule. Paris, the ravisher of the Grecian Helen and the cause of all his country's woes, has the honor of slaying Achilles and survives the war, while the upright, pious, and patriotic Hector falls beneath a cruel and irresistible destiny; and Achilles, reverential and obedient to the gods as he is, is envied by them for his brilliant career, like the faultless Bellerophon (Il. vi. 200, cf. 155), and goes down to an early grave on a foreign shore, leaving the enterprise in which he had embarked still unaccomplished. It is, however, a significant fact, that the protagonists of the two poems, on whom the genius of Homer has shed its brightest glories, are both the special favorites of the goddess of wisdom and of the all-wise, all-powerful Zeus; and this alone is enough to make any man a host (Il. ix. 116).

We find in Homer no trace of that divorcement of morality from piety which usually distinguishes false systems of religion. The gods are, indeed, peculiarly quick to resent an insult or neglect in the worship of themselves; but they punish also violations of the moral law. They punish poor mortals for crimes of which they themselves are guilty, and reward virtues in men which they themselves do not practise. They punish with especial severity social and political crimes, such as perjury (Il. iii. 279), oppression of the poor (Od. xvii. 475), and unjust judgment in courts of justice (Il. xvi. 386). And, with all the imperfections of society, government, and religion, the poems present us, on the whole, a remarkable picture of primitive simplicity, chastity, justice, and practical piety, under the threefold influence of right moral feeling, mutual respect, and fear of the divine displeasure; such at least are the motives to which Telemachus makes his distinct appeal when he endeavors to rouse the assembled people of Ithaca to the performance of their duty (Od. ii. 64).

9. THE RELATION OF THE HOMERIC DOCTRINE OF THE GODS TO THE TEACHING OF THE SCRIPTURES.

According to the received chronology, the Trojan war synchronizes with the scriptural epoch of the Judges. And whatever may have been the precise era of Homer's life, it is admitted on all hands that he was a faithful voucher, or (to put the statement in a form less objectionable to the advocates of the sceptical theory) the Homeric poems, if not a substantially true history, are at least a faithful representation of the manners, ideas, and traditions of the heroic age — the age of the war. Moreover, according to their own traditions and all ethnological evidence, the original inhabitants both of Greece and Troy came from those same mountainous regions of Western Asia from which the Hebrews took their origin. It would be strange, then, if we did not find in the Iliad and Odyssey some vestiges at least of the same patriarchal and primitive facts, doctrines, and usages of which we have an inspired record in the Pentateuch and the books of Joshua and Judges. Homer, like Joshua and the book of Judges, makes frequent mention of Sidon, the mother city of the Phenicians (Il. vi. 290; Od. xiii. 285: Josh. xix. 28; Judg. i. 31); also of Thebes, the ancient capital of the Egyptians (Il. ix. 381), whose "strength" ("and it was infinite") had already been brought low in the days of the prophet Nahum (iii. 8-10), that is, as early as the eighth century before the Christian era. The domestic and social manners of the Pentateuch are reproduced almost unchanged in the Homeric poems.[1] In like manner, not a few of the religious ideas and practices of the Old Testament reappear in the Iliad and Odyssey. Enoch walked with God; and he was not, for God took him (Gen. v. 24). So the Homeric gods, particularly Zeus, translate and immortalize their favorites; though beauty of person, and not excellence of character, seems to have been the attraction, and sensuous (not to say sensual) delight, rather than spiritual complacency, was the bond of union (Il. xx. 233; xi. 1). God appears on earth in human form, and converses with the Hebrew patriarchs, face to face (Gen. xviii. 17; xxxii. 30), and he was on terms of still more frequent and familiar intercourse with our first parents in the garden of primeval innocence. So the gods manifest themselves to the heroes in the war of Troy; and they even intermarried with men and women of former generations. The Israelites are a chosen people, to whom God reveals himself in a peculiar way; the Phaeacians and the Ethiopians are the favorite nations with the Homeric gods, who visit them in their own proper form and person, especially at their feasts. The Lord goes down to the cities of Sodom and Gomorrah in person, or in the person of his angels, to see whether they have done according to the cry that has come up to him, and when he finds them sunk in moral corruption, destroys them from off the earth; so the gods, in the likeness of strangers from foreign lands, often visit cities (*ἐπιστρωφῶσι πόληας*) to see the character and conduct of their inhabitants, and reward or punish accordingly (Od. xvii. 485). The supreme god of the Iliad and the Odyssey, as well as the

[1] Cf. Coleridge's Introduction to the Study of the Greek Poets.

God of the Bible, is the god of the stranger and of the poor (Od. vi. 208). Homer, as well as Moses, recognizes the principle, that hurricanes and floods may be, and are, heaven's vengeance sent upon the earth when the wickedness and ungodliness of nations and their rulers are very great (Il. xvi. 384). The titans and giants of Homer are a reproduction of the rebel builders of Babel, and of those antediluvian giants who were the offspring of the sons of God and the daughters of men. Ate, cast out from heaven as a deceiver, and now ever intent upon destroying the children of men, answers in very many particulars to Satan, the great adversary of God and man; while, on the other hand, the Litae, Jove's daughters, who with slow and toilful step, follow the adversary, to repair the mischief and intercede both with their Father and with the erring sons of men (Il. ix. 502), are a beautiful illustration of the principle, and to some extent also of the plan, of reconciliation through a Mediator; and even the rainbow, the appointed symbol of mercy and peace to the world after the flood, reappears in Iris, the rainbow goddess and messenger of heaven.

We have already adverted to the traces of a primitive monotheism in the vast supremacy of Jove over all the other gods, and also to a kind of trinity of persons, manifestations, and agencies in Zeus, Athena, and Apollo, who are so often addressed together in prayer in the triune invocation:

Αἲ γὰρ, Ζεῦ τε πάτερ καὶ Ἀθηναίη καὶ Ἄπολλον·

These three are worshipped, alike by Greeks and barbarians, in every part of the world. These three surpass all the gods in moral character,[1] as much as they do in

[1] On this point, and the whole subject of the Homeric trinity or triad,

their providential power and care over the universe. And these three sustain such intimate and endearing relations to each other that they may be said, in general, to "agree in one."

The father of gods and men in Homer is, of course, the Universal Father of the Scriptures, though sadly defaced and degraded from the infinite Creator and the thrice holy Moral Governor of the universe as he is revealed in the Scriptures. Apollo, the son of Jupiter and Latona (who is scarcely known except as the mother of Apollo), is the seed of the woman, the bruiser of the serpent's head, the source of oracles, and inspirer of prophets, the Logos or Word of God (*Λοξίας*), the bright and shining light (*Φοῖβος*). He is, as his name has been differently explained, both the *ἀπέλλων* and the *ἀπολλύων*, at once the healing or averting and the destroying deity, the god of medicine and the god of the bow; but even as god of the bow, what is most characteristic of him is, that he inflicts death in such a manner as to take away its sting, by his loving and gentle arrows (*οἷς ἀγανοῖς βελέεσσιν*, Od. xv. 411). In the Greek tragedies he enjoys, in common with Zeus, the title of saviour (*Σωτήρ*, Aesch. Ag. 512). Athena is, at least she resembles and suggests, the personal and divine wisdom with whom and by whom God founded the earth and prepared the heavens—the Spirit of God that brooded upon the face of the original chaos, and breathed into it order and beauty; "rejoicing always before him, and rejoicing also in the habitable parts of the earth." Her especial "delight is with the sons of men," and her providential care is over them. She is the guide and

Gladstone is very full, and in the main satisfactory. See the second section of his second volume.

teacher of wise and good men. In short, she is the executive on earth of all the most spiritual functions of the providence and government of the Most High.

The attributes ascribed to Apollo and Athena cannot be explained as the spontaneous development of nature-worship or hero-worship in the mind of the Greeks, still less as the offspring of pure invention.

"They are such as to bring about cross-divisions and cross-purposes, which the Greek force of imagination and the Greek love of symmetry would have alike eschewed. How could invention have set up Pallas as the goddess at once of peace and its industries, of wisdom, and of war? How, again, could it have combined in Apollo the offices of destruction, music, poetry, prophecy, archery, and medicine? Again, if he is the god of medicine, why have we Paieon? if of poetry, why have we the Muses? If Minerva be (as she is) goddess of war, why have we Mars; if of the work of the artificer, why have we also Vulcan; if of prudence and equity, and even craft, why Mercury?

"It seems to be the distinctive character of Minerva in the Homeric theo-mythology, that though she is not the sole deity, yet the very flower of the whole office and work of deity is everywhere reserved for her. ..... The whole conception is therefore fundamentally at variance with the measured and finite organization of an invented system of religion, and, by its own incongruities with that system, it proves itself to be an exotic element.

"Apollo, too, has much of that inwardness and universality of function which belongs to Minerva, as well as a diversity of offices peculiarly his own. ..... The tangled thread runs out without knot or break, when we unravel it by primitive Messianic tradition, because it was fundamental to that tradition, that the person who was the subject of it should exhibit this many-sided union of character and function."[1]

The strange incongruity between the attributes theoretically ascribed to the gods and their character and conduct as it appears in actual life — an incongruity of which we have already spoken, and which strikes every reader of the Iliad and Odyssey — is perhaps to be explained on the same principle. The omniscience, the omnipotence, the universal providence, and the absolute sovereignty which, in theory, belong to the gods, seem like an inheritance of truth transmitted from a wiser and better age, and preserved, like heirlooms, in the memory; while the character and conduct which imply such ungodlike limitations of knowledge and power, and such gross derelictions, not only from divine, but even from human standards of moral excellence, are the inventions of the poet, and therefore in harmony, or certainly not at variance, with the taste and imagination of his contemporaries. Or shall we say that the pure theology is the intuitive and almost unconscious testimony of the reason and conscience of man (wherever it is not wholly smothered by sin) to the truth of God, while the corrupt mythology is the voluntary and conscious invention of an imagination and a heart that does not like to retain the knowledge of the true God, and therefore changes him into the image and likeness of his creatures. Whatever may be the explanation, the contradiction between the theoretical doctrine and the practical representation of the Homeric gods is palpable, and stands out in marked contrast with the harmony

[1] Gladstone, Vol. ii. sec. ii.

and consistency of the divine character even in the Old Testament, how much more with the purity, beauty, and glory of that character as it appears in the New.

In conclusion, then, we say, the poems of Homer illustrate and honor the Bible both by contrast and by resemblance. They bear witness, as it were, in spite of themselves (and it is the testimony not of an individual but of an early cultivated people in a primitive age), to the unity, trinity, omnipotence, omniscience, universal providence, and absolute sovereignty of God, and to his frequent special interpositions in human affairs, and his various methods of revealing himself to the knowledge of men. At the same time, they show how little tradition can be trusted to transmit the knowledge of God and the true religion among the most enlightened people; they burlesque sacred themes, and not only reduce the gods to a level with men, but even make them objects of pity and of derision to their worshippers. The more we study the theology of Homer, the less easily can we believe that the theology of the Bible is the offspring either of tradition or of human invention.

IV.

THE HOMERIC DOCTRINE OF SIN,

ITS EXPIATION, AND ITS PENALTY.[1]

Homer has no word answering in comprehensiveness or depth of meaning to the word sin, as it is used in the Bible; and that for the obvious reason that the consciousness of sin was awakened, the idea of sin was developed, under the peculiar discipline of the Jewish and the Christian dispensations as they never were among the Greeks or any other people of ancient times. The noun *ἁμαρτία*, which is appropriated to express this idea in the Greek of the New Testament, does not occur in the Homeric poems. The verb *ἁμαρτάνειν* is used often in the sense of missing a mark (Il. v. 287) or failing of an object (Od. xxi. 155), but rarely of a sin against the gods, as in Il. ix. 501. The same verse is also the only instance in which *ὑπερβαίνειν*, the etymological equivalent of our *transgress*, is used in the sense of transgression or trespass: *ὅτε κέν τις ὑπερβήῃ καὶ ἁμάρτῃ*, *whenever any one may chance to have transgressed and sinned*, etc., against the gods. The corresponding noun *ὑπερβασία*, *transgression*, occurs infrequently, but always in a moral sense, of the violation of some law of God or man, as, for instance, the crimes of the suitors (Od. iii. 206; xxii. 168), the violation of an oath, which is an offence especially against Jupiter

[1] [Reprinted from the American Theological Review. Vol. iv. No. 2. April, 1862.]

(Il. iii. 107 ; *μήτις ὑπερβασίῃ Διὸς ὅρκια δηλήσηται*), and the sins and follies of youth in general (Il. xxiii. 589).

But the word which is most frequently employed to express wrong-doing of every kind, is *ἄτη*, with its corresponding verb. As this word shows most clearly the light in which sin was viewed by the early Greeks, it demands a somewhat careful examination. The radical signification of the word would seem to be a *befooling*,[1] a depriving one of his senses and his reason, as by unseasonable sleep (Od. x. 68; xii. 372) and excess of wine (Od. xxi. 295), joined with the influence of evil companions (Od. x. 68) and the power of destiny or the deity (Od. xi. 61, cf. xii. 372). The idea of some supernatural power or influence seems always to be associated with this befooling, and its ultimate source is always conceived to be the gods or the fates. Hence the Greek imagination, which animated and impersonated every great power, very naturally conceived of *Ἄτη* as a person, a sort of omnipresent and universal cause of folly and sin, of mischief and misery, who, though the daughter of Jupiter, yet once fooled or misled Jupiter himself, and thenceforth, cast down from heaven to earth, walks with light feet over the heads of men, and makes all at times go wrong (Il. xix. 91 cf. ix. 505). Hence, too, when men come to their senses, and see what folly and wrong they have perpetrated, they cast the blame on *Ατη*, and so ultimately on Jupiter and the gods (Il. xix. 86–90); for the same folly and wrong which in the latter part of this remarkable passage Agamemnon ascribes to the agency of *Ἄτη*, at the beginning he refers to *Ζεύς* and *Μοῖρα* and *Ἐρινύς*.

[1] I here follow very nearly in the footsteps of Nägelsbach, to whose section on this subject (in his Homeric Theology) I am indebted for valuable thoughts, and still more for illustrative passages.

The passage is thus imperfectly rendered by Pope:

> "Nor charge on me, ye Greeks, the dire debate;
> Know, angry Jove and all-compelling Fate,
> With fell Erinys, urged my wrath[1] that day,
> When from Achilles' arms I forced the prey.
> What then could I against the will of heaven?
> Not by myself but vengeful Até driven;
> She, Jove's daughter, fated to infest
> The race of mortals, entered in my breast.[2]"

In like manner Priam, blinded by his fondness for the beauteous Helen, and for her paramour, his false and faithless son, relieves her of all responsibility for the war, by laying the blame on the gods (Il. iii. 164–165):

> "No crime of thine our present sufferings draws;
> Not thou, but heaven's disposing will, the cause."

Yet Helen, in her reply, condemns and despises herself, and makes no attempt to cast the responsibility on the gods (Il. iii. 180 cf. 241; vi. 344). And Agamemnon elsewhere confesses his folly and wrong, repeating the confession (*ἀασάμην*, ix. 116 and 119) and making no attempt to shift the blame on a higher power; and the very same act of injustice to Achilles which in one place is imputed to an irresistible overruling power, is expressly referred in another to the monarch's own pride and self-will (Il. i. 133, 185, et passim). So the riotous suitors and the inconsiderate comrades of Ulysses went under a kind of judicial blindness — nay, under an immediate divine impulse — to their doom (Od. xviii. 346); and yet they went yielding to their violent and

[1] Literally, *folly*, wrong, ἄτην.

[2] The Greek is very expressive: Ἄτη ἣ πάντας ἀᾶται. The agent, the action, and the effect are all expressed by the same root. *Folly which fools all, infused wild folly* (ἄγριον Ἄτην) *into my bosom*. And this Folly is only the executioner of Jove and Fate, and another name for Erinys.

wanton passions, following their own strong inclinations (Od. xvii. 431; ὕβρει εἴξαντες, ἐπισπόμενοι μένεϊ σφῷ). And the two ideas are sometimes brought into immediate juxtaposition, in striking resemblance to the Scriptures. The suitors, says Homer, were destroyed by the appointment of the gods and by wicked deeds. Even so the betrayer of the Lord Jesus went as it was written of him, and yet went under the impulse of his own blind passions, to his own place; and though the Redeemer was delivered up according to the determinate counsel and foreknowledge of God, yet it was with wicked hands that his murderers crucified him and put him to death.

In Homer then, as in the Bible, sin is folly, blindness, madness, so strange that it seems explicable only on the supposition of some external, supernatural, blinding and bewildering agency, and yet so fully and so consciously in accordance with the sinner's own inclinations, and in obedience to his own impulses, that he cannot shake off the responsibility. The wicked suitors have no knowledge; they are as unwise as they are unjust (Od. ii. 282):

ἀφραδέων ἐπεὶ οὔτι νοήμονες οὐδὲ δίκαιοι.

they have wrought folly in Ithaca, as great sinners wrought folly in Israel (Josh. vii. 15; Gen. xxxiv. 7), and the whole people will reap the consequences (Od. ii. 239) unless they purge themselves of the iniquity. And this suggests another point of resemblance. In Homer, as in the Bible, sin is misery, calamity of the most dreadful kind; in other words, sin and its punishment are so inseparable, nay, so identical, that they are expressed by the same word. Readers of the Hebrew and Greek Scriptures are familiar with this so-called Hebraistic usage. But it is even more striking in the Iliad and Odyssey. Ἄτη is both sin and suffering, both folly and calamity, sometimes the one idea and sometimes the other being more prominent, but neither at any time wholly excluded.[1] If the chief idea in any passage is that of folly, yet it is folly leading to calamity, perchance to utter ruin. If, on the other hand, calamity seems in any passage to be the principal idea, it is still only that calamity which results from folly and moral blindness. The whole history of the suitors is a standing illustration of the great fact in the government of God, that moral blindness leads to deeper blindness, and sin is punished by more aggravated wickedness, *till at length persuasions and entreaties are useless* — such is the very language of the poet (Od. xvi. 278) —*for their appointed day of vengeance has already come.* "And even as they did not like to retain God in their knowledge, God gave them over to a reprobate mind, to do those things which are not convenient" (Rom. i. 28).

Man is a frail, feeble, erring, and sinful creature; weakest and most to be pitied of all the animals that live and move upon the earth; easily elated by prosperity, and as easily depressed by adversity; impatient under the latter, proud, self-righteous, and self-confident under the former, and too often rebellious under both (Od. xviii. 130–140).[2] As his tempter (Ἄτη) goes about all over the world (πᾶσαν ἐπ' αἶαν, Il. ix. 506), harming men (βλάπτουσ' ἀνθρώπους), and tempts all and leads them astray (πάντας ἀᾶται Il. xix. 91), so sin and misery are universal in the world. In speaking of the race, however, or of themselves, or of their neighbors and

[1] Hence the mistake of Buttmann in making *calamity* the original and principal meaning of the word (cf. Butt. Lex. sub. v.). That it is a mistake, is sufficiently clear from the usage of the word as illustrated in the text.

[2] This striking passage is quoted below, p. 192.

acquaintance generally, Homer's heroes are much more ready to deplore the misery than to condemn the sin. They never say such evil and bitter things of themselves as David, Isaiah, and Job; and nowhere in the Iliad and Odyssey do we read such pictures of human depravity as we read everywhere in the Law and the Prophets and the Psalms, and not less in the Gospels and the Epistles. "By the law is the knowledge of sin," even as by the gospel is its remedy.

But the Gentiles are not without law. Even in the bible of the ancient Greeks, sin is the transgression of law (ὑπερβασία). Law is that which is laid down (θέμις from θε- root of τίθημι, as *law* from *lay*), settled, established, as the course of nature, the custom of society, the usages of mankind, the rights of individuals, families, communities, and nations; in short, the whole natural, social, and moral order of the universe. All this is included in the oft-repeated phrase θέμις ἐστίν, or ἥ θέμις ἐστίν, which in different connections means, as it is right, as the custom is, as is proper between man and man, as is due to the host or the guest, as is befitting the king and commander, or the subject and the soldier. These various laws of nature and custom, of right and fitness, are all laws of Jupiter (Διὸς μεγάλοιο θέμιστες, Od. xvi. 403), and counsels or purposes of the gods (θεῶν βούλας, ibid. 402), which the wise and good man, like Ulysses, will carefully consult before he proceeds to action, and then scrupulously obey (ibid.) while the foolish and wicked, like the unreasonable and unjust suitors (οὔτι νοήμονες ουδὲ δίκαιοι) or the madcap Ares himself, know no law (οὔτινα οἶδε θέμιστα, Il. v. 761, cf. Od. ii. 281). Jupiter, with the co-operation of the other gods, is the author and executioner of these laws—their guardian and avenger. Moreover, human laws and governments proceed from him as their original source. He gives the sceptre to whom he will (Il. ii. 205, 206); and by him kings reign and princes decree justice; literally before him (πρὸς Διός, Il. i. 239) they guard and execute the laws. So that all laws, human as well as divine, are clothed with something of divine authority, and all violations of them are sins in the sight of the gods.

The duties that spring from this natural order and divine constitution fall naturally under the threefold division common to all ethical systems, and distinctly recognized by Homer (Od. ii. 64–67), of duties to self, duties to fellow-men, and duties to God.

Among the duties which the Homeric hero owes to himself, or the laws which he feels bound to obey, especial prominence is given to the law of self-respect, the sense of personal worth, the pride of ancestral dignity, the desire to excel in bravery, the love of glory, the law of honor, the law of conscience, and the duty of self-control. "Be men, be mindful of yourselves" (Il. xv. 487); "be men, respect yourselves" (ibid. 561); "be indignant at the wrong yourselves, while you also regard the good opinion of others" (Od. ii. 64); or as Pope has the two former passages:

"Be mindful of yourselves, your ancient fame,
And spread your glory with the navy's flame."

"O Greeks, respect your fame,
Respect yourselves, and learn an honest shame."

Such are some of the most frequent and stirring appeals which the leaders address to their troops on either side.

"To stand the first in worth, as in command,
To add new honors to my native land;
Before my eyes my mighty sires to place,
And emulate the glories of our race."

Such is the education which the Lycian Glaucus boasts to have received from his royal father (Il. vi. 206); and the Trojan Hector declares in the same book (442 sqq.) that he cannot withdraw from the deadly fight even to please his wife, for he not only dreads the reproach of his countrymen and countrywomen, but his own soul scorns the ignoble deed, since he was taught to be always brave, and fight among the foremost ranks for his own glory and the glory of his royal father.

"Juno, my son, and Pallas, if they please,
Can make thee valiant; but thy own big heart
Thyself restrain. Sweet manners win respect."

These are the last words of counsel which the aged Peleus addressed to the youthful Achilles when he set out for the war—words which that impetuous hero did not heed, and so want of self-government blighted all the happiness of his brilliant but brief career. It is just this relinquishing of the helm to the control of the passions instead of the supremacy of reason and conscience, which gives Ate the opportunity to bewilder and blind the soul still more, and thus work its ruin. And if the man, blinded and maddened by passion, refuses to listen to entreaty, the very ministers of mercy and mediation between heaven and earth at length turn against him, and plead for vengeance (Il. ix. 510). So that even the sins and follies which the man perpetrates under her blinding influence are voluntary and responsible in their origin, and the calamities which he suffers, and which, like the sins, are called Atae, are self-caused, being the result of the voluntary abdication of the throne by reason and conscience to unrestrained passion, uncontrolled self-will, or, it may be, excessive pride and self-glorification.

Among the relative duties none is more earnestly inculcated or more beautifully exemplified than duty to parents. See the filial love and respect with which the the manly and heroic Hector, the bulwark at once of his family and of his country, still treats his honored mother (Il. vi. 264 sqq.). See the filial spirit of Telemachus, bound up in the fortunes of his long absent father, performing long journeys by sea and land, to glean tidings of his fate, weeping on his neck at the lodge of Eumaeus, defending him, under the guise of a beggar, from the insults of the suitors in the palace, affectionate, confiding, watchful, and obedient to his every word, look, and action, till at length he receives the welcome sign:

> " Slings his keen falchion, grasps his spear, and stands,
> Armed bright for battle, at his father's side."

And in living demonstration of the maxim of one of the Seven Sages, that parents may expect from their children that obedience which they themselves paid to their parents, look at that scene near the conclusion of the Odyssey, than which there is scarcely anything more touching in the whole range of history or fiction, where Ulysses, now victorious over all his enemies, re-established on his throne, and restored to the embrace of his beloved Penelope, cannot rest till he has sought out the aged Laertes, finds him in his garden, clad in rags and toiling at menial employments, weeps in concealment over the sad spectacle, plies his faded memory with facts in their early history to convince him that it is indeed no other than his own long lost Ulysses, and holds him clasped to his bosom, till the old man recovers from the swoon which so unexpected and joyful an event has brought over his bewildered faculties. The boy Telemachus hardly treats his mother with as much respect and deference as the man Hector (for there is scarcely any age at which one submits to maternal authority with so little grace as when he is passing out of his teens); yet he refuses compliance with the demand of the suitors to send her back against her will to her own father's house, and paints in glowing colors the scorn of men (νέμεσις ἐξ ἀνθρώπων) and vengeance of the gods (στυγερὰς Ἐρινῦς) which Providence (δαίμων) will visit on an undutiful son:

> "While thus he speaks, Telemachus replies:
> Even nature starts, and what ye ask denies.[1]
> Thus, shall I thus repay a mother's cares,
> Who gave me life, and nursed my infant years?
> How from my father should I vengeance dread!
> How would my mother curse my hated head!
> And while in wrath to vengeful fiends she cries,
> How from their hell would vengeful fiends arise!
> Abhored by all, accursed my name would grow,
> The earth's disgrace, and human kind my foe!"

In Homer, then, as well as in the Scriptures, "Honor thy father and mother" is "the first commandment with promise"; and the primal curse rests on filial ingratitude and rebellion.

Nearly allied to filial duty is that reverence which is due to age, and which in Homer, as in the Pentateuch,

[1] Literally *it is not possible* to banish her from the house. Compare the similar but still more lofty answer of the youthful Joseph when solicited to sin (Gen. xxxix. 9): How can I do this great wickedness, and sin against God.

is rendered in the most touching and graceful forms. Priam relies on the united power of both these motives to move the heart of the slayer of his son, and urges the plea with a pathos which even the implacable Achilles cannot resist (Il. xxiv. 486 sqq.):

> "Ah, think, thou favored of the powers divine,
> Think of thy father's age, and pity mine!
> In me that father's reverend image trace,
> Those silver hairs, that venerable face;
> His trembling limbs, his helpless person see!
> In all my equal, but in misery!
> These words soft pity in the chief inspire.
> Touched with the remembrance of his sire,
> The reverend monarch by the hand he raised,
> On his white beard and form majestic gazed,[1]
> Not unrelenting; then, serene, began,
> With words to soothe the miserable man."

The Iliad and the Odyssey have each its own matchless picture of conjugal affection and fidelity, the one a Trojan, the other a Grecian pair; the former doomed to a sad parting in the very beginning of their married life, soon after Providence had blessed them with a pledge of their mutual love; the latter destined, after long separation and sorrow, to meet, and, in a serene old age, to enjoy the reward of their mutual faithfulness, but both, though dead, yet speaking to the hearts of millions of the honor and blessedness of pure, unchanging wedded love. Hector and Andromache, Ulysses and Penelope, when will those names ever be forgotten? And who that remembers them can ever forget the lessons which they teach? Over against them in the Homeric gallery stand another pair, blackened and scathed by the indignation of gods and men, standing monuments of the

[1] Οἰκτείρων πολιόν τε κάρη πολιόν τε γένειον.

guilt and ruin of conjugal infidelity — Aegisthus and Clytemnestra; a foul adulterer and a faithless friend, who with murderous hand stabbed their lord and king at the friendly feast, and whom, even in Hades, whither they have been sent by the avenging hand of Orestes, the injured and murdered husband still follows with his curses (Od. xi. 409 sqq.):

> "O wife, thy deeds disgrace
> The perjured sex, and blacken all the race;
> And should posterity one virtuous find,
> Name Clytemnestra, they will curse the kind."

While in Homer, as in the Bible, there is thus a peculiar sacredness about the domestic relations, the violation of which brings down the special vengeance of the gods and the Erinyes, the stranger, also, is under the especial protection of Jupiter, who rejoices in the title of *Ζεὺς ξένιος*, the god of the stranger and the guardian of the rights of hospitality (Il. xiii. 624; Od. xiv. 389), and who will surely avenge any wrong done to the stranger beneath the roof (Od. ix. 266–271; cf. Deut. x. 18), as well as to the host, who affords him hospitable entertainment, (Il. iii. 351–354). The fate of Troy and the catastrophe of the Iliad turn on the violation by Paris of the rights at once of the husband and the host, for which double crime the Trojan king and people have rendered themselves responsible by refusing or neglecting to make reparation (Il. xiii. 625 sqq.), and must therefore suffer a dreadful overthrow.

With the stranger, the poor and needy, the beggar and the suppliant are often associated as under the special guardianship of Jupiter (Od. ix. 266–271):

> "Low at thy knee, thy succor we implore,
> Respect us, human, and relieve us, poor.

At least some hospitable gift bestow,
'T is what the happy to th' unhappy owe;
'T is what the gods require — those gods revere;
The poor and stranger are their constant care:
To Jove their cause and their revenge belongs,
He wanders with them, and he feels their wrongs."

It is a violation of established law (οὐ θέμις ἔστι) to dishonor the stranger; for all strangers and beggars are under the protection of Zeus (πρὸς Διός εἰσιν), a sentiment often repeated in the Odyssey (vi. 207; xiv. 57); and the gods and Erinyes are their avengers (xvii. 475).[1]

An implacable, unmerciful, unforgiving spirit is often censured as unlike the gods, and unbecoming helpless, dependent mortals. The suitors are as unmerciful as they are unjust; and the gods do not love cruel and oppressive deeds (Od. xiv. 82). The aged friend of Achilles warns him to be merciful as he would obtain mercy, and not to scorn the entreaties of men, lest the gods spurn his prayers (Il. ix. 496).

"Now be thy rage, thy fatal rage resigned;
A cruel heart ill suits a manly mind:
The gods, the only great, the only wise,
Are moved by offerings, vows, and sacrifice.
Prayers are Jove's daughters," etc.

"When man rejects the humble suit they make,
The sire revenges for the daughters' sake."

The argument is of the same kind as in the sermon on the mount: Be merciful, for God is merciful; and forgive, that you may be forgiven.

Human laws are not only called by the same name as divine laws (θέμιστες), but are administered under

[1] The like sentiment is repeated with emphasis in the Old Testament (Exod xxii. 21; Lev. xix. 33; Deut. x. 18; Mal. iii. 5).

the same divine sanction. Kings and judges execute law and justice as in the presence and with the authority of Jove (πρὸς Διός, Il. i. 239). The sceptre and the laws are his gift (Il. ii. 205). Heralds are the messengers of Jove as well as of men (Il. i. 334). The oaths by which treaties are ratified and justice administered are witnessed by Zeus (Il. iii. 276), and are even called his oaths (Διὸς ὅρκια, Il. iii. 107); and though he may fail immediately to punish the violation of them, he will sooner or later accomplish the vengeance to which he is pledged (Il. iv. 161), and Pluto, Proserpina (Il. iii. 278), and the Erinyes (Il. xix. 260) will be his unfailing executioners:

"Not thus our vows, confirmed with wine and gore,
Those hands we plighted and those oaths we swore,
Shall all be vain; when heaven's revenge is slow,
Jove but prepares to strike the fiercer blow.
The day shall come, the great avenging day,
Which Troy's proud glories in the dust shall lay.
I see th' Eternal all his fury shed
And shake his aegis o'er their guilty head.
Such mighty woes on perjured princes wait."

Those who, like the suitors, disregard the rights of men, are also charged, as in the form of indictment for murder in the English law, with having no fear of God before their eyes:

"Laws, or divine or human, failed to move,
Or shame of men or dread of gods above."

Such is the indictment of Ulysses against the suitors, who had long promised themselves impunity, but who now at length, are overtaken with sudden vengeance (Od. xxii. 39).

The chief duties to the gods are respect for their

persons, worship at their altars, obedience to their commands, and submission to their will.

The penalty of a direct insult to any divine personage, though it be an infant god or a god disguised in human form, is death. At least those who dare offer such a personal affront to deity never prosper, and never live long upon the earth (Il. v. 406–409; vi. 136 sqq.):

> "Know thou, whoe'er with heavenly powers contends,
> Short is his date, and soon his glory ends;
> From fields of death when late he shall retire,
> No infant on his knees shall call him sire."

> "Not long Lycurgus viewed the golden light,
> That daring man who mixed with gods in fight,
> . . . .
> Nor failed the crime th' immortals' wrath to move,
> Th' immortals blessed with endless ease above;
> Deprived of sight by their avenging doom,
> Cheerless he moved and wandered in the gloom;
> Then sunk, unpitied, to the dim abodes,
> A wretch accursed and hated by the gods."

A sentiment not unlike the woe which the Scriptures denounce on him who striveth with his Maker; but how inferior in moral dignity and sublimity!

Men may expect to enjoy the favor of the gods in proportion to the frequency, abundance, and richness of the vows and prayers, sacrifices and offerings, which they bring to their altars. Throughout the Iliad and Odyssey the gods are represented as moved by such offerings at their respective temples very much as earthly sovereigns are won by presents and obeisances offered in their courts, insomuch that Poseidon rescues Aeneas on the score of his constant and acceptable offerings (Il. xx. 298), and Zeus is almost tempted to contravene the decrees of destiny in favor of Hector because he has burned so many fat bullocks on his altar (Il. xxii. 170, cf. 179). When we read of Nestor sacrificing to Poseidon at nine altars, and nine bullocks on each altar (Od. iii. 7), we are reminded of the thousands of victims which Solomon sacrificed in the middle of the court, as well as on the brazen altar, at the dedication of the temple, though the latter far exceeds the former in the costliness of his sacrifices, as well as in the grandeur and sacredness of the occasion. The neglect to honor any god or goddess with sacrifices which they regard as their due, especially the slight implied in his or her omission while other divinities receive their due honors, is an unpardonable offence. Thus the far-famed Calydonian boar was sent upon the Aetolians in vengeance for neglected sacrifice, because, while the other gods were rejoicing in their hecatombs, to Artemis alone Oeneus, king of the Aetolians, had brought none of the first-fruits of his fields and vineyards; whether the slight was intentional or not, it was a great mistake and a great sin (ἀάσατο δὲ μέγα θυμῷ, Il. ix. 537); and the fields and vineyards of Oeneus must pay the penalty, and the whole nation must be involved in a calamitous war to expiate the offence (Il. ix. 535 sqq.).

An affront offered to a priest or other representative of a god, like an offence against his person or his altar, provokes the divine vengeance. It was Agamemnon's insult to the priest of Apollo and refusal to restore his daughter that brought the pestilence on the Grecian host, and gave occasion to the wrath of Achilles, which was more fatal than the pestilence itself to the Grecian cause; for in this case, as in the somewhat similar case of David, the sin of the monarch was visited primarily on the people, and the king was punished, and punished sorely, through the calamities that fell on them (Il. i. passim, cf. 2 Sam. xxiv).

Robbed of his own captive prize in revenge for proposing the return of Agamemnon's, Achilles is ready to draw his sword and slay the monarch in the very midst of his assembled army. But Athena, sent by the queen of the gods, presents herself before him and bids him restrain his anger, "command his passions, and the gods obey." Achilles instantly obeys, and assigns this good reason for obedience:

> "Hard as it is, my vengeance I suppress;
> Those who revere the gods, the gods will bless."

There is no conviction more deeply inwrought into the minds of all the leading men of both sides in the Trojan war, than this: not so much the right of the gods to command as their power to bless or curse; not so much the duty of obeying the gods, but the sure reward of obedience and the certain punishment of disobedience; and there is scarcely a book in the Iliad or the Odyssey that does not furnish a practical commentary both on the belief and its realization.

From this same superiority of power on the part of the immortal gods over short-lived and changeful mortals, results the wisdom and necessity as well as the duty of fear, of reverence (*αἰδεῖο θεούς*, Od. ix. 269; Il. xxiv. 503), of silent and unquestioning submission to their will: Do not by any means, yielding to folly and rashness, talk large (*μέγα εἰπεῖν*), but leave the matter to the gods,[1] since they are far more powerful (Od. xxii. 287). Such is the sage counsel of the disguised Ulysses to one of the haughty suitors, while in giving the like advice to another, he indulges still

[1] *θεοῖσιν μῦθον ἐπιτρέψαι*, cf. Ps. xxxvii. 5: Commit thy way unto the Lord.

more his natural vein of reflection and argument (Od. xviii. 130 sqq.):

"Of all that breathes or grovelling creeps on earth,
Most vain is man! calamitous by birth:
To-day with power elate, in strength he blooms;
The haughty creature on that power presumes:
Anon from heaven a sad reverse he feels;
Untaught to bear, 'gainst heaven the wretch rebels.
For man is changeful as his bliss or woe;
Too high when prosperous, when distressed too low.
Then let not man be proud; but, firm of mind,
Bear the best humbly and the worst resigned;
Be dumb[1] when heaven afflicts, unlike yon train
Of haughty spoilers insolently vain."

But his warnings are unavailing. Spoiled by prosperity and self-gratification, they all perish, guilty at once of robbery towards man and rebellion against the gods. And not a few of the Grecian heroes triumph over the Trojans in the war only to fall victims to their own pride, folly, and self will on their return to their native land, thus lending the sanction of the greatest of Greek poets to the proverb of the wisest of Hebrew kings: "The prosperity of fools shall destroy them." Ajax, the son of Oïleus, is the most conspicuous warning, who, though wrecked and cast upon a rock, sinned greatly (*μέγ' ἀάσθη*,[2] Od. iv. 503) by declaring that he would escape in spite of the gods, and so Poseidon smote the rock with his trident, and soon sunk the rebel in the depths of the sea. And Agamemnon and Achilles, though neither of them directly rebels or opposes the will of heaven, yet both of them encroach too nearly,

[1] *σιγῇ*; literally, let him keep in silence the gifts of the gods, whatever from time to time they may give (appoint).

[2] This expressive phrase is repeated half a dozen times on the same subject, and occurs often in Homer.

though in very different ways, on the prerogatives of the gods; and the brilliant, self-willed, and passionate career of the latter comes to a speedy conclusion before the fall of Troy, while the former triumphs over his enemies only to perish ingloriously in the embrace of his friends.

The paramount fundamental principle, then, which Homer inculcates in regard to sin is, that it is sure to meet with deserved punishment. For this both parties habitually pray (Il. iii. 320; iii. 351):

> " Who'er involved us in this dire debate,
> Oh give that author of the war to fate."

> " Give me, just Jove, to punish lawless lust,
> And lay the Trojan gasping in the dust;
> Destroy the aggressor, aid my righteous cause;
> Avenge the breach of hospitable laws!
> Let this example future times reclaim,
> And guard from wrong fair friendship's holy name."

This they confidently expect. Jove will not be an abettor of falsehood and perjury (Il. iv. 235). Solemn treaties and sacred oaths cannot be violated with impunity (Il. iv. 158):

> " When heaven's revenge is slow,
> Jove but prepares to strike the fiercer blow.
> The day shall come, the great avenging day,
> Which Troy's proud glories in the dust shall lay,
> 'T is not for us, but guilty Troy to dread,
> Whose crimes sit heavy on her perjured head."

And these prayers are heard, these expectations are realized; in the progress of the war and in the final issue, justice usually prevails, and crime generally meets with its deserved punishment.

These passages illustrate also the object or end of

17

punishment. It is partly to satisfy divine justice or hatred of sin, and partly to deter others from transgression. Zeus is angry with fraud and wrong, and therefore shakes his dreadful aegis over the wicked (Il. iv. 167), and others will fear to repeat the crime, even in future generations (Il. iii. 353).

Punishment is the penalty due to sin; or, to use a favorite expression of Homer, not unusual in the Scriptures also, it is the payment of the debt incurred by sin. When he is punished, the criminal is said to pay off, or pay back (*ἀποτίνειν*) his crimes; in other words, to expiate or atone for them (Il. iv. 161, 162):

> σύν τε μεγάλω ἀπέτισαν,
> σύν σφῇσιν κεφαλῇσι, γυναιξί τε καὶ τεκέεσσιν.

that is, they shall pay off, pay back, atone, etc., for their treachery, with a great price, with their lives, and their wives and children. Or rather, to show the certainty of this atonement, the past tense is used, and they are represented as having already made the atonement.[1] The same verb is used of the suitors, with an accusative of the crime to be expiated or atoned for (Od. xiii. 193):

> πρὶν πᾶσαν μνηστῆρας ὑπερβασίην ἀποτῖσαι.
>
> "Till the suitors shall have atoned for all their transgression."

The middle voice of the same verb is employed in the sense to get payment for an offence, to take satisfaction for a crime, in other words, to take vengeance on the offender and punish the criminal (Od. iii. 206, 216). The prevailing sentiment of the Iliad and Odyssey is,

[1] Cf. Rom. viii. 30: οὓς δὲ ἐδικαίωσεν, τούτους καὶ ἐδόξασε: "Whom he justified, them he also glorified," though the glorification was not yet accomplished, but it was the certain result of the justification.

that punishment is the proper, and only proper, expiation of sin.

At the same time the doctrine is expressly taught that the gods may, and sometimes do, remit the penalty, when duly propitiated by prayers and sacrifices accompanied by suitable reparation (Il. ix. 497 sqq.):

"The gods, the only great and only wise,
Are moved by offerings, vows, and sacrifice;
Offending man their high compassion wins,
And daily prayers atone for daily sins.
Prayers are Jove's daughters, of celestial race,
Lame are their feet, and wrinkled is their face;
With humble mien and with dejected eyes,
Constant they follow where Injustice flies;
Injustice swift, erect, and unconfined,
Sweeps the wide earth, and tramples o'er mankind,
While Prayers, to heal her wrongs, move slow behind.
Who hears these daughters of almighty Jove,
For him they mediate to the throne above:
When man rejects the humble suit they make,
The sire revenges for the daughters' sake.
From Jove commissioned, fierce Injustice then
Descends to punish unrelenting men."

There are many points of great interest in this remarkable passage. In the first place, *Sin* (*Ἄτη*, rendered Injustice by Pope) is here made to be the punishment of sin unrepented and unforgiven. In the second place, it is expressly taught that the gods are sometimes propitiated, and turned from their purpose (*παρατρωπῶσ'*) to punish sin, by prayers, vows, and sacrifices offered by the sinner. In the third place, prayers are impersonated, and represented as mediators between heaven and earth, daughters of Jove and divine, yet meek and lowly, feeble and marred, who, when accepted by the sinner, intercede in his behalf with the king of gods and men, but, if rejected, plead for double vengeance on his head.[1]

We have a practical illustration of this doctrine in the first book of the Iliad, where Apollo averts the pestilence from the army, when the daughter of his priest is returned without ransom, and a sacrifice (ἑκατόμβη, vs. 447) is sent to the altar of the god at sacred Chrysa. Here, too, there is an intercessor, whose prayers accompany the offerings, and make sure their acceptance with the god, and that no other than the injured priest whose wrongs had first brought the pestilence upon the Grecian host. Apollo hearkens to the intercession of his priest, accepts the sacred hecatomb, is delighted with the accompanying songs and libations, and sends back the embassy with a favoring breeze and a favorable answer to the army, who meanwhile have been purifying themselves (ἀπελυμαίνοντο, vs. 314) and offering unblemished hecatombs of bulls and goats on the shore of the sea which washes the place of their encampment.

The question has been raised whether in this and the like cases in the Iliad and Odyssey we have a proper sin-offering, which is supposed to have a truly atoning and piacular efficacy, or whether it is only in the nature of a gift accompanying the prayers, like presents to an earthly sovereign, and intended to add efficiency to the reconciling power of the petitions. It is not easy to meet this question with a decisive answer. The manner in which the gods speak of these sacrifices as their prerogative and portion (τὸ γὰρ λάχομεν γέρας ἡμεῖς, Il. iv. 49 et passim) and the personal, not to say animal,

[1] Hence these Prayers (Ἀραί) become Curses in other passages in the Iliad (xii. 334), and in the Attic tragedies, another name for the Erinyes (Soph. Eum. 417).

rather than moral, satisfaction with which they receive and enjoy the δαιτός ἐΐσης λοιβῆς τε κνίσσης τε (ibid. 48), favor the latter supposition. At the same time, the accompanying rites and ceremonies, the forms of expression and sometimes the expressed object of the sacrifice bear a striking resemblance to those of the Israelites in the Old Testament, and suggest a similar original intention, though they have already lost not a little of their high and sacred moral significance. The object of the propitiatory embassy to Apollo in the first book, for example, is thus stated by Ulysses: Agamemnon, king of men, has sent me to bring thy daughter, Chryses, and to offer a sacred hecatomb for (ὑπέρ) the Greeks, that we may *propitiate* (ἱλασόμεσθα) the king who now sends woes and many groans upon the Argives (442 sqq.); and the language certainly approximates at several points very closely to that of the Pentateuch, and of the Epistles to the Romans, and the Hebrews. Again, the sacrificial lambs and cups of wine, which were offered in ratification of a solemn treaty, represented the parties to the treaty, and symbolically bore the curse of its violation; hence they could not be eaten and drunk, but the wine was poured out on the ground as an offering to the gods, with the accompanying imprecation: so let their brains be poured upon the ground who first break the treaty; and the lambs, if sacrificed by the people of the country, were buried in the ground; if by strangers, were thrown into a sea or river (Il. iii. 210 sqq.; xix. 267).[1]

As to the punishment of sin in another world, Homer is explicit only in regard to great criminals, such as

[1] Cf. Owen's Iliad, iii. 310, and Smith's Dictionary of Antiquities, under "Oath."

perjured persons and those guilty of unnatural crimes towards men or rebellion against the gods. Pluto, Proserpina, and the Erinyes are habitually invoked as the powers that, under the earth, punish departed souls who have sworn falsely (Il. iii. 278; xix. 259). And Ulysses, in his visit to Hades, sees Tityus, Tantalus, Sisyphus, and the like monsters of iniquity, suffering perpetual tortures corresponding to their crimes (Od. xi. 576, sqq.).

"There Tityus, large and long, in fetters bound,
O'erspreads nine acres of infernal ground;
Two ravenous vultures, furious for their food,
Scream o'er the fiend and raven in his blood,
Incessant gore the liver in his breast,
The immortal liver grows, and gives th' immortal feast.
"There Tantalus, along the Stygian bounds,
Pours out deep groans (with groans all hell resounds);
Even in the circling floods refreshment craves,
And pines with thirst amidst a sea of waves;
When to the water he his lip applies,
Back from his lip the treacherous water flies."

Next he beholds Sisyphus:

"With many a weary step, and many a groan,
Up the high hill he heaves a huge round stone;
The huge round stone resulting with a bound,
Thunders impetuous down, and smokes along the ground.
Again the restless orb his toil renews,
Dust mounts in clouds and sweat descends in dews."

In general, the lower world as represented by Homer in his famous Nekyia, is not so much a state of retribution, as an image and shadow of the present life, where mortals all live again, or rather live on, and live forever, retaining the same character and habits, and following the same or similar pursuits, as they followed and possessed in the upper world — an idea of future existence which seems to have prevailed among simple people, and in barbarous tribes, in all ages, from the earliest inhabitants of the East to the aboriginal tribes of our western wilderness, as is evidenced by the articles which they bury with their dead and the offerings which they bring to the graves of departed friends. Thus Orion is a giant hunter still, and still drives the savage beasts before him with his ponderous club, while Minos still bears a golden sceptre, and administers justice to the dead, and Agamemnon, Ajax, and Achilles, each preserves unchanged and unchangeable the essential character which he had when he trod the earth and breathed the upper air. Positive punishment seems to be inflict-only on heinous offenders. Others reap the natural consequences of their conduct in this life; only their character is there as unalterable as their state, and their ruling passions are intensified at the same time that they are removed beyond the reach of those objects which on earth afforded them gratification. It is at best a gloomy picture which the poet draws of the other world. It is situated on the extreme border of the ocean at the remotest south. Near it dwell the Cimmerians, enveloped in perpetual mist and cloud, never visited by one ray of the rising or the setting sun (Od. xi. 13 sqq). It is described by Ulysses and by those who dwell there as a joyless land (*ἀτερπέα χῶρον*, 94), far from the light of the sun, beneath misty darkness and thick gloom (155). The inhabitants of that world are usually spoken of as souls (*ψυχαί*, x. 530; xi. passim), repeatedly as powerless heads (*ἀμενηνὰ κάρηνα*, x. 536; xi. 29); they are also called images (*εἴδωλα*, 83, 476) and are compared with a shadow or a dream (207). They cannot embrace the living, because they no longer have flesh and bones, which were consumed by the funereal fire (219); yet they have muscles or sinews (ἶνες, ibid.), and the sweat rolls down the members (μελέων) of Sisyphus as he rolls the huge round stone, just as if he were still in the body. Moreover, a kind of animal appetite draws them in crowds, whole tribes and nations (ἔθνεα νεκρῶν, 34), to drink the offerings of honey, wine, and water, and especially of sacrificial blood, and it is only by drinking the blood that they are enabled to recognize Ulysses and converse with him. They all weep over their wretched state, and sigh for departed and lost objects of affection. When Ulysses congratulates the shade of Achilles on ruling with powerful sway among the dead, as he had ruled on earth among the living, he replies that he would rather live (489 sqq.),

> "A slave to some poor hind that toils for bread,
> Than reign the sceptred monarch of the dead."

He speaks disparagingly of the mental faculties as well as of the physical powers of the departed, calling them the witless dead (νεκροὶ ἀφραδέες), mere images of departed mortals (βροτῶν εἴδωλα καμόντων, 476). Yet the very purpose for which the hero of the Odyssey goes to Hades, is to learn facts about his family and his own future, which not even the goddess Calypso could unvail to him; and most of those with whom he converses know more than he does of the present state of their mutual friends on earth; indeed they derive their poor pleasures chiefly from their knowledge of the upper world, even as their many woes flow chiefly from its remembrances, resentments, and regrets. The highest pleasure, not to say the only pleasure, of which the son of a goddess and the greatest hero of the heroic age seems to be capable, is the exultation which he feels when Ulysses extols the bravery of his son; and poor Ajax is still tortured with the same resentment which, in a fit of madness, sent him down to Hades, and, still implacable, refuses to speak to his successful competitor, while that competitor, though still in the body and subject to all the passions of earth, softened by the sad spectacle, wishes he had never won the prize. Thus full of errors and contradictions is the poet's picture of a future state. Still Homer bears unequivocal testimony to the great doctrine of retribution, and the soul of man everywhere intuitively believes not only in its own immortality, but in that fundamental doctrine of revelation as an eternal and immutable law of its being: "Whatsoever a man soweth, that shall he also reap."

V.

THE THEOLOGY OF AESCHYLUS.[1]

THERE could be no greater misapprehension of the ancient Greek drama, than to judge of it by the modern theatre. They have little in common but the name. The points of contrast are more numerous and more striking than the points of resemblance. The modern drama is exhibited within doors, in the night, and by gas-light or candle-light. The ancient was by day, in the open air, and beneath the broad, pure light of heaven. The modern theatre is a common building; and though of extraordinary size and splendor, yet enclosed by walls and roof, and capable at most of containing only two or three thousand people. The Greek theatre was hewn out of the solid rock in the side of the Acropolis, or built up with quarried stone on a scale of similar magnificence; and it counted its audience by tens of thousands. The spectators in a Parisian theatre can see nothing but the theatre, with its temporary and insignificant adornings. The Acropolis, the Agora, the porticoes, the temples and altars of the gods, all the architectural splendors of Athens, clustered around those who gathered in the theatre of Dionysus; all the natural and historical glories of Attica were spread before them. As they had no covering but the blue sky, and no light but the bright sun — the singularly deep, liquid, blue

[1] [Reprinted from the Bibliotheca Sacra, Vol. xvi. No. 62, April 1859.]

sky, and the wonderfully bright sun of Greece — so the horizon was the only limit to their field of vision.

The modern theatre is a private speculation, patronized it may be by royalty, and sometimes attended by the aristocracy, where monarchy and aristocracy exist, but for the most filled and supported by the lowest and the worst of the population. At Athens, the theatre was a public institution, the expenses were paid, directly or indirectly, out of the public treasury; the government was the proprietor and manager, and the audience was the enlightened, the refined, the sovereign people of Athens, together with the *élite* from all the principal cities of Greece. The theatre, as it now exists in the cities of Europe and America, is generally, if not universally, a school of vice and crime, in which bad men and women teach other men and women, not quite so bad as themselves, to gratify their appetites and passions, and to become the pests of society. The theatre, as it was in its palmy days in the Grecian cities, was a school of good morals and religion, taught by the wisest and best men of their times; for such were the tragic poets in the age of the immortal triumvirate of Greek tragedy; and the poets themselves were not only the authors but the actors, or at least the trainers of the actors, of their own dramas; and as tragedy was the consummate flower of Greek poetry,— the epic and the lyric, the objective and the subjective, united in one perfect blossom,— so was it also the opening bud of ethical philosophy and theology. As it was taught in the school of Homer and Pindar, so was it the teacher of Socrates and Plato, and of the great Athenian orator, in whom the ethics as well as the eloquence, the practical philosophy as well as the elegant literature, of Greece culminated. Such is the rank which Milton assigns the tragedians in his splendid description of Athens in the Paradise Lost:

> "What the lofty, grave tragedians taught
> In chorus or iambic, teachers best
> Of moral prudence, with delight received,
> In high sententious maxims, while they treat
> Of fate and chance, and change in human life,
> High actions and high passions best describing."

The modern drama aspires only to amuse the theatre-going multitude. The ancient was designed not more for entertainment than for instruction. Modern theatrical entertainments, if not in open hostility to religion, are habitually irreligious. Greek tragedy grew up in connection with religious worship, and constituted not only a popular but a sacred element in the festivals of the gods.[1] "The theatre was invented," says an old Roman writer, "for the worship of the gods, and for the delight of men."[2]

In short, strange as it may sound in modern ears, the Greek stage was, more nearly than anything else, the Greek pulpit.[3] With a priesthood that sacrificed but did not preach, with few books of any kind and no Bible, the people were, in a great measure, dependent on oral instruction for knowledge; and as they learned their rights and duties as citizens from their orators, so they hung on the lips of the "lofty, grave tragedians" for instruction touching their origin, duty, and destiny as moral and immortal beings. As the Pnyx was their

[1] In may be said, that the modern drama had a similar origin in the Mediaeval "Mysteries." But it has quite forgotten its original.

[2] Theatra excogitata cultus deorum et hominum delectationis causa. Valerius Maximus, as quoted by Blackie, who places the passage on the title-page of his translation of Aeschylus into English verse.

[3] [The word pulpit is derived from the Latin pulpitum, *stage*.]

legislative hall, and the Bema the source of their deliberative eloquence, so their demonstrative eloquence, the eloquence of the pulpit, proceeded from the stage and resounded through the theatre. Greek tragedy is essentially didactic, ethical, mythological, religious. It was the express office of the chorus, which held the most prominent place in the ancient drama, to interpret the mysteries of Providence, to justify the ways of God to men, to plead the cause of truth, virtue, and piety. Hence, it was composed usually of aged men, whose wisdom was fitted to instruct in the true and the right, or of young women, whose virgin purity would instinctively shrink from falsehood and wrong. The chief end of tragedy, according to Aristotle, is to purify the heart and regulate the passions; to which end, the rhythm of the choral dance, the harmony of the music, and the metre of the verse conspired with the moral lessons more directly taught by the characters, the chorus, and the plot. Tragedy, in its very nature, as conceived by the Greeks, transported the hearer out of himself and away from the present. It carried him back towards the origin of our race, up nearer to the providence and presence of the gods, and on toward the retributions of another world. With few exceptions, the subjects are mythological. The characters are heroes and demigods, monsters, it may be, in crime, but their punishment is equally prodigious: sin and suffering always go together. They illustrate, by their lips and in their lives, the providence and the retributive justice of God. The plot turns on some great principle of the divine government, which is further explained and enforced in the sublime strains of the chorus. The myth, out of Homer or Hesiod — no myth, but a sacred reality, to the audience — is the text; the corypheus is the preacher; and the choir repeat the doctrine, investing it with all the sanctity and majesty of their sacred lyrics. Nor is prayer wanting in these ancient *liturgies* (λειτουργίαι), since the choruses consist, in no small part, of direct addresses to the deity.

While this is more or less true of all the great masters of Greek tragedy, Aeschylus is pre-eminently the theological poet of Greece. The gods themselves, the inferior gods, are not unfrequently the actors as well as the subjects of his dramas; and they handle the grand themes of theology very much as they are handled by the good and evil angels in the Paradise Lost. His human characters, even though stained with blood, breathe sentiments of piety; or if they dare utter proud or rebellious words, it is but a prelude to their certain and dreadful overthrow. The great problems which lie at the foundation of religious faith and practice — the same problems which are discussed by Job and his three friends — are the main staple of nearly all his tragedies. With him, these were not idle speculations. They were practical questions, with which his own mind had manifestly struggled, on which his own destiny was suspended, and into the solution of which he enters with not a little of the earnestness of a personal religious experience. The earlier poets — Homer, Hesiod, the sacred poets, and the authors of the so-called Homeric hymns — had looked at them in their more purely poetical aspects, had believed the myths, perhaps, with a more literal and implicit faith. The subsequent philosophers — Plato, Aristotle, Plutarch — developed them more fully in a system of doctrines. Aeschylus stands on the dividing line between them, no less poetical than the former, scarcely less philosophical than the latter, but more intensely practical, personal, and theological than either. The poet who most resembles him in modern times, is the Puritan poet of Old England. A believer in metempsychosis might well maintain that the same soul dwelt in them both. To say nothing of the obvious resemblance between the Prometheus of the former and the Satan of the latter — which was in part, doubtless, the result of intentional imitation — and not to speak of a similar license in coining, or rather forging, ponderous poetical epithets, both were characterized by the same matchless sublimity, both possessed by the same strong political and patriotic sympathies, and both fired with the same intense earnestness of religious feeling. Dante was another kindred spirit. The Inferno, the Paradise Lost, and the Prometheus Bound, should be read and studied together. The Agamemnon is often and justly compared with Macbeth. But the English tragedy illustrates more the workings of the human soul, while the Greek leads us to think almost entirely of the providence of God. In this respect, perhaps, the tragedies of Aeschylus find their nearest counterpart in the Book of Job. On the whole, there is no other book of which the reader of Aeschylus will be more frequently reminded: the form of both is dramatic; the scene in both is primitive; the characters are the patriarchs and princes of an early age; the interlocutors discuss the same subjects; the same sublime and awful mystery casts its dark shadow over them; they grapple with themes too vast for their comprehension; they wrestle with beings too mighty to be resisted; they are overwhelmed with the contrast between the littleness and vileness of man, and the majesty and glory of God; and they cry out: "What is man, that he should be pure? How shall man be just with his Maker? Who, by searching, can find out God? Lo, these are parts of his ways; but the thunder of his power who can understand?" It is not, then, a misnomer, to speak of the theology of Aeschylus; nor can it fail to be a question of deep interest: What were the theological opinions of such a mind, so far removed from the light of revelation?

1. SOURCES OF RELIGIOUS KNOWLEDGE.

One of the first questions which naturally arise in considering such a subject, is the source or sources from which the thoughtful and devout who lived before the dawn of revelation derived their religious faith, and what the authority on which it rested.

The most fruitful of all these sources is tradition; tradition, however, having its origin, according to the common opinion, in a primeval revelation or direct communication from God. They received their religious opinions and observances — the religion of the family and the religion of the state — as an inheritance from their fathers, who, in like manner, had received the same bequest from theirs; and thus it had come down, like the heir-looms in their families, like the blood in their veins, from their earliest progenitors. Nor did they deem this mere blind credulity, trusting in a long line of ancestors, each as ignorant as themselves, and therefore the entire chain hanging without any support. They claimed not to rest on human authority as their ultimate reliance. The higher and better classes, the aristocracy of wisdom and goodness as well as of birth, traced their religion, as they did their race, back ultimately to the gods, or to men who walked with the gods and talked with them face to face, like our first parents and the patriarchs of the Old Testament. The universality of this persuasion would, of itself, entitle it to no small credit as an instinctive belief, if it were not expressly sanctioned by revelation; and corrupt and erroneous as many of the superstitions (that is, surviving relics of the earliest times) are, which the different heathen nations thus hold in common, yet there is enough of general resemblance, both in the form and substance of these traditions, to justify the belief that they did originally proceed from the same source, and that a primeval revelation or direct communication from heaven:

> "Such thoughts, the wreck of Paradise,
> Through many a dreary age,
> Upbore whate'er of good or wise
> Yet lived in bard or sage."[1]

On the subject of future punishment especially, the Greek poets and philosophers are in the habit of appealing to tradition. Thus Plato habitually throws his descriptions of a future state into the form of a *myth*, as he sometimes calls them, though at others he is careful to declare, that they are not μῦθοι but λόγοι (cf. Gorgias, 523), whose truth he does not indeed know, but he believes them to be true, and insists that they are entitled to universal belief.[2] In reference to the gods, also, he says (Timaeus, 40, D.), that "the subject is too great for us, but we must believe those who have spoken of it aforetime, who, being, as they said, the offspring of

[1] Keble's Groans of Nature.

[2] Compare the Seventh Epistle, where it is said: "We ought always to believe those ancient and sacred words, which declare the soul to be immortal," πείθεσθαι δὲ οὕτως αἰεὶ χρὴ τοῖς παλαιοῖς τε καὶ ἱεροῖς λόγοις, οἳ δὴ μηνύουσιν ἡμῖν ἀθάνατον ψυχὴν εἶναι.

18*

the gods, doubtless knew their own sires, and must not be disbelieved when they tell us, as it were, things pertaining to their own household." And so Aeschylus, when he speaks of a great truth in reference to the unseen world, or a great law of the divine providence and existence, very often refers to it as a λόγος (Suppliants, 230; Eumenides, 4, etc.),[1] or a μῦθος (Choephoroe, 312, etc.), and often applies to it an epithet, such as γέρων, τριγέρων, παλαίφατος (Ibid.; Agamem. 750), expressive of its antiquity and sacredness.

Nearly allied to these sacred traditions are those world-old and world-wide maxims of wisdom, virtue, and piety, which being the voice of mankind, are also the voice of God: vox populi, vox Dei; which Aeschylus delights to honor, like the old English poet,[2]

> "The people's voice the voice of God we call,
> And what are proverbs but the people's voice,
> Coined first, and current made by public choice?
> Then sure they must have weight, and truth withal."

Oracles are another source of religious knowledge, and especially of guidance in religious duty, to which Aeschylus often alludes, and generally in terms of profound respect. Thus Inachus, father of Io, sends frequent messengers to Pytho (Delphi), and to Dodona, to learn what he must do or say to please the gods, and receives in return "ambiguous answers, obscurely worded and hard to be understood" (Prometheus Vinctus, 660 sq.). But at last there came a clear and distinct response, commanding the father to banish his daughter from home and country, and let her wander

[1] The citations are made according to the Leipsic edition of Tauchnitz. The arrangement differs much in different editions.

[2] Cited by Trench in his Lessons on Proverbs.

an exile to distant lands, under penalties so frightful as to enforce an instant though reluctant obedience. Jupiter is the original source of oracles. They are communicated, however, for the most part, through Apollo, Jupiter's son and prophet (Eumenides, 18), who derives his surname Loxias from his prophetic office, being as it were the λόγος, word of Jove,[1] and who, from his prophetic seat, never gives forth a response which his father, and the father of the Olympian gods, has not commanded him to give (Eumen. 616).[2] Apollo, of course, ordinarily speaks through the lips of his inspired priestess, who is his voice, as he is Jove's; though in the Eumenides, Apollo is represented as appearing in his own person as one of the characters of the drama, and pleading with his own lips the cause of Orestes. Aeschylus never intimates a doubt of the inspiration of the priestess. He is manifestly a sincere believer in the divine authority of oracles. So were all the wise and good in the wisest and best ages of Grecian history. And ambiguous as they often were, perverted as they sometimes were to partizan and selfish purposes, their influence was, on the whole, on the side of truth and justice. Greece, and the ancient world, were the better for their existence. What forbids us to suppose that they were in some sense directed and overruled by Providence, and instead of being under the control of evil spirits, which was the prevailing theory among the Christian Fathers, were intended to be the forerunners among the heathen, as the prophets were among the Jews, of the Christian revelation? With this suppo-

[1] According to another interpretation, this surname denotes the ambiguity of the oracles. See Liddell and Scott, *sub voce.*

[2] Cf. John vii. 16; viii. 28.

sition accords the fact, observed and explained by Plutarch as best he could, that the heathen oracles died away as that revelation was dawning upon the world.[1]

Lots (Septem contra Thebas, 55); auguries (oracular birds with unerring art, Ibid. 26), and other omens; dreams and visions (Prom. 646; Persae, 176 et al.):

> "For the mind's eye looks clearly out from sleep;
> But mortals have no foresight in the day";

(Eumen. 104); these are all so many different means by which the gods reveal the future, or make known their will to men.

There are also prophets — Calchas (Agamem. 248), Cassandra (Ibid. 1073), Amphiaraus (Theb. 568), whom Apollo inspires directly, without the intervention of omens, oracles, or sacrifices, breathing into them his own prophetic spirit, which, like a tempest, tosses their agitated minds, or burns like a fire in their bones (Agamem. 1256, 1215):

> "Ah, what a sudden flame comes rushing on me!
> I burn, I burn! Apollo, oh Apollo!"

> "Woe, woe is me! Again the furious power
> Swells in my laboring breast; again commands
> My bursting voice, and what I speak is fate."

Such are the cries of Cassandra, as she comes again and again under the frenzy of inspiration, and sees, as if they were before her eyes, all the past and future calamities and crimes of the house of Atreus.

[1] See Plutarch, De Defectu Oraculorum; and also De Sera Numinis Vindicta (ed. Hackett and Tyler), p. 150.

[2] I have used the metrical versions of Potter, Blackie, and Chapman (in Blackwood's) at pleasure, as they seemed most faithfully to represent the original.

2. EXISTENCE. NATURE, AND ATTRIBUTES OF THE GODS.

Aeschylus is not always consistent with himself in his representations of the gods, especially of the supreme divinity. In his Prometheus Bound he seems to fall in with those anthropomorphous conceptions of the deity, which so disfigure the poems of Homer and Hesiod. The Jupiter of this tragedy is an arbitrary despot, who has usurped the throne of his father, and is destined in turn to be dethroned by one of his descendants, who is ignorant of the future, which is known only to Prometheus, oppresses the inferior deities, and is intent on the destruction of miserable mortals,—lustful, tyrannical, unjust, and cruel alike to the victims of his appetite and the objects of his displeasure, and lording it over the universe with the morals and the manners of a lawless usurper. But it is not quite fair or safe to take these as the sentiments of the poet himself. We do not gather the theology of Milton from the rebellious ravings of Satan in the Paradise Lost, nor the doctrines of the Bible from the mouth of the adversary in the Pentateuch and the book of Job.[1]

The character of the supreme deity, as it is generally represented in the other tragedies, and as it appears especially in the epithets by which he is addressed by the chorus, corresponds much more nearly with our ideas of the true God. He is the universal father—father of gods and men; the universal cause (παναίτιος, Agamem. 1485); the all-seer and all-doer (παντόπτης,

[1] This one-sided view was doubtless balanced and corrected in the concluding piece of the trilogy, the Prometheus Unbound, which was exhibited at the same time with the Prometheus Bound, and served to complete it, but which is now lost.

πανεργέτης, Ibid. and Sup. 139); the all-wise and all-controlling (παγκρατής, Sup. 813.); the just and the executor of justice (δικηφόρος, Agamem. 525); true and incapable of falsehood (Prom. 1031)

Ψευδηγορεῖν γὰρ οὐκ ἐπίσταται στόμα
τὸ δῖον, ἀλλὰ πᾶν ἔπος τελεῖ·[1]

holy (ἁγνός, Sup. 650), merciful (πρευμένης, Ibid. 139); the god especially of the suppliant and the stranger (Supplices, passim); the most high and perfect one (τέλειον ὕψιστον, Eumen. 28); "king of kings, of the happy most happy, of the perfect most perfect power, blessed Zeus" (Sup. 522):

ἄναξ ἀνάκτων, μακάρων
μακάρτατε, καὶ τελείων
τελειότατον κράτος, ὄλβιε Ζεῦ.

Such are some of the titles by which Jupiter is most frequently addressed; such the attributes which are most commonly ascribed to him. How unlike the acts of lust and violence which are imputed to the same divinity by the Greek mythology, and which are alluded to by Aeschylus, and that not merely in the Prometheus, but in the very same chorus which commences with the above sublime invocation! Does not this palpable inconsistency lend confirmation to the idea of a primitive revelation? Must not these truly divine epithets have proceeded originally from a higher and purer source than the corrupt and corrupting fables which have attached themselves, like barnacles, to the wrecks of primitive truth that have floated to our shores across the sea of ages?

The general resemblance, suggested by these attri-

[1] Cf. Tit. i. 2: "Which God, that cannot lie, promised."

butes, between the supreme god of the Greek tragedies and of the Hebrew Scriptures, derives additional force from the frequency with which, as we shall see, he is spoken of as a jealous God, visiting the iniquities of the fathers upon the children; one who will by no means clear the guilty; whose mysterious providence is an unfathomable abyss, and before whose irresistible power the heavens and the earth are shaken, and gods and men are as nothing.

As Moses inquires the name of the Being who commissions him to deliver Israel, so the chorus of Argive senators in the Agamemnon (160) hesitates by what name to invoke the supreme deity:

Ζεὺς, ὅστις ποτ' ἐστίν, εἰ τόδ' αὐ-
τῷ φίλον κεκλημένῳ
τοῦτό νιν προσεννέπω·

And in accordance with these early tendencies of the Hebrew and the Greek, or, if you please, the Shemitic and Japhetic mind, Paul finds at Athens an altar inscribed "To an unknown God," and substantially justifies our mode of interpreting these resemblances by saying to the Athenians: "Whom therefore ye worship unknowing, him declare I unto you" (Acts xvii. 23).

We are, however, effectually prevented from placing the notions and traditions of Aeschylus on the same level with revelation, by the low and unworthy, the degrading and demoralizing conceptions of the Deity, which intermingle, even in the best tragedies, with these just ascriptions of truly divine honor and majesty; such for instance as his dethronement of his father (Eumen. 641), his quarrels with his own wife, and amours with the wives and daughters of men (Sup. 162–174 et al.), and the fraud and treachery with which he flatters poor mortals, and lures them on to their own destruction (Pers. 93):

δολόμητιν δ' ἀπάταν θεοῦ
τίς ἀνὴρ θνατὸς ἀλύξει; κ.τ.λ.

"But when the gods deceive,
Wiles which immortals weave,
Who shall beware?
Who, when their nets surround,
Breaks with a nimble bound
Out of the snare?
First they approach with smiles,
Wreathing their hidden wiles:
Then with surprise
Seize they their prey; and lo!
Writhing in toils of woe,
Tangled he lies.

Jupiter is the invisible deity of the Aeschylean pantheon. The other gods — Apollo, Athena, Hermes, Hephaestus, etc. — appear as personages of the drama, and take part in the dialogue; Jupiter, never. In accordance with the popular ideas of the good old times in which the scene is laid, they walk the earth in human form, and participate directly in the affairs of men; he sits on his throne and rules over all; or if he comes down to earth it is in a more disguised form, as in some myth which we hear from the lips of the actors, or in the display of his mighty power, as we see it in the storm and the earthquake with which he overwhelms Prometheus. Indeed, as Müller has well remarked in his learned and profound dissertations on the Eumenides:[1] "With Aeschylus, as with all men of profound feeling among the Greeks, from the earliest times, Jupiter is the only real god, in the higher sense of the word.

[1] Cambridge edition, 1835, p. 223.

Although he is, in the spirit of ancient theology, a generated god, arisen out of an imperfect state of things, and not produced till the third[1] stage of the development of nature, still he is, at the time we are speaking of, the spirit that pervades and governs the universe." As in the epithets applied to him we seem to see the relics of a primeval revelation, so in his immense superiority to the other gods we see the primitive monotheism often breaking through the clouds of polytheistic error and superstition.

Besides the most high and universal father, the Greek mythology recognizes an indefinite number of inferior deities subordinate to his supreme authority, the messengers of his will, and the agents of his universal providence. These appear in the tragedies of Aeschylus in the most real and practical light, now as direct actors in the drama, now as objects of fear or trust, supplication or deprecation to mortals, and now as the acting deities of this lower world; and we seem to see the process still going on before our eyes, by which they came into so real an existence.

The analogy of human life is the fruitful source from which many of them sprang. They wear the human form. They exhibit human appetites, desires, and passions, at the same time that they are invested with more or less of the attributes of divinity. They stand in the ordinary relations of human life to each other and to the supreme god. It is not good for man or god to be alone; so Jupiter must have his wife and children, — daughters as well as sons, — who, of course, partake of his nature; and they, in turn, have their children, who

[1] The reigns of Uranus and Cronus have preceded; Jupiter's is the third. Cf. Agamem. 168 sqq.

are at a still greater remove from the perfection of their first father. He is a sovereign, and must have his court, his messengers, and his ministers, though this is represented much less *pro more humano*, in Aeschylus than in Homer. Among the "scraps from the banquet of Homer," to which the father of Greek tragedy modestly likens his plays, he gives us none of those tragi-comic, those almost burlesque scenes on Mount Olympus, at which the readers of the Iliad and Odyssey scarcely know whether to laugh or weep. When the gods are the actors, the scene is laid on earth; and they appear chiefly as the direct agents and visible representatives of the invisible government of Zeus. As his realm is vast, he must not be burdened with the immediate administration. His brothers may preside over the sea and the under-world, and his children and children's children may have each their particular province among men; while he exercises a general superintendence from his throne on high. The characters of the several subordinate deities, must of course, correspond with their offices, and so be as various as the departments of the divine government. There must be gods of the sea and gods of the land; gods of the forest and gods of the field; gods of war and gods of the several peaceful occupations. There must be a god of commerce, a goddess of agriculture, a goddess of science and the arts, a god of music, poetry, and prophetic inspiration. There must especially be a god of war, a god of wine, a goddess of love, and gods or goddesses of the sensual, selfish, and malign passions; since to refer these directly to the supreme were scarcely compatible with his goodness, and yet to exempt them from all control by him, or connection with him were inconsistent with his universal sovereignty. By a still more natural and obvious process, those human virtues and all those moral elements in the soul of man, which are but the offspring and image of the divine attributes, assume a concrete form, and put on a more than human authority and power. Dike, Themis, Nemesis, the Eumenides, and the Moerae (Justice, Law, Retribution, the Furies, and the Fates) are not mere abstractions, not mere personifications, but truly divine beings and dread realities to the ancestors and the contemporaries of Aeschylus. Even Kratos and Bia (Strength and Force) are brought upon the stage in the Prometheus, and are seen in the process of deification; and this process, passing so visibly, as it were, before our eyes, helps us to understand how the fertile imagination of the Greeks, which not only clothed and adorned, but animated, whatever it touched, gradually peopled heaven, earth, and hell, with the innumerable deities of the Athenian Pantheon.[1]

These last are pre-eminently the divinities of Greek tragedy. With the exception of the sea-nymphs, who constitute the chorus in the Prometheus, we see nothing in the extant pieces of Aeschylus, of the gods of the outer, material world. But these gods of the moral universe, whose seat is by the throne of Jupiter or in

[1] Petronius says, it was easier to find a god at Athens, than a man. Hence the *κατείδωλον* and the *δεισιδαιμονεστέρους* of Paul in his address to the Athenians on Mars' Hill (Acts xvii). The Greeks regarded different countries as having different gods; and as Pharaoh refuses to obey Jehovah, because he is the God of the Hebrews and not of the Egyptians, saying: "Who is Jehovah, that I should obey his voice? I know not Jehovah"; so the herald of the sons of Aegyptus does not fear the gods of Argos (Sup. 890, 919), though he reverences the gods of the Nile. Cf. Exod. v. 2; also 1 Kings xx. 23, where the servants of the king of Syria say to him: "Their gods are gods of the hills, therefore they were stronger than we," etc.

the world of spirits, whose sceptre is the conscience, and whose province is the soul of man, — these are the ruling powers in the realm of tragedy. Themis (Law), daughter of heaven and earth, and goddess of law and order in both worlds, companion of Jupiter and sharer in his counsels, primeval prophetess and voice of God to man, gives right counsels, protects the needy and the defenceless, and maintains the harmony of the moral universe (cf. Prom. 18, 509; Eum. 2; Sup. 358, et al.).[1] Dike (Justice), the renowned and triumphant (*νικηφόρος*) daughter of Jupiter and Themis, stands on a lofty and immovable foundation, holding in one hand a balance, wherein she weighs impartially the character and conduct of men, and in the other a sword, wherewith, sooner or later, she strikes through the heart of the wicked; while Fate (*Αἶσα, Μοῖρα*) and Wrath or Vengeance (*'Ερινύς*) stand on either side of her, the former to forge and whet her sword, and the latter to insure the infliction of deserved punishment (cf. Choeph. 59; 146; 644–650; Agamem. 1535). Nemesis, kindred in name and nature to *Νόμος*, is the goddess of retribution, or more literally of distributive justice,[2] who visits upon mankind their just deserts, and since there is no escape from the penalties which she visits upon the guilty, she bears the name of *'Αδράστεια* (the Inevitable, the Unescapable); they therefore are wise who do her reverence (Prom. 935). The Furies and the Fates (*Ερινύες, Μοῖραι*) are sisters (Eum. 962), and joint rulers (gubernatores, *οἰακοστρόφοι*, Prom. 515) of the moral universe. They are daughters of Night (Eum. 416), and have their

[1] Compare Hooker's magnificent and oft-cited personification of law, "her voice the voice of God, her seat the throne of the universe," etc.

[2] Νόμος distributes, or allots to men their duties; Νέμεσις, their dues.

abode in the dark world below (κατὰ χθόνος θεαί, Eum. 115, et al.); yet have they great power in heaven and on earth, as well as under the earth (Ibid. 950). They are represented as old, black — like Gorgons and Harpies (though without wings) — hags, hateful to gods and men (Eum. passim). Yet, like their mother Night (Νὺξ φιλία, Agamem. 355), they have their bright and cheerful side towards the good and those who propitiate their favor; hence the name Eumenides, and the epithets σεμναί and εὔφρονες, by which the Furies were known, especially at Athens (Eum. 373; 992 et. al.), as not only euphemistically, but when appeased, truly the kind and gracious as well as the venerable and awful deities. By a conception as just as it is profound, the Fates and the Furies are habitually associated with Justice as her companions, ministers, and executioners.[1] The Fates are δαίμονες ὀρθονόμοι (Eum. 963), justice-dispensing deities; they personify and preside over the unchangeable moral laws and necessities of the universe, and unite with the Furies and with Justice herself in securing the certain inevitable punishment of transgressors. There is, however, this difference, that while Dike weighs character and discriminates motives, the Fates and the Furies are blind powers, capable of discerning only overt acts, and demanding the punishment of the perpetrators, without regard to justifying motives or palliating circumstances. The Fates are triform, though Aeschylus does not, like Hesiod, distinguish them by their several names. The Furies are indefinite in number. Each distinct relation, if not each individual person who is wronged, has his separate Erinys; there is the Erinys of the father and of the mother, the Erinys

[1] See passages c'ted in reference to Dike above, and very many others.

of the son and of the daughter, the Erinys of the fellow-citizen and of the stranger, who pursues the wrong-doer to the death and into the eternal world; the Alastor,[1] who drives the guilty person like Cain, a fugitive and a vagabond on the face of the earth, and even follows him into the dark realm of Hades (cf. Agamem. 1433, 1501; Theb. 70, 720 et passim). In their subterranean abode, the Erinyes are called Arae (Eum. 417), since just indignation at sin often vents itself in imprecations, and the curse of an injured father, mother, or other friend, is often the bitterest ingredient in the punishment of the injurer.

Ate, in the tragedies, is essentially another name for Ara and Erinys. This name, however, denotes especially the bewitching and bewildering power of sin, and that judicial blindness, that almost supernatural frenzy, which sometimes impels individuals, and sometimes whole families, generation after generation, as if by an irresistible and fatal necessity, to the perpetration of enormous crimes, and thus involves them in irretrievable and overwhelming calamities. In this point of view, the blinding and avenging deity is often conceived of as an evil demon (*ἀλάστωρ ἢ κακὸς δαίμων*,[2] Pers. 354), hateful and powerful, falling upon guilty individuals, families, and nations, taking possession of them, depriving them of their senses, and preying upon them, like a blood-thirsty tiger upon his victim, or an odious raven upon a carcass, till there is nothing left to prey upon (Pers. 472 et passim; Agamem. 1468, etc.), till

[1] Ἀλάστωρ (from ἀλάομαι, *to wander*). The avenging deity, that causes to wander, and the wretched Cain-like wanderer himself, are both called by the same name. Cf. Agamem. 1501, and Eum. 236.

[2] Cf. also *στυγνὲ δαῖμον* 472; *δυσπόνητε δαῖμον*, 515; *δολίαν ἄτην*, Agamem. 1523, etc.

the ill-starred, or rather evil-demoned (κακοδαίμων), family or race is extinct. It was by the association of such ideas as these with the word δαίμων, which was originally almost synonymous with θεός, that the way was gradually prepared for its appropriation by the sacred writers in the New Testament, to express those demons which possessed the bodies as well as the minds of men at the opening of the new dispensation, and for its use by Christians generally as nearly a synonyme with devils. The κακὸς δαίμων of Aeschylus and the Greek tragedians, however, is never the διάβολος of the Scriptures, the accuser of the saints, the universal tempter, and the prince of a kingdom of darkness hostile to the kingdom of light; but always an avenging, cursing, and bewildering deity.

There is, however, a class of gods who are represented as hostile to Zeus: the gods of the old *régime*, who were dethroned by Jupiter when he first came into possession of supreme power, or who conspired against his government when it was already established, or who resisted his will though he was acknowledged sovereign. But all alike are now overthrown, and suffer the vengeance of the conqueror. Prometheus is chained to a cliff or chasm in the Scythian desert, while a vulture preys perpetually on his vitals (Prom. 1020). His brother Atlas, bound in adamant, is doomed to sustain the heavens on his shoulders, while the ocean boils around him, and the dark vault of Hades groans beneath his feet (Prom. 425). The hundred-headed and impetuous Typhon, stricken with the thunder-bolt of Jove, lies scorched and crushed beneath the roots of Etna (Ibid. 353). And the ancient Kronus, with all his Titan allies, is sunk in the deep and dark abyss of gloomy Tartarus (Ibid. 220). So we are told in the epistles of Peter and of Jude, "God spared not the angels that sinned, but cast them down to Tartarus (ταρταρώσας, 2 Pet. ii. 4), in everlasting chains under darkness."

Not unlike these Titanic sons of heaven and earth, and sometimes classed with them, though of less prodigious power, and not so dreadful a doom, are the heroes and demigods, offspring of gods and men, some of whom, indeed, are the good angels of their age and race and the benefactors of mankind; but others are demons, monsters at once in crime and in calamity. Such are not a few of the Theban heroes (Theb. passim), the descendants of Tantalus (Agamem. 1468), and the other mythical characters, who form the favorite subjects of tragic verse. They remind the reader of the Jewish Scriptures very forcibly of the description given of the world before the flood in the book of Genesis (vi. 4, 5). "There were giants in the earth in those days; and also after that, when the sons of God came in unto the daughters of men, and they bare children unto them, the same were mighty men, which were of old, men of renown. And God saw the wickedness of man, that it was very great upon the earth." Many of the heathen fables are doubtless the facts of revelation and of primeval history in disguise. The Pantheon of the Greeks takes the place of the angelic hierarchy. The Titans are the fallen angels. The inferior deities of Olympus perform not a few of the offices of the good angels, though they partake much more largely of human passions and frailties; and yet — a fact which indicates how much the Scriptures have done to elevate our ideas of Deity — the occupants of Olympic seats were gods, while those who stand and serve around the Most High in heaven, are his creatures; and though they rise rank above rank, angels and archangels, thrones, dominions, principalities, and powers, still the highest archangel, who stands nearest the eternal throne, presumes not to accept the worship of men, but says: "See thou do it not, for I am thy fellow-servant: worship God."

3. THE CHARACTER AND CONDITION OF MEN.

The Prometheus of Aeschylus represents mankind as having been in the condition of helpless infants and degraded savages (443 sqq.), without fire and without houses, dwelling in caves of the earth, ignorant of the arts and destitute of the comforts of life, with reason, speech, and the senses themselves so imperfectly developed, that seeing, they saw in vain, and hearing, they heard not (447, cf. Mat. xiii. 13):

βλέποντες ἔβλεπον μάτην,
κλύοντες οὐκ ἤκουον·

And in this sad condition they continued, till Prometheus stole for them fire from heaven, taught them the useful arts, inspired them with hopes, — delusive hopes, however, as he himself confesses, — and revealed to them the way of divining the future and propitiating the favor of the gods (Ibid. 460–507). Whether this was their original state, the state in which they were created, Aeschylus does not expressly say; but he implies, and doubtless held, the doctrine of Hesiod and other poets, that under the reign of Kronus, the golden age of the world, a better race inhabited the earth, the companions of the gods and the favorites of heaven; and the present race of men were fallen, degenerate, depraved, and hence obnoxious to the displeasure of the deity. Accordingly Jupiter was, for a time, bent on their extirpation,[1] and the creation of a better race in their stead (232). Hence, too, he punishes Prometheus for imparting to them knowledge, and strikes with thunder Aesculapius for having restored mortal man to life (Agamem. 1022); even as our first parents were forbidden to eat the fruit of the tree of knowledge, and, when they had sinned, were driven out of the garden, and cherubim were placed at the entrance, and a flaming sword, which turned every way, to guard the way to the tree of life (Gen. iii. 24). "Alas, the fates of men!" exclaims the prophetess (Agamem. 1327):

> "Alas, the fates of men! their brightest bloom
> A shadow blights; and in their evil day
> An oozy sponge blots out their fleeting prints,
> And they are seen no more. From bad to worse
> Our changes run, and with the worst we end."

Such, not unfrequently, are the strains in which the chorus laments the deeds and the sufferings (ἔργα καὶ πάθος, Choeph. 1014 sqq.) of men, and the whole series of tragic plots is but an illustration and expansion of this melancholy idea; as the history of the Bible is but a running commentary on the sad strains in which the prophets and singers of Israel deplore the brevity, sinfulness, and wretchedness of human life.

4. THE PROVIDENCE AND GOVERNMENT OF GOD.

We have already seen that Jove is conceived of as the original cause and author of all. All events proceed from his will, and are brought to pass by his agency. "Wo! wo! 't is by the will of Jove, cause of all, worker of all. For what is accomplished among mortals with-

[1] Cf. Gen. vi. 6.

out Jove? What of these things (the crimes and calamities of the house of Atreus) is not wrought of God?" (Agamem. 1485):

> ἰὼ ἰὴ διαὶ Διὸς
> παναιτίου, πανεργέτα·
> τί γὰρ βροτοῖς ἄνευ Διὸς τελεῖται;
> τί τῶνδ' αὐ θεόκραντόν ἐστιν.

Nay, his word is deed; he speaks, and it is done (Sup. 595): *πάρεστι δ' ἔργον ὡς ἔπος*; (Sup. 97–100):

> "No force he wields; his simple will,
> His quiet sentence, blasteth."

He is sole monarch, and irresponsible, and gives no account of his matters; to resist his will is only to kick against the pricks (Prom. 323). Men strive in vain to disturb the execution of his purposes (Prom. 852).

> "Their counsels never can transgress
> The settled harmony of things,
> The wisdom of the king of kings."

At the same time, everything is declared to be subject to the control of an invincible destiny (Prom. 105). "Things are as they are, and are surely brought to their destined issue" (Agamem. 67). In answer to the question, Who is the guide (gubernator, *οἰακοστρόφος*) of necessity, Prometheus says, "The triform Fates and the vengeful Furies." When further asked, if Jove is less powerful than these, he answers, that Jove cannot escape destiny (Prom. 515). According to the prevailing doctrine of the other tragedies, however, the will of Jove is superior to, or identical with fate, and that with justice;[1] and this is made a reason for worshipping him: "Let us worship the God of strangers, the great, the

[1] See above, p. 221.

supreme Jove, who by hoary law directs fate:" ὃς πολιῷ νόμῳ αἶσαν ὀρθοῖ (Sup. 679). Hence, while the Fates are invoked as justice-dispensing deities (Eum. 963), Jupiter also is represented as having justice with himself (Prom. 187). So, not unfrequently, justice and fate are used interchangeably, as almost synonymes (Agamem. 1535), and both are spoken of as the appointment of the gods, τεταγμένα ἐκ θεῶν (Agamem. 1025), or τὸ μέλλον ἐκ θεῶν (Pers. 373). And Jupiter is invoked with Might and Right, as a threefold power, of which Jupiter is the greatest (Choeph. 242), whose will, guided by justice and clothed with power, will infallibly bring out the right issue: "Whatever is fated, that will take place; the great unbounded mind of Jove cannot be overpassed" (Sup. 1045):

> "Comes fated good or ill,
> Wait we in patience still,
> No power may thwart his will,
> Jove, mighty Jove.

Such is the juxtaposition into which the three ideas of fate, justice, and providence are constantly brought to each other.

As to the relation of the divine purposes, or the decrees of destiny, to the freedom of human actions, Jupiter alone is, in the highest sense, free (Prom. 50). Still the divine purposes are not altogether irrespective of human agency. Sooner or later, in some way and by some person, they are certain to be fulfilled. But the time and manner of their accomplishment, and if they relate to families, races, and nations, the individual by whom they are accomplished, may depend on the wisdom or the folly, the piety or the impiety, of men. "Ah!" mourns the shade of Darius, as he sees how soon after his death his son Xerxes brought destruction on the armies, and almost on the empire of Persia (Pers. 739 sqq.):

"Ah! on wings how swift, the issue of the ancient doom hath sped!
Thee, my son, great Jove hath smitten. Long-drawn years I hoped
would roll,
Ere fulfilment of the dread prophetic burden should be known.
But when man to run is eager, swift is the god to add a spur."

The spirit of this last line is, as Blackie well suggests essentially the same with the old Latin proverb: Quem Deus vult perdere, prius dementat; and it is the prevailing sentiment of the Greek tragedies: men go to destruction under the impulse of their own folly and madness, and an angry deity has only to "add the spur."

If you say the sin is fated, and fate is responsible, the answer is, the punishment is fated too:

ἡ μοῖρα τούτων, ὦ τέκνον, παραίτια.

So pleads Clytemnestra (Choeph. 910) in extenuation of her crimes, but Orestes replies:

καὶ τόνδε τοίνυν μοῖρ' ἐπόρσυνεν μόρον.

No prayers or tears can avail to break the chain that links suffering to sin (Agamem. 67 sqq.)

"But things are as they are; the chain
Of fate doth bind them; sighs are vain.
Tears, libations, fruitless flow,
To divert from purposed ire
The powers whose altars know no fire."

Yet the very thing which is fated may come in answer to prayer; and this belief is urged as an encouragement to pray (Choeph. 462):

"The tremulous fear creeps o'er my frame to hear
Thy words; for though long-dated,
The thing divinely fated
Shall surely come at last, our cloudy prayers to clear."

Or more literally rendered, "that which is fated abides from of old, and may come to you, praying"; that is, on condition of, or in answer to, your prayers. The dramas of Aeschylus are, in their whole structure and contents, a standing witness to a belief in the efficacy of prayer, as a general thing, notwithstanding the fixed decrees of fate or providence. No Calvinist was ever a more strenuous assertor of the "doctrine of decrees," than the chorus in these dramas. At the same time, no Methodist ever offered more frequent or more fervent prayers. Prayer, however, does not supersede the necessity of exertion, or the use of suitable means. "Pray,"—such is the spirit of the reproof which Eteocles administers to the chorus, as they pray for the safety of beleagured Thebes (Theb. 216)—"pray indeed, but look well to the fortifications;" or, in the language of a modern proverb, first addressed by Cromwell to his Ironsides, "trust providence, but keep your powder dry."

The mystery of divine providence is a frequent subject of remark. The ways of the Deity are dark, thickly shaded, difficult to trace, past finding out (Sup. 92):

"Oh, would that Jove might show to men
His counsel as he planned it;
But ah, he darkly weaves the scheme—
No mortal eye hath scanned it"

His purposes are an unfathomable abyss (Ibid. 1055). Clouds and darkness are round about him. But the poet, like the Psalmist, connects with this the assurance that justice and judgment are the habitation of his throne (Ibid. 86–99). He sits upon his holy seat (ἑδράνων ἐφ᾽ ἁγνῶν, 103), and thence executes all his righteous and steadfast purposes. He holds in his hands the scales of equal and universal justice (Ibid. 819), and, causing the balance to preponderate according to his righteous will, distributes evil to the evil and good to the good (Ibid. 401):

> "Where kindred with kindred contendeth in war,
> Jove looks on the strife and decides from afar,
> Where he holdeth the scales even-handed;
> Oh, why wilt thou doubt to declare for the right?
> He blesseth the good, but in anger will smite
> Where the sons of the wicked are banded."

He awards to every man that which is due (τοὐφειλόμενον) for his deeds, measure for measure, speech for speech, blow for blow, according to that thrice-hallowed and venerable saying, "He that has done evil must suffer for it" (Choeph. 304–313).[1] It is from Jove that this great law of moral necessity proceeds; and it is for him to provide that things end in accordance with this rule of exact distributive justice (Ibid. 304–306). And so long as Jove remains, it remains an eternal law that the doer shall receive according to what he has done (Agamem. 1563). The choral song, or rather prayer, above referred to (Choeph. 304 sqq.), brings together so many of the ideas respecting fate, justice, providence, and prayer which we have been endeavoring to illustrate, that we quote it entire, in the spirited and substantially correct translation of Blackie:

> "Mighty Fates, divinely guiding
> Human fortunes to their end,
> Send this man, with Jove presiding,
> Whither Justice points the way.

[1] Comp. Matt. vii. 2, "With what measure ye mete," etc.

Words of bitter hatred duly
Pay with bitter words: for thus,
With loud cry triumphant shouting,
Justice pays the sinner's debt.
Blood for blood and blow for blow —
Thou shalt reap as thou didst sow:
Age to age with hoary wisdom
Speaketh thus to man."

Jupiter is especially jealous for his own honors and prerogatives. Wo to the man, or the god, who invades or encroaches on them. Prometheus, chained to the rocks and torn by vultures, pays the penalty not only of assuming too much to himself, but of lavishing undue knowledge and power on mortals (Prom. 29) Xerxes, though a mortal, thought to surpass Poseidon and all the gods, and soon met with a dreadful overthrow (Pers. 749). Agamemnon has been fortunate quite beyond the ordinary lot of men. The choir therefore fear for him the envy of the gods. "To have an exceedingly high reputation is exceedingly hazardous; for the thunderbolt from Jove smites such in the face." Hence, they prefer only that degree of happiness which does not excite envy, and pray never to be sackers of cities (Agamem. 468–472). Agamemnon himself is conscious of the danger, and strives to avert it by humility and moderation. He refuses at first to tread on the purple which Clytemnestra has spread before his feet, and bids the obsequious attendants to honor him as a man, and not as a god (*κατ' ἄνδρα, μὴ θεόν*). But his treacherous and crafty wife, who seeks in this very way to provoke the jealousy of the gods against him, lures him on, through pomp and pride, to destruction. The Theban heroes, undaunted by the omens and prohibitions of the gods, go against the city boasting that they will destroy it with or without the consent of Jove; and, with a single exception, they all perish before the gates (Theb. 440, 529, etc.). This envy of the gods — for such is the ordinary meaning of the word (τὸν θεῶν φθόνον, Pers. 362 et passim) — is one of the most tragic elements in the tragic drama of the Greeks, often remarked upon by the characters and the chorus, and often the pivot on which the catastrophe turns. Hence it became a proverb among the Greeks, τὸ θεῖον φθονερόν (Herod. iii. 40) — God is envious. As it is expressed by a word of lower moral significance, so is it a less pure and elevated characteristic, having more reference to mere outward prosperity, and less to the feelings of the heart, than that jealousy which Jehovah asserts for himself in the Decalogue. Still it is manifestly a kindred attribute to that which guards the incommunicable prerogatives of the Most High, and which says: "I will not give my glory to another."

Another attribute, which is asserted with great frequency of Jupiter, and which is also a special characteristic of the God of Israel, is his regard for the poor and needy, the suppliant and the stranger. Not a few of the epithets most frequently applied to Jupiter express this character. He is Ζεὺς ἀφίκτωρ, ἱκέτης, ἱκεσίος, ἱκτήρ; and "dreadful is the anger of Zeus, the protector of suppliants" (Sup. 344). "It is necessary to dread the anger of Zeus, the protector of suppliants, for it is the highest fear among mortals" (Ibid. 566). He is also Ζεὺς ξένιος (Agamem. 362), ξυνέστιος (Agamem. 703), the guardian of the stranger and the rites of hospitality; and they who do violence to the stranger on the one hand, or to the host who renders hospitality on the other, shall see his bow and feel his thunder-stroke

(Agamem. 364). The whole drama of the Suppliants is an intentional illustration of this principle in the divine government. The daughters of Danaus, fleeing from the abhorred nuptials which were to be enforced upon them at home, land on the shores of Argos, and cast themselves on the altars of the country for protection; and their prayer is: "Behold me a suppliant, a fugitive, a wanderer (347). Spurn not my petition, lest you rouse the anger of the gods." For not Jupiter alone, but the other gods befriend the suppliant stranger. Themis is the goddess of suppliants (358). Apollo, an exile once himself, will pity exiles (215). The land will be defiled and cursed of all the gods, if it refuse shelter to those who have fled to it for safety in the hour of need. And though the Argive king foresees a war with Egypt as the consequence of harboring the fugitives, yet a war with the gods is more to be dreaded (437); though the enemy plunder the house, yet the god of the hearth and the household (*Ζεὺς κτησίος*) can more than make up the loss; and he resolves to be their protector.[1]

The delay of the Deity in punishing the wicked — a subject which occasioned not a little perplexity to the sacred writers — was also the subject of one of the most instructive and profound theological treatises that have come down to us from pagan antiquity.[2] "The mills of the gods grind late, but grind to powder" — *ὀψὲ θεῶν ἀλέουσι μύλοι, ἀλέουσι δὲ λεπτά* — is a proverb which is often repeated by the moralists of Greece;

[1] So according to the Odyssey (xiv. 57), all strangers and poor beggars are from Zeus.

[2] See Professor Hackett's Analysis of Plutarch De Sera Numinis Vindicta (ed. Hackett and Tyler), p. 65 sqq.

and the subject is one of frequent recurrence in the tragedies of Aeschylus. There is in the Choephoroe (58–60) a striking passage illustrative of the different times and ways in which punishment comes upon transgressors; "some in the light of day, others in the dark twilight of life, a lingering but overflowing flood of pains; while for others is reserved the endless night of future retribution." Paul, in his Epistle to Timothy, draws a similar distinction. "Some men's sins are open beforehand, going before to judgment, and some they follow after." But in time (χρόνῳ; ἐν χρόνῳ; ἐν χρόνοις)[1] justice steals upon the wicked, and exacts of them the full penalty of their crimes (Choeph. 650, 954):

> "Her from his shrine sent the rock-throned Apollo,
> The will of her high-purposed sire to obey,
> The track of the blood-stained remorseless to follow,
> Winged with sure death, though she lag by the way."

At the set time, yes, on the appointed day (χρόνῳ τοι κυρίῳ τ' ἐν ἡμέρᾳ, Sup. 729), whoever dishonors the gods shall pay the penalty to divine justice.

Prosperity, whether individual or national, is the gift of God (θεοῦ δῶρον, Theb. 625). Prayer is not without efficacy in procuring it (Ibid. 626); it is also the reward of justice and piety (Eum. 550):

> "The man without compulsion just,
> Who by these rules preserves his trust,
> Unprosperous shall never be;
> At least, ne'er ruined utterly."[2]

Who fears the gods is fearful to oppose (δεινὸς ὃς θεοὺς σέβει, Theb. 596); the city which they preserve is im-

[1] These words are the standing limitations of the rule of retribution; well rendered by Blackie: "though she lag by the way."

[2] Cf. Ps. xxxvii. 24, "Though he fall, he shall not be utterly cast down."

pregnable (Pers. 247); it is taken only when the gods forsake it (Theb. 218); they send forth the conqueror, and they bring him back again victorious (Agamem. 1853); and in the conquest and destruction of empires, he is but the agent of divine justice (Ibid. 812); but when success becomes a god, and more than a god, to mortals, then divine justice watches its opportunity to descend upon them (Choeph. 57). Jupiter is ever at hand, as the severe judge and punisher of proud thoughts (Pers. 827). It is an old saying, uttered in ancient times, that great and entire prosperity does not die childless, but begets as its legitimate offspring insatiate calamity (Agamem. 750). Hence the chorus are led to offer a prayer kindred to that of Agur, that neither poverty nor riches, neither conquest nor captivity, may be their lot (Ibid. 472, cf. 1341):

"Who of mortals will not pray,
From high-perched Fortune's favor far,
A blameless life to spend."[1]

As prosperity has its dangers, so the idea is not unknown, though less familiar, that adversity has, or may have, its blessings. It, too, is of divine appointment. It must be borne with patience, when the gods give it (*θεῶν διδόντων*, Pers. 294). It teaches wisdom to the wise, and sometimes purifies even the polluted (Eum. 276). "It is good to grow wise under sorrow" (*ξυμφέρει σωφρονεῖν ὑπὸ στένει*, Eum. 520). It is the prerogative of God, who has attached instruction to suffering (*τὸν πάθει μάθος θέντα*), thus to guide them, though against their wills (*ἄκοντας*), to wisdom (Agamem. 176 sq.):

"For Jove doth teach men wisdom, sternly wins
To virtue by tutoring of their sins;

[1] Cf. also Eum. 529: "By God's decree the mean is best," etc.

Yea, drops of torturing recollection chill
The sleepers; 'gainst man's rebellious will
Jove works the wise remorse:
Dread powers, on awful seats enthroned, compel
Our hearts with gracious force."[1]

There are not wanting, in Aeschylus, indications of a belief in special providences, reaching even to the elements and the changes of the weather. The messenger who announces to the queen mother at Susæ the overthrow of the forces of Xerxes, in describing the return of the shattered remnant, says, that on the very night when they reached the banks of the sacred Strymon, the deity raised a wintry storm out of season, and froze the whole stream, so that as many as availed themselves of the providence before the rising sun, passed over safely on a bridge of ice; but when the sun rose, it soon melted the ice, and "man upon man, in crowded ruin fell"; thus men, who had never before believed in the existence and providence of the gods, believed and worshipped (Pers. 498 sqq.).[2]

5. SIN, ITS PENALTY AND EXPIATION.

The sins, with which the tragic poets have to do, are chiefly, as might be expected, such violations of the law of nature as murder, incest, undutifulness to parents,[3] inhospitality to strangers, sacrilege, superhuman pride, and arrogating divine prerogatives. These are, emphatically, the crimes that characterize the Greek drama;

[1] Χάρις is the Greek word, and it is used in a sense strikingly similar to the usage of the New Testament.

[2] As to the credibility of this miracle, as a matter of fact, compare Thirlwall, and Grote, Vol. v. p. 191.

[3] "Honor thy parents," is the third, or as we should say the first, the prime commandment (Sup. 704), and is often accompanied with a promise.

these, and such as these, the sins which stain with their guilt, or involve in their consequences the individuals and families set apart as the favorite themes of the tragic muse; these the very atmosphere and element, darkened with clouds and agitated by storms, in which tragedy lives and moves and has its being. The drama, called the Suppliants, starts from that aversion to intermarriage with near blood relations (cousins in this instance), which is so nearly universal that it may be called an instinct, an intuition, and turns for its peripeteia on the sacredness of the domestic and the public altar, and the inviolability of those who have fled for refuge to these sanctuaries of the gods. Murder, incest, violation of filial and fraternal duty, and other unnatural crimes, are fundamental ideas in the Seven against Thebes. The divine displeasure at those who arrogate to themselves that which belongs to God only, which is also prominent in the Seven against Thebes, is the main subject, or at least the chief tragic element in Prometheus and the Persians. And in the remaining three of the seven extant tragedies of Aeschylus, the Agamemnon, the Choephoroe, and the Eumenides, which together constitute a magnificent trilogy, the only trilogy that has come down to us entire—hands red with blood, with kindred blood, are ever before the spectator's mind; and the great question which agitates spectators and actors is, How can that stain be washed away? If there were any room to doubt the genuineness and authenticity of the Pentateuch, the doubter might find an antidote to his scepticism in the bare fact, that the same subjects which constitute the staple of the epic and tragic mythology of the Greeks are also among the earliest and most prominent subjects of Mosaic history and legislation. The histories of Cain and Lamech,[1] the laws of murder and incest, the altars and the cities of refuge, the sacrifices and rites of purification, the ideas of expiation and reconciliation, which make up so large a portion of the Old Testament, reappear on the tragic stage, and constitute the very warp of the Greek drama.

And the first great law which the tragedians recognize—a law written in the hearts of men and sanctioned by divine authority—is, that the sinner must suffer for his sin (Choeph. 311):

> δράσαντι παθεῖν
> τριγέρων μῦθος τάδε φωνεῖ.

"For him that hath done the deed to suffer for it—thus cries a proverb (or tradition) thrice-hallowed by age."

Moreover, the great primary law of retribution is expressly the *lex talionis:* like for like and measure for measure. "Ye have heard that it hath been said by them of old time, An eye for an eye and a tooth for a tooth." We have this ancient saying, standing out with great prominence, and repeated again and again, on the pages of Aeschylus (Agamem. 1562):

> "'T is robber robbed, and slayer slain; for, though
> Oft-times it lag, with measured blow for blow,
> Vengeance prevaileth
> While great Jove lives. Who breaks the close-linked woe
> Which heaven entaileth?"

The Greek of this passage reads as follows:

[1] Ixion, the first murderer (Eum. 718), was purified by Jove himself, but proving ungrateful, was doomed to endless punishment. Cf. Gen. iv. 15, 16. The lament of Lamech (Ibid. 23, 24) is the lament of Orestes and of many an unwilling homicide in the Greek poets. He had slain a man in self-defence; and if Cain was protected by divine interposition from the avenger of blood, much more Lamech; "if Cain shall be avenged sevenfold, truly Lamech seventy and seven fold."

φέρει φέροντ', ἐκτίνει δ' ὁ καίνων·
μίμνει δὲ μίμνοντος ἐν χρόνῳ Διός,
παθεῖν τὸν ἔρξαντα· θέσμιον γάρ, κ. τ. λ.

And it may be literally rendered thus: "He spoils the spoiler, and the slayer pays the full penalty. It remains so long as Jove remains, that he must suffer who has done the deed; for it is an established law." Who can read this, and the many kindred passages of our poet, without being reminded of that primeval law of the divine government, which was promulgated to the second universal ancestor of the human race, as he went forth from the ark to repeople a depopulated world: "Whoso sheddeth man's blood, by man shall his blood be shed." And the principle is not repealed, but repeated and recognized as a general law of providence in that saying of our Lord: "They that take the sword shall perish by the sword."

This law is recognized as a law of nature, and therefore (so far as any of the laws of nature may be said to execute themselves) self-executing. The connection between sin and suffering is constantly represented as a natural and necessary connection, like that between sowing and reaping, parent and offspring (Choeph. 310; Pers. 821):

Blood for blood and blow for blow, —
Thou shalt reap as thou didst sow.

A haughty spirit,[1] blossoming, bears a crop
Of woe, and reaps a harvest of despair.

Lust and violence beget lust and violence, and vengeance too at the appointed time (Agamem. 763).[1]

[1] In one of these passages, ὕβρις is the root or the seed, and ἄτη the fruit or the harvest. In the other, ὕβρις is the parent, and ὕβρις the immediate, and ἄτη the remote offspring. See a similar genealogy of lust, sin, and death, in James i. 15.

Impiety multiplies and perpetuates itself (Ibid. 788). The sinner pays the debt he contracted, ends the career that he began (*τίσας ἅπερ ἦρξεν*, Ibid. 1529), and drinks to the dregs the cup of cursing which he himself had filled (Ibid. 1397). But so far from the atheistic idea that these laws are in such a sense self-executing as to dispense with a personal God, a divine governor and judge, the laws themselves become real, living, divine persons, the agents and executioners of the Most High; so far from the conscience being the sole power of judgment and retribution, the conscience itself is only an instrument in the hands of Justice and Vengeance, and the Most High directs and controls all these inferior agents and instrumentalities. It is in reference to this very matter of punishment for sin that the question already cited is asked: "What is accomplished without Jupiter? What of these things is not wrought of God?"

With the general doctrine, "The soul that sinneth it shall die," the Scriptures connect another, which seems at first view to conflict with it, namely, that God visits the iniquities of the fathers upon the children, unto the third and fourth generation. These same apparently inconsistent doctrines lie, side by side, at the very foundation of Greek tragedy. Aeschylus repeats, again and again, with all the earnestness of the prophet Ezekiel (ch. xviii.), the law, *δράσαντι παθεῖν*. But he is equally explicit in declaring that an old transgression sometimes abides to the third generation, as illustrated in the unhappy family of Laius (Theb. 742):

> παλαιγενῆ γὰρ λέγω
> παραβασίαν ὠκύποινον·
> αἰῶνα δ' ἐς τρίτον μένει.

With urgent force the Fury treadeth
To generations three,
Avenging Laius' sin on Laius' race.

In all cases, however, in which the children suffer for the sins of the parents, they are themselves not innocent. The sin is hereditary as well as the suffering. The guilt and the punishment are propagated together, from generation to generation. It runs in the blood. Like begets like (Agamem. 758–762; Ibid. 1564, 1565):

"One base deed, with prolific power,
Like its cursed stock, engenders more;
But to the just, with blooming grace,
Still flourishes a beauteous race."

"Thus by the laws of nature son succeeds
To sire; and who shall drive him from the house?"

Or, to render this passage more literally, as it is amended by Hermann and Bloomfield, "Who can expel the brood of curses from the family! The race is wedded (glued) to Ate." A kind of judicial blindness and madness not only comes over the heinous transgressor himself, but cleaves to the accursed race. They are given over to the power of an avenging demon, the demon, the Ate, the Ara, the Erinys of the race, who involves them, one after another by their own acts, and yet almost in spite of themselves, in guilt and ruin. To illustrate this were simply to unfold the plot of the several dramas, and to repeat the history of blood and crime, familiar to every one who knows anything of classical mythology, of the house of Pelops, and (to carry it back to its root) of Tantalus himself (Agamem. 1469). The Agamemnon is a *locus classicus* on this subject. It paints the power and sway of the avenging deity, in the same dark and fearful colors in which the retributive power of conscience is drawn in Macbeth; and while the resemblance between the two plays is thus striking, a careful comparison would also illustrate most clearly the difference between the theology of Aeschylus and the theology, or more strictly the anthropology, of Shakespeare. Under Jove, Ate or Erinys, two names for one and the same power, is the divinity of the Agamemnon; and the characters of the play are but her ministers. "Say not," cries Clytemnestra, with a grandeur and steadfastness in wickedness surpassing even that of Lady Macbeth, and with an element of justice to which that lady had no claim (1498; 1432):

> "Say not that I, that Agamemnon's wife
> Did it. The Fury fatal to this house,
> In vengeance for Thyestes' horrid feast,
> Assumed this form, and, with her ancient rage,
> Hath for the children sacrificed the man."
>
> "By that revenge
> Which for my daughter I have greatly taken;
> By the dread powers of Ate and Erinys,
> To whom my hand devoted him a victim,
> Without a thought of fear I range these rooms."

Aegisthus, too, puts on a moral dignity foreign to his nature, claims to be but the avenger of his father's wrongs, and heaven's executioner of justice, and welcomes the doom which in turn awaits him (1578):

> "Now I know that the just gods
> Look from their skies, and punish impious mortals,
> Seeing this man rolled in the blood-wove woof,
> The tissue of the Furies, grateful sight!
> And suffering for his father's fearful crimes."

And then he goes on to describe the horrid banquet of Thyestes, spread for the sacrilegious Atreus beneath his own roof, for his own brother (the father of Aegisthus), and the curse which Thyestes, when he discovered that he had been feasting upon the flesh of his own children, pronounced upon Atreus (father of Agamemnon) and all his race: "Thus perish all the race of Pleisthenes" (1602). And the chorus, possessed with the same thought of a race doomed to calamity and crime, and hunted by an avenging deity, exclaims (1468):

> "O god, that o'er the doomed Atridan halls
> With might prevailest,
> Weak woman's breast to do thy headlong will
> With murder mailest!
> O'er his dead body, like a boding raven,
> Thou tak'st thy station,
> Piercing my marrow with thy savage hymn
> Of exultation."

To which Clytemnestra responds:

> "There's sense in this; now hast thou touched the key
> Rousing the Fury, that from sire to son
> Hath bid the stream of blood, first poured by her,
> Descend. One sanguine tide scarce rolled away,
> Another flows in terrible succession."

And the chorus in reply, while acknowledging the agency of Erinys, recognizes also the hand and will of the Highest:

> "Ah, 'tis a higher power
> That thus ordains; we see the hand of Jove,
> Whose will directs the fate of mortal man."

The consequences of great crimes, especially in high places, extend to every person and every thing that has any connection with them. The country and country's gods are polluted (Agamem. 1645: *χώρας μίασμα καὶ θεῶν ἐγχωρίων*). The army and the people share in the curse (Pers. passim). The earth itself is defiled by pollutions of ancient blood (Sup. 265) Even the innocent and the virtuous who share in the enterprises of the wicked may be involved in their ruin, as the pious man must sink with the ungodly when he embarks in the same ship with them (Theb. 602). This doctrine of social liability is illustrated by this striking simile in the case of Amphiaraus, of whom a character is drawn, than which nothing more beautiful has come down to us from ancient times — "a discreet, upright, good, and pious man, who wished not to *seem* but to *be* good," and "a great prophet," who foresaw the disastrous issue of the Theban expedition, and forewarned the leaders; but led on by a high sense of honor, he went with them, and fell like them (Theb. 601):

> "Death's unblest fruit is reaped
> By him who sows in Ate's fields. The man
> Who, being godly, with ungodly men
> And hot-brained sailors mounts the brittle bark,
> He, when the god-detested crew goes down,
> Shall with the guilty, guiltless perish."

The pollution and curse of sin (*μίασμα, μύσος, ἄγος*), when once contracted by an individual, or entailed upon a family, will rest upon them and pursue them, till the polluted individual or the hated and accursed race (*στυγηθέν, δύσποτμον γένος*, Theb. 691, 813) is extinct, unless in some way the sin can be expiated,[1] or some god interpose to arrest the penalty. Some sins are inexpiable. Prayers, tears, sacrifices, are all in vain. The criminal must die by the hand of justice, and even in Hades, vengeance will still pursue him (Sup. 227). Others may in time be washed away by ablutions, worn away by exile and pilgrimage, and expiated by offerings of

[1] The expiation requires the intervention of some friend, a god or a prince, who is clothed with more or less of divine authority.

blood (Eum. 445 seq. et al.). "It is enough," pleads the chorus in the Seven against Thebes, "for Thebans to come to blows with Argives, for such blood admits of expiation (*καθάρσιον*); but the death of own brothers thus mutually wrought by their own hands, this pollution never grows old" (Theb. 678). Indeed, the presumption in regard to great crimes is, that they cannot be expiated. The blood cannot be washed away (*αἷμ' ἄνιπτον*, 1459); (Choeph. 518):

> "All ocean poured in offering
> For the warm life-drops of one innocent man
> Is labor lost: old truth thus speaks to all."[1]

"For what expiation is there for blood when once it hath fallen upon the ground?" (*τί γὰρ λύτρον πεσόντος αἵματος πέδῳ*, Choeph. 47); (Choeph. 398):

> "What hath been, and shall be ever,
> That when purple gouts bedash
> The guilty ground, then *blood doth blood*
> *Demand, and blood for blood shall flow.*
> Fury to Havoc cries; and Havoc,
> The tainted track of blood pursuing,
> From age to age works woe."

Thus the law (*νόμος*), for so it is expressly called, rolls on reverberating its thunders and threatening vengeance from act to act and chorus to chorus of that grand trilogy of which we have spoken, through the Agamemnon, through the Choephoroe, and far into the Eumenides. And the history of blood and crime follows close upon the law, like the rain-storm after the boding thunder. In the Agamemnon — the first of the trilogy — the crimes of former generations — of Tantalus,

[1] Compare Shakespeare's Macbeth:
> "Will all Neptune's ocean wash this blood
> Clean from my hand?"

of Pelops, and of Atreus, — gathering blackness as they descend, are often alluded to by the chorus as ground of fearful foreboding. Then Cassandra sees them in frightful visions, and sings them in prophetic frenzy as a bloody prelude to the vengeance which is just ready to fall upon the proud Achaean king. Moreover, that monarch's own crime in the sacrifice of his weeping, pleading daughter, though committed under the heavy yoke of necessity, and the hardening influence of frenzy (218), still haunts the memory of the people as the sure precursor of coming evil, while it goads on the bereaved and outraged mother to her long-cherished and now soon to be accomplished vengeance. She lures him on over purple tapestries to the luxurious bath, where she throws a net over him, and slays him with repeated strokes of her own hand; and this play ends with threats of vengeance on the murderess at the hand of his and her son, the absent Orestes.

In the Choephoroe those threats receive their accomplishment. Orestes returns under the guise of a messenger sent to announce his death, unites with his sister Electra in tears, prayers, and vows at the tomb of their father, and then slays Clytemnestra and Aegisthus, who perish by treachery, just as they had treacherously slain Agamemnon (886). But no sooner has he imbrued his hands in his mother's blood — though he did it by command of the oracle, under threats of dire calamity if he disobeyed — than his thoughts begin to wander like horses without a charioteer; doubt, fear, and frenzy seize upon him; and he sees the Furies — the angry hell-hounds of his mother (*μητρὸς ἔγκοτοι κύνες*, 1052) — in Gorgon form, in sable vestments, and entwined with snakes, who pursue him as he flees to find a refuge at the altar of Apollo.

But after the law comes the gospel. First the controversy, then the reconciliation. Such is the natural order of the ideas; such the actual sequence of events; and a dim consciousness of the former as a fact, and of the latter as a want, if not also as an object of faith and hope, seems to have revealed itself to the human mind, even in the darkest period of its existence. Something like this seems to underlie not a few of the Greek trilogies. The Prometheus Bound was followed by the Prometheus Unbound, reconciled and restored to the favor of Jove through the intervention of Jove's son (Prom. 767–769).[1] The Oedipus Tyrannus of Sophocles was completed by the Oedipus at Colonus, where he dies in peace amid visible tokens of divine favor. And so the Agamemnon and Choephoroe reach their consummation only in the Eumenides, where the Erinyes themselves are appeased, and the Furies become the gracious ones. This is not, however, without a special divine interposition, and then only after a severe struggle between the powers that cry for justice and those that plead for mercy. The law still thunders its dreadful sentence; the avenging goddesses come into the very sanctuary, and threaten vengeance in the very presence of "great Loxias," Orestes' advocate, "the healing prophet and the seer," and "the cleanser (*καθάρσιος*, 63) of the house."

[1] Hermes declares to Prometheus, that he shall not be released till some god appear a successor (*διάδοχος*) to his sufferings, and willing to go down to Hades and Tartarus for him (Prom. 1026); Apollodorus says, that Hercules, after freeing Prometheus, delivered up the centaur Chiron to Jove, willing, though immortal, to die in his stead (*θνήσκειν ἀντ' αὐτοῦ*, Apol. ii. 5, 11, 12). See Blackie's note in loc., where also see the extent to which the idea of vicarious sacrifice has prevailed among the heathen nations. The Druids, according to Caesar, held the doctrine: Pro vita hominis, nisi hominis vita reddatur, non posse aliter deorum immortalium numen placari arbitrantur (Bell. Gall. vi. 16).

The scene opens at Delphi. Orestes is seen sitting on the Omphalos (40):

> "His hands with gore are dripping, and he holds
> A sword drawn newly, and an olive branch
> Chastely enwrapt with wool of whitest fleece."

Apollo stands by his side, and Hermes, messenger of Jove, in the background. The Furies sit all around him, sleeping and snoring under the power of the suppliant-protecting god. Their form is the same in which they first appeared to Orestes, immediately after the murder of his mother. Hideously grim and black, from their eyes they distil a deadly dew. Hags, antique maids, they are fit only to dwell in subterranean Tartarus. Apollo encourages Orestes, sends him under the conduct of Hermes to the feet of Athena at Athens, and there promises to find out means for his deliverance. No sooner has he gone out than the ghost of Clytemnestra rises, and rebukes the Furies for their inertness. Thus awakened to their duty, and quickened by the scent of blood, they pursue after him, muttering as they leave the temple of Apollo (160, 177):

> "Such things our young gods do, by might
> Prevailing ever over right:
> Apollo, stern to me, shall never save him,
> Nor under earth shall he be free;
> Another blood-avenger there shall have him,
> And cling unto him after me."

The scene is now shifted from Delphi to the temple of Athena Polias at Athens. Scarcely has Orestes arrived at the house and image of the goddess, and offered his prayer for reception and protection, as a suppliant, polluted indeed, but whose pollution has been worn away by long and weary wanderings, when the

Furies overtake him, and renew their threats of vengeance in language and imagery most frightful (264–275):

"But thou must give thy living limbs to me
To suck the marrow out; may I from thee
The odious draught as food receive;
Thee, while alive, I will bereave
Of all thy pith, and take thee downward hence;
This the tributary recompense
Thou art in thy person paying
For thy impious mother-slaying.
And thou shalt see if any other,
To god or stranger, sire or mother,
Hath done despiteous wrong, how he
Must pay the penalty, like thee.
For Hades, underneath the ground,
A strict examiner is found;
And all the deeds of mortal kind
He sees, and writes them in his mind."

To which Orestes replies (280 sqq.):

"My mother's blood, that was upon my hand,
'T is there no more, — the stain, washed out, is gone.
While fresh, it was removed at Phoebus' hearth,
By purifying blood of slaughtered swine."

The Furies, to whom Aeschylus with characteristic boldness has assigned the sacred and venerable office of the chorus in this piece, now close in, as it were, around their victim, and join in singing a hymn of curses, in which they magnify their own powers and functions as the avenging deities appointed by the eternal law of Fate, and imprecate the direst woes on all offenders, and especially on those who shed kindred blood (354 sqq.; 381 sqq.):

"When Mars, grown tame to touch and sight,
In social life shall slay a friend,

Then we pursue him to the end,
And hunt him down, though he be stout,
Nor leave him till we blot him out."

"For we are skilful to devise,
And can effect whate'er we plan;
Of ill deeds, awful memories,
And hard to be appeased by man;"

Athena soon appears in person, and the two parties plead their cause before her, Apollo appearing openly as the advocate of Orestes. The Furies urge the overthrow of ancient laws as the inevitable consequence of acquittal. Orestes, in person and through his advocate, pleads duty to his father, the sanction of Apollo, and the expiation, which under Apollo's teaching, he has made. Athena summons about her a council of the oldest and wisest of the citizens — the original of the famous council and court of Areopagus — and takes their votes; and when, so difficult and doubtful is the question, they are equally divided, she throws her casting vote in favor of Orestes. For a season, the Furies are frantic at the indignity, and threaten dire revenge on the people and the very soil of Athens (778 sqq.):

"Ye younger gods have trampled down
Old laws, and wrested them from me;
Amerced of office and renown,
I will, for this indignity,
Drop from my heart's wrath-bleeding wound
A blight, a plague-drop, on the ground:
A lichen fatal to the trees,—
To children, shall invade the soil,
Hear, Justice!) and inflict disease
On men — the blotch and deadly boil."

But Athena finds means to appease and reconcile them, and gives them a sanctuary at the very base of Mars'

Hill, hard by the court of Areopagus. The dreadful goddesses, having now become the venerable and the gracious-minded, invoke their sister Fates to join them in blessing, instead of cursing, the land; and as they are conducted with great pomp to their new seats of just but benignant power, all the people unite in a general song and shout of rejoicing.

Such is an imperfect outline of this most interesting and instructive drama. It is not denied that much of all this is earthly, civil, and political in its primary intention. But the presence of the gods, and the constant references to a future state of just and inevitable retribution, forbid any restricted application. The ideas are founded deep in the religious nature of man. They set forth the theology of Aeschylus and the better part of his contemporaries. And it must be confessed that that theology is surprisingly healthy, sound, and truthful in its essential elements. The great doctrines of hereditary depravity, retribution, and atonement are there in their elements, as palpably as they are in the Sacred Scriptures. Would that much of modern poetry were equally true to the soul of man, to the law of God, and to the gospel of Christ!

The offices and work here ascribed to Apollo, taken in connection with what has been said of the same god under a former head, must strike every Christian reader, whatever may be his explanation of them, as remarkable resemblances, not to say foreshadowings, of the Christian doctrine of reconciliation. This resemblance or analogy becomes yet more striking when we bring into view the relation in which this reconciling work stands to *Ζεὺς Σωτήρ*, Jupiter the Saviour—*Ζεὺς τρίτος*, Jupiter the third, who in connection with Apollo and

Athena, consummates the reconciliation. Not only is Apollo a Σωτήρ (Agamem. 512) who, having himself been an exile from heaven among men, will pity the poor and needy (Sup. 214); not only does Athena sympathize with the defendant at her tribunal, and, uniting the office of advocate with that of judge, persuade the avenging deities to he appeased (Eum. 970); but Zeus is the beginning and end of the whole process. Apollo appears as the advocate of Orestes, only at his bidding (Eum. 616). Athena inclines to the side of the accused, as the offspring of the brain of Zeus, and of like mind with him (664, 737). Orestes, after his acquittal, says that he obtained it:

> "By means of Pallas and of Loxias,
> And the third Saviour who doth sway all things."[1]

And when the Furies are fully appeased by the persuasion of Athena, she ascribes it to the power of *Ζεὺς ἀγοραῖος*, Zeus, the master of assemblies:

> "Jove, that rules the forum, nobly
> In the high debate hath conquered.
> In the strife of blessing now,
> You with me shall vie forever."[2]

In short, "throughout the Oresteia, Aeschylus exhibits dimly and mysteriously in the background, but with all the more poetical effect on that very account, the idea of Zeus Soter, the third, as the power that pervades the universe, and conducts the course of things, gently (slowly ?) indeed, but eventually to the best possible issue."[3]

[1] Τοῦ πάντα κραίνοντος τρίτου σωτῆρος (975).

[2] Chapman's version is more striking, but less true to the original:

> But Zeus prevails; the power of mercy still
> Predominates — good doth o'ermaster ill.

[3] C. O. Müller on the Eumenides, p. 219; where see also his remarks on

6. A FUTURE STATE OF REWARDS AND PUNISHMENTS.

The immortality of the soul is nowhere taught by Aeschylus as an abstract and general truth. Still less does he know anything of the doctrine of the resurrection. That struck the philosophers at Athens as a novelty and an absurdity when Paul preached it five or six centuries later on Mars' Hill. But a future state of existence is everywhere taken for granted, as it is in the Old Testament. It is implied in prayers and offerings to the dead. Thus Electra invokes Agamemnon to send blessings on herself and Orestes, and to appear as an avenger of his murderers (Choeph. 140; 480 et al.) And Atossa, by advice of the chorus, makes her prayer to her departed husband Darius, whom she had seen in vision the previous night, that he would avert all evil omens and bring to pass all that was good (Pers. 220, etc.). It is implied also in the evocation of departed spirits, who even make their appearance on the stage in the tragedies of Aeschylus. Thus Clytemnestra comes up from the abodes of the dead to goad on the Furies to avenge her murder, and declares that she wanders in disgrace, not only unavenged, but perpetually dishonored and reproached among the dead for the murder of her husband (Eum. 95). Darius, evoked from the under-world by the queen-mother and the Persian nobles, appears to counsel them after the overthrow of Xerxes (Pers. 680). And the living Clytemnestra, with hands yet dripping with her husband's blood, with biting sarcasm avers that Iphigenia, the victim of her father's unnatural cruelty, shall meet him, as is fit, at

the wide diffusion through Greece of the conception and cultus of Jupiter Soter, as the third.

"the Ferry of Sighs," greet him lovingly, throw her arms about him, and kiss him (Agamem. 1555).

The place of the departed is called Hades, or the unseen world. It is ὁ νεκροδέγμων, the receiver of the dead (Prom. 153); ὁ πάνδοκος, the all-receiver (Theb. 860); it is the realm of the most hospitable Zeus (τὸν πολυξενώτατον Ζῆνα, Sup. 157), the entertainer of most numerous guests. It is situated under the earth (Prom. 152 et al.). It is a dark and gloomy abode (ἀναύγητος, Prom. 1027), untrodden by Apollo, uncheered by the light of the sun (Theb. 859). Men are conveyed to this sunless, all-receiving, invisible shore, across Acheron, by an ill-omened boat with sable sails, filled by a breeze of sighs (Ibid. 854–860). It seems to be conceived of often as one vast sepulchre, where are gathered all the dead of all ages; often as a subterranean world, the image of this, only excluded from the light of day; an empire with its infernal sovereignties (νερτέρων τυραννίδες, Choeph. 403); a city with its counsellors sitting at the gates (Agamem. 1291), and its inhabitants with characters and pursuits not unlike those in the present life.

Tartarus is a part of Hades, or rather a dark, deep dungeon (μελαμβαθὴς κευθμών, Prom. 219) sunk far beneath it (νέρθεν Αΐδου, Ibid. 152) in whose dismal depths (κνεφαῖα βάθη, 1028) the enemies of Zeus are kept in indissoluble chains (δεσμοῖς ἀλύτοις, 154), and from which there is no way of escape (ἀπέραντον, 153, cf. 1077).

The character and condition of the departed corresponds in a great measure with their character and condition here. The same distinctions of rank hold there as here. Darius rules in Hades; nay, ranks among the gods of the lower world (Pers. 691), even as the Persians honored their kings as gods on earth (Pers. 156). And Agamemnon, not less distinguished below than above, is honored and reverenced as a king and a minister of the greatest subterranean powers (Choeph. 253 seq.); for (such is the argument of Electra) thou wast a king when thou wast living. Yet wealth is of no avail to the dead, and earthly pleasures are not there to be enjoyed; and on this ground Darius exhorts the Persian nobles, even in their defeat, to make the most of the pleasures of the present life (Pers. 840).

Still more certainly will the distinctions of character which exist on earth continue also in another world. The good and happy here will be good and happy hereafter, though comparatively little is said in Aeschylus of the blessedness of the righteous. It is the punishment of the wicked on which the tragedians chiefly insist, for the obvious reason that this falls in more with the plan and idea of tragedy. Death is no escape to the wicked from their sins or the consequences of them. Their crimes will follow them into another world. The same Furies that pursue them on earth, unless appeased and reconciled, will follow them in Hades, nay, in Tartarus, which is their fit and favorite abode (Eum. 72). In Hades also there is a tribunal which the wicked cannot escape, and a faithful record of their lives, and a just judge, who will certainly bring them to judgment and punish them according to their deeds. For example, Danaus encourages his frightened and desponding daughters with the assurance that the wretch who would fain force upon them an incestuous marriage, without their own or their father's consent, cannot be pure in the sight of God. Not even in Hades can he who does such things escape guiltless and unpunished. For there, as the saying or tradition is (ὡς λόγος), another Zeus judges crimes, and awards to the departed their final sentence (Sup. 227):

> "Who does these deeds
> Will find no refuge from lewd guilt in Hades;
> For there, as we have heard, another Jove
> Holds final judgment on the guilty shades."

And the Argive king fears to deliver up the fugitive suppliants, lest he bring upon himself as an avenger, the all-destroying god, who does not even let go free the dead in Hades (Ibid. 414):

> ὃς οὐδ' ἐν Αἵδου τὸν θανόντ' ἐλευθεροῖ.

In the Eumenides, as we have seen on a former page, the Furies declare to Orestes that they will not only waste his body and suck his blood here, but after having hunted him through life, they will drag him away to the lower world, there to pay the full penalty for his mother-slaying. And like certain and condign punishment awaits every other sinner, whether against God or man (273–275):

> "For Hades, underneath the ground,
> A strict examiner is found;
> And all the deeds of mortal kind
> He sees, and writes them in his mind.
>
> μέγας γὰρ Αἵδης ἐστὶν εὔθυνος βροτῶν,
> ἔνερθε χθονὸς,
> δελτογράφῳ δὲ πάντ' ἐπωπᾷ φρενί.

And this punishment is not only certain, but remediless and endless. Though he flee beneath the earth, he shall never be set free from the demands of justice (175). "And where shall be the end of the murderer's punishment?" "Where joy is never known" (422). Such are the ideas of future punishment which are perpetually recurring in the Eumenides. From the beginning almost to the end of this magnificent drama, eternal retribution hangs like a gloomy cloud in the distance; and it is on this dark background that the poet has painted, in bright and beautiful contrast, the bow of reconciliation.

In conclusion, should we attempt to express our views of the Greek drama, and the old Paganism generally, in its relation to Christianity, we could hardly sum them up better than in the words of the learned and devout American historian of the church, Dr. Schaff: "Its polytheism rested on a dim monotheistic background, subjected all the gods to Jupiter, and Jupiter himself to a mysterious fate; it had at bottom the feeling of dependence on higher powers and reverence for divine things; it preserved the memory of a golden age and of a fall; it had the voice of conscience, and a sense, obscure though it was, of guilt; it felt the need of reconciliation with deity, and sought that reconciliation by prayer, penance, and sacrifice. Many of its religious traditions and usages were faint echoes of the primal religion; and its mythological dreams of the mingling of the gods with men, of Prometheus delivered by Hercules from his helpless sufferings, were unconscious prophecies and fleshly anticipations of Christian truths."

Is not the summary we have given of the theology of Aeschylus sufficient to demonstrate the above conclusions as a matter of fact? And why should we fear or reluctate to receive them as a matter of doctrine? Paul, while he censured the idolatry of the Athenians, did not hesitate to recognize an element of truth in their ideas, of devoutness in their spirit, and even of authority in their poets, and to build upon this foundation his masterly discourse on the Areopagus. So likewise in his epistles, whenever he can seize upon anything truthful, which the heathen "prophets" have said, he presses it into the service of Christianity. There certainly is in the poets and philosophers of ancient Greece not a little of truth and of resemblance to the great central facts of Christianity, mixed up with gross superstitions and hurtful errors; and why should not this, like all other truth, be referred to God as its source? Does not God rule in history? Has he not always had his witnesses in the world and in human hearts? Does God, in his word, contradict his works; or are his works of creation and providence the scaffolding wherewith he built — the mould wherein he cast — his word? Is Christianity at variance with history, or is it rather the consummate flower and fruit of all God's dealings with mankind? And if it is, must there not be some type and promise of its coming in all his previous dealings with men, even as in every tree which he has made, the type of the flower and fruit is found in every leaf and twig and branch, and the whole stock, even to the root? He who made the pre-Adamic earth an "unconscious prophecy" of man, and formed the lower orders of animals types of the higher, and planted the seeds of each succeeding age of human history in that which preceded it, and filled the outward world and the soul of man with types and shadows of coming events, even as he filled the Old Testament with types and shadows of the New — has he planted no seeds of Christianity in human hearts; caused no types of the highest truth and life to grow in the literature and religion of the ages; cast no shadow of the greatest event that is ever to transpire in our world on the previous history of that world; created no unconscious prophecies of his last and best dispensation in the brightest and best minds of antiquity? If we believed this of Christianity, we could not believe it came from God, because it would want the stamp of all his other works. But when we see all literature and history, as well as external nature and the soul of man, full of prophecies and preparations for its coming, then we cannot resist the evidence that he who made and governs the world is the author of Christianity.

There are two extreme views of the theology of the old Greek poets and philosophers. The one is held without due consideration by too many mere theologians, who regard every ray of truth and excellence discovered in classical literature as so much subtracted from the brightness of Christianity. As if the Logos were not the light which lighteth every man that cometh into the world! As if, in order to add to the glory of the sun, the stars must be extinguished!

The other, assumed without proper examination by too many mere scholars and free-thinkers, denies, like Buckle in his History of Civilization, that Christianity has added anything to the sum of moral and religious truth known to the ancients. As if our very children did not understand the chief end of man and the way of salvation better than the wisest of pagan philosophers!

> "What sages would have died to learn,
> Now taught by cottage dames."[1]

As if there were in pagan literature and biography any

[1] [Keble on the Catechism.]

near approximation to the life and teachings of Jesus of Nazareth. As if unbelievers themselves could really know him without exclaiming, "Never man spake like this man;" "his life was more than human;" "his death was the death of a god!"

Between these extremes there is a middle ground, taken after the fullest and freest investigation by such Christian philosophers and scholars as Schaff, Trench, Neander, and Cudworth, not to say such sacred writers as Paul, who see in Christ "the desire of all nations," and in Christianity that towards which human history has been tending, and for which human hearts have been longing, in all ages. In medio tutissimus ibis.

VI.

THE THEOLOGY OF SOPHOCLES.[1]

In the museum of the Lateran at Rome there is a statue — discovered within the last quarter of a century among the ruins of ancient Anxur — whose faultless symmetry of form and harmony of expression suggest to the uninstructed beholder the thought that it must be some Greek artist's ideal of perfect manly beauty, executed in the best period of Grecian art, and preserved by a kind providence for the instruction of an age whose prerogative it is to collect and interpret the wisdom of the ancients. But by its resemblance to all the known likenesses that have come down to us from antiquity, it is proved to be a portrait statue of the master who carried Greek tragedy, which is the culmination of Greek poetry, to its highest perfection. Not only the general features, and the outshining soul bespeak this most favored of the sons of the muses; but the smallest details of dress and manner are highly characteristic. While wisdom sits enthroned on the brow, and eloquence on the lips; while every limb seems to have been shaped according to the nicest laws of proportion, and rhythm regulates every attitude and movement, the mouth seems formed for the utterance of musical harmonies; the drapery displaying, rather than veiling, the fine

[1] [Reprinted from the Bibliotheca Sacra, Vol. xvii. No. 67, July 1860, and Vol. xviii. No. 69, Jan. 1861.]

structure of the body, images the transparent purity and refinement of his style; and the light fillet which confines the natural and graceful tresses of this, in common with all the other statues of the poet, indicates the almost uninterrupted series of triumphs which crowned his long and prosperous life.[1]

With these plastic representations the descriptions of ancient writers fully accord. Literature and art agree in representing Sophocles as one of the most gifted and fortunate of mortals, the favorite alike of men and gods. Born of wealthy parents, in the most beautiful of the suburbs of Athens; educated under the best masters of gymnastics and music in that harmonious system of culture which aimed to develop a healthy mind in a healthy body; endowed with every gift of nature, and adorned with every grace of art, when the Greeks were assembled in Salamis to celebrate their victory over the barbarian hosts of Xerxes, in the sixteenth year of his age he was chosen among all the children and youth of Athens, naked and lyre in hand, to lead the chorus in dance and song around the trophy. Triumphing over the acknowledged master of tragedy at his first appearance on the stage at the age of twenty-five; carrying off the first prize in more than twenty of his pieces, the second in many more, and never falling into the third rank; raised to the highest honors, civil and military, as the reward of his genius, and never for a moment losing the favor of the capricious multitude; enjoying the friendship of all the great and good at Athens; the intimate friend of Herodotus; receiving

[1] See an appreciative and graphic description of this statue in Braun's Ruins and Museums of Rome. See also Müller's Anc. Art with Welcker's Additions (London, 1852), p. 598.

his first prize at the hands of Cimon and his colleagues; himself the colleague of Pericles and Thucydides; admired by the lyric poets, envied by the tragic, and spared even by the comic Aristophanes;[1] outliving as well as outshining not only his older, but also his younger rival, and at the age of ninety turning a charge of dotage into the most magnificent of all his triumphs, by simply reading before his judges one of the choral songs of a recently-written tragedy; and dying, at a sacred festival, a death as enviable, and almost as remarkable, as that of his own Oedipus; he deserved, as few mortals have ever deserved, the felicitations that were pronounced upon him from the stage by a contemporary comic poet:

> "Μάκαρ Σοφοκλέης, ὃς πολὺν χρόνον βιοὺς
> Ἀπέθανεν, εὐδαίμων ἀνὴρ καὶ δεξιός,
> Πολλὰς ποιήσας καὶ καλὰς τραγῳδίας·
> Καλῶς δ' ἐτελεύτησ' οὐδὲν ὑπομείνας κακόν."[2]

And he was not more happy in his person and life than he was in the circumstances in which his lot was cast. It was his good fortune to come upon the stage of active life just in season to take a leading part in celebrating the triumphs of united Greece over the wealth and power of Persia, and to leave it a little while before Athens succumbed to Sparta, in that deplorable strife of parties and nations in which the Grecian states exhausted their resources, and paved the way for their common subjugation to the yoke of Macedon; and, if we may credit some anonymous ancient memoirs, and the traditions preserved by Pausanias,[3] the din of war

[1] Cf. Frogs, 76 sqq.

[2] From the Μοῦσαι of Phrynichus.

[3] Cf. Pausan. i. 21, 2.

and battle was hushed a moment at his death and burial: Dionysus, the father-god of tragedy, having twice appeared in vision to the Spartan general Lysander, and commanded him to allow the interment of the poet's body in the family tomb outside the walls of Athens. He saw the astonishing growth of Athenian power after the Persian wars, the forsaken and ruined city rebuilt with far more than its previous splendor, the *Ἄστυ* and the Piraeus fortified by strong walls, the Agora surrounded by porticos and public edifices, the Acropolis crowned with temples and statues of the gods, Athens acquiring the hegemony by sea and land, and bringing all the nations under the more powerful sway of her literature and art; and, as from year to year the Dionysiac festivals drew together crowds, not only of citizens but of strangers, from every part of Greece to admire the magnificence of the city, and to enjoy the splended entertainments of the theatre, Sophocles, more than any other man, was the host in this feast of reason, "the observed of all observers."

The Iliad and Odyssey had long since been written, and the poems of the mythic and the epic cycle were complete. Anacreon and Pindar had already sung; the poets of the lyre had already perfected that infinite variety and richness of metre and music which has never been equalled by any other people. Aeschylus had transformed the car of Thespis into the fixed and amply-furnished stage, the troop of itinerant players into the chorus of accomplished actors and singers, the goat-song of satyrs into the regular drama, which had taken its place among the established institutions of the state, and aspired to the honor not only of amusing but instructing the people. It remained for Sophocles —

and for this his well-balanced mind was admirably adapted — to combine and harmonize the several elements of dialogue and song, action and scenic representation, and carry tragedy to its highest perfection. It was that happy period in the national existence when wealth had superseded the primitive rudeness, but had not yet passed over into luxury; when tyranny had given place to liberty, and liberty had not degenerated into licentiousness; when blind tradition or dogmatic prescription no longer ruled with absolute sway, and yet unbridled speculation had not loosened the bonds of morality and religion. The despotism of the *τύραννοι* had been abolished; the despotism of the *δῆμος* was not yet established. The age of ignorance and barbarism had passed away; the age of the sophists and rhetoricians had not yet fully come. The retiring shadows of the former still lingered upon Aeschylus; the false and artificial lights of the latter already dazzled and misled Euripides; Sophocles dwelt in the sunlight of the golden age of Athenian government, literature, and religion. Aeschylus, like some ancient prophet or oracle-declaring priest, ascended the tripod and, in strains of awful sublimity, proclaimed the laws of God and the destinies of men, pointed criminals to the everlasting Erinyes, that were sure to overtake them, and arraigned heroes and demigods before the tribunal of divine justice. Euripides seated himself in the chair of the philosopher, and, interspersing his dialogues with discussions, reasoned, refined, doubted, sometimes almost scoffed, and perpetually mingled the myths of the ancients with the declamations of the sophists and the speculations of the schools. Sophocles walked the *stage* as if it were emphatically his own, sung in the orchestra, as if music and verse were the language of his birth; and represented the past, the present, and the future, the providence and government of God, and the character and destiny of men, idealized but not distorted or discolored, just as they were mirrored in the pure and tranquil depths of his own harmonious nature. Aeschylus, as we have before said, was the theological poet of ancient Greece. Euripides may be characterized as the philosophical and rhetorical poet. Sophocles was, emphatically, the dramatic poet, whose home was in the theatre; and who, from that central and elevated position in the midst of the city, on the sunny side of the Acropolis, looking up to the temples of the gods, and around on all the diversified scenes of nature and pursuits of men, saw them all canopied by the blue sky and bathed in the bright sunlight of Athens. We must not expect, then, to find the theology of Sophocles so strongly marked in its character, nor so ubiquitous in its presence as that of Aeschylus, nor, perhaps in some respects, so faithful a transmission of the universal and primeval traditions of our race; but it may, for that very reason, furnish a fairer representation of the average sentiments of the Athenian people.

Only seven out of more than a hundred tragedies which the ancients ascribed to Sophocles have come down to us. But among those, fortunately, and by a very natural law of preservation, are the very tragedies which were most admired by his contemporaries. Of these seven, all but one (the Trachiniae) cluster about those fruitful themes of ancient epic and tragic verse — Thebes and Troy; three (Philoctetes, Ajax, and Electra) attaching themselves to the latter, and three (Oedipus Tyrannus, Oedipus at Colonus, and Antigone) centring in the former. The scenes of the tragedies, however, conduct us, not only to Thebes (Oedipus and Antigone) and Troy (Ajax), but to Lemnos (Philoctetes), Trachis (Trachiniae), Argos (Electra), and Athens (Oedipus at Colonus), the chief cities of historical Greece. As the perfection of his plots is among the chief excellences of Sophocles, we shall pursue a different method from that adopted in the treatment of Aeschylus, and instead of a classified synopsis of doctrines, we shall present our readers with a brief analysis of each tragedy. There will be less of logical unity in this method, but, we trust, more of variety and interest. Besides, this difference of treatment is due to the difference between the authors. The Theology of Aeschylus is uttered more fully in words and single passages, while that of Sophocles is acted out in the characters and the plots.

THE TRACHINIAE.

The scene of this drama is laid in Trachis, near Thermopylae, and there is a distinct allusion (632 seq.) to Thermopylae as the place of meeting for the Amphictyonic Council. It derives its name from the fact that the chorus consists of Trachinian women. The subject is the Death of Hercules; and the Dying Hercules would be a more characteristic title. Schlegel pronounces it so inferior to the other pieces of Sophocles, that he wishes he could believe it spurious; and "many critics have remarked that the introductory soliloquy by Deianira, without any motive, is very unlike the prologues of Sophocles." The scene opens with the wife of Hercules (Deianira) soliloquizing on her unhappy lot as having been wooed by the frightful, hateful river-god, Achelous, and since she has been won by Hercules, doomed to perpetual loneliness and anxiety, while her lord is involved by the Fates in endless labors; and though now his allotted labors are all performed, she is peculiarly distressed by his absence for fifteen months, during which she, an exile at Trachis, has received from him no intelligence. The soliloquy begins with an anachronous allusion to the famous maxim[1] of Solon: "Call no man happy before his death," in which the poet intends, perhaps, to shadow forth the tragic end of Hercules, but which his wife alludes to only by way of contrast with the palpably unhappy life which she has led from her birth, and is likely to lead till she rests in her grave. An attendant maid suggests that she relieve her anxiety by sending a messenger in quest of Hercules. Hyllus, her son, opportunely presents himself, and, after some conversation with his mother, departs to seek his absent father. The first chorus invokes the aid of the sun-god (Helius) in discovering the abode of the hero, approves the sympathy and fidelity of his half-widowed wife, and yet reproves her for not reposing more confidence in the overruling providence of the all-controlling king, the son of Kronus (*ὁ πάντα κραίνων βασιλεὺς, Κρονίδας*, 127), who does not intend unmixed good for mortals, and yet never forsakes his children (139, 140):

ἐπεὶ τίς ὧδε τέκνοισι
Ζῆν' ἄβουλον εἶδεν.

"Spangled night, with sable sway,
Frowns not on the world for aye;
Sorrow wounds not — golden store
Doth not bless to change no more;

[1] λόγος ἀρχαῖος ἀνθρώπων, vs. 1.

Joy and woe in turns succeed:
Hearts, in turn, must bound and bleed.
Lady, on my counsels dwell,
Trust that all may yet be well;
When, oh when did lofty Jove
Reckless of his children prove?"[1]

Deianira responds by assigning as a special cause of her anxiety, an old tablet (παλαιὸν δέλτον ἐγγεγραμένην,[2] 157) which Hercules put into her hands at his last departure (quite unlike his wont on former occasions), in which was inscribed his destiny (εἱμαρμένα) as revealed to him by the Oracle at Dodona, and his last will and testament (ξυνθήματα) in case he should not return at the end of fifteen months, for that was to be the crisis of his fate, when he must either die, or thereafter live an untroubled life; and that time had already expired. While she is yet speaking, a crowned messenger appears, and announces that Alcides lives and conquers, that he is bringing out of the battle the first-fruits for the gods of the country (ἀπαρχὰς θεοῖσι τοῖς ἐγχωρίοις, 183), and will soon return home in triumph. Deianira renders thanks to Zeus, who dwells in Oeta's unshorn meads for this welcome, though late news, and calls on the Trachinian maidens to join with her in celebrating the unexpected intelligence. A brief choral song follows

1 Dale's version, which we follow chiefly in the choruses; though we shall make use of Francklin and Potter, when they seem to be more true to the sense and spirit of the original. It will be seen that these last lines do not include all men as the children of the universal father, but refer exclusively to the natural children of Jove, born of mortal women, like Hercules.

2 Cf. 685: χαλκῆς ὅπως δύσνιπτον ἐκ δέλτου γραφήν; also 1169. These passages illustrate Sophocles' idea as to the early existence of alphabetic writing. It is not a mere unconscious anachronism; for he details the form and manner.

— a general paean to Apollo, Artemis, and Dionysus. A train of captives is now seen approaching, sent forward by the conquering hero to attest his victory, and herald his speedy return; though for the present he remains on the extreme northern promontory of Euboea to erect altars, consecrate a grove (*τέλη ἔγκαρπα*,[1] 238), and offer purifying sacrifices (*ἁγνὰ θύματα*, 287) to paternal Jove. The sight of the captives awakens the compassion of Deianira, and excites her fears, lest, as an offset to her present great prosperity, similar calamities may come upon her; and she prays to *Ζεὺς Τροπαῖος* (303), the giver of victory and the averter of calamity, that she may die, rather than live to see such a day, thus foreshadowing her own actual doom. Among the captives one of noble mien and patient spirit excites her special pity, and she inquires who the stranger is. The messenger who would fain conceal the hero's moral infirmities, affects ignorance, but is at length compelled by a spectator who has heard the whole story from him in the Agora, to disclose the fact that she is the daughter of Eurytus, king of Oechalia, and that a passion for her was the sole cause of the long delay of Hercules, and the sole motive for the slaying of Eurytus, and the destruction of Oechalia. Grieved, but not maddened, by these facts, the unhappy but still loving wife puts the best construction on her husband's unfaithfulness. Love rules in her own breast; love lords it over the immortal gods; why then should she not be indulgent towards her husband if he has fallen beneath the power of this disease (*τῇδε τῇ νόσῳ*, 445), and still more towards the innocent vic-

[1] In doubtful readings we for the most part follow Wunder; though the verses are cited as numbered in the Leipsic edition.

tim of his passion. This is not the first time that the son of Jove, like Jove himself, has been thus overcome:

> "Hath not Hercules
> Of other consorts been the only lord,
> Yea, and of many; and did one receive,
> At least from me, harsh words or keen reproach?
> Nor shall she meet them; though for her his breast
> Glows with impassioned love.
> . . . . .
> Nor will we court a voluntary ill,
> Contending with the gods."

The chorus, which follows, celebrates the matchless might of Aphrodite, alluding cautiously to her triumphs over the three gods who divide the sovereignty of the world—Zeus, Poseidon, and Hades (Pluto); and dwelling at length on the strife of the river-god (Achelous) and the son of Jove (Hercules) for the hand of Deianira.

That princess now reappears from the palace, with bleeding but submissive heart, bewailing chiefly the almost certain loss of her husband's affections, yet relating to the Trachinian maidens the means which she proposes to use in order, if possible, to retain them. In obedience to the instructions of the dying centaur—slain by Hercules for undue liberties with his bride on their bridal tour—she had carefully preserved, in a brazen vase, the clotted blood from the arrow's point—of which the centaur said:

> "Forever shall it bind to thine
> The soul of Hercules, that ne'er his love
> Shall burn to others as it burns to thee."[1]

[1] It is not difficult to see the sardonic grin with which the centaur thus "paltered with words in a double sense," deceiving the woman, as Satan did Eve, when he said: "Ye shall be as gods, knowing good and evil." Hercules never lived to love another woman, after putting on the fatal robe.

And now she has moistened (ἔβαψα, 580)[1] or anointed (ἔχριον, 677) with it a tunic, which she proposes to send by the returning messenger to her absent lord. Encouraged by the approval of the choir, she sends it, with a charge that none be suffered to put it on but himself, and that he should let no light of sun or fire fall upon it, till, in accordance with her vow, on the day of sacrifice (611--612):

> "He should stand forth, and to the gods display
> A new adorer clad in new attire."

With that blindness which is one of the most tragic elements in the character and destiny of men, the chorus now exult in the near prospect of Hercules' return. Meanwhile, however, Deianira has made a discovery, which has thrilled her with horror and fearful forebodings. The lock of wool with which she applied the poison to the robe, thrown upon the ground, in the sunshine had crumbled to pieces like sawdust; and, from the spot on which it fell, clotted foam bubbled up, as when new wine of the vintage is poured upon the ground (700 sqq.). And now, wise only when it is too late, she marvels that she did not see that the dying centaur could bear no good will to his slayer; and she has only this consolation, that if Hercules shall thus lose his life, she is resolved to die with him.

[1] Ἔβαψα is not only interpreted by its synonyme (ἔχριον) here; but the process of applying the poison is explained at length in vs. 690–699. It was applied to the tunic with a lock of wool. Ἔβαψα is plainly used here as a generic word, equivalent to *wet*, or *moistened*, and the more specific word ἔχριον, 677, ἔχρισα, 691, is repeatedly used to explain the process. Compare the βαπτισμοὺς . . . . . χαλκίων καὶ κλινῶν, Mark vii. 4, where the application must have been made in a similar way. Sophocles uses the word frequently of the sword stained with blood, and in Ajax, 30, uses βαίνειν in the same way: νεοῤῥάντῳ ξίφει; cf. 95: ἔβαψας ἔγχος εὖ πρὸς Ἀργείων στρατῷ.

While she is thus speaking, Hyllus her son returns from Euboea, and tells the tragic story, how Hercules, while sacrificing to his father Jove, at the Cenaean promontory, received the deadly robe (*θανάσιμον πέπλον*, 760) at the hands of the messenger; arrayed himself in it, slew the victims — twelve unblemished (*ἐντελεῖς*, 762) bulls, the firstlings of the spoil (*λείας ἀπαρχήν*, 763), together with a hundred smaller cattle from the common herd; and, exulting, poured forth his prayers, till the sacrificial flame kindled the dormant virus, when the sweat started from his body, the robe clung as if it had been glued to his sides and every limb, and anguish shot through all his bones. Frantic with pain, he hurled the unsuspecting messenger from the precipice upon the wave-encompassed rocks, dashed himself upon the around, and made the rocks and woods ring with his cries of agony. Then borne, helpless and distracted, by his son and attendants, he was placed on board a ship, and they would soon see him, living or dead, brought to his home (809 sqq.):

> "Such were thy counsels, mother, such thy deeds
> To my poor father; for which traitorous acts
> May penal justice and the avenging Fury[1]
> Meet recompense award thee. Thus I pray,
> If it be lawful — lawful it must be,
> Since every law towards me thyself hast spurned,
> And slain the best and bravest of mankind,
> One on whose like thou ne'er shalt look again."

Without a word in reply, the wretched woman, cursed by her own son as the cause of death to her husband, steals away to put in execution her threat against her

[1] Ποίνιμος Δίκη Ἐρινύς τε (810–811). This dreadful prayer is softened by the filial limitation: *if it is right*, εἰ θέμις γε.

own life; while the choir break forth in lamentations, and reflections on the true meaning of the oracle and its now hastening fulfilment (823 sqq.):

"Behold, dear virgins, with what fatal speed
The ancient oracle of heaven
Hastes, to its dread fulfilment driven:
'When the revolving months,' so Fate decreed,
'Had crowned the twelfth long year,
Rest from his toils severe
The son of Jove should win'; firm to its end
Doth the sure presage tend:
Who wakes to life and light no more,
His earthly toils are closed, his earthly bondage o'er."

At the close of the chorus, a nurse comes forth from the house and announces the death of Deianira by her own hand. Another choral song ensues, in which the singers know not which to deplore most, the past, or the evils that are yet to come:

"To feel or fear is equal pain."

Borne by attendants, Hercules now comes upon the stage, racked with pain, murmuring at Jove for the ill return he has received for his altars and sacrifices, invoking death to relieve his pangs, imprecating vengeance on her head, whom he supposes to be the guilty cause; and dwelling with bitter and prolonged emphasis, on the contrast between his past heroic achievements and his present helpless and suffering state (1105–1108):

"Yet remember how, with torn and wasted frame,
I pine, devoted with this dark, dark curse:[1]
I, who a mother of the noblest vaunt!
I, who in heaven was styled the son of Jove!"

[1] Τυφλῆς ὑφ' ἄτης, under that blind bewildering Ate, with whose dread power we have become so familiar in the theology of Homer and of Aeschylus.

Hyllus, who has learned the innocence of his unhappy mother, ventures a word in her defence; which, at first, rouses the hero almost to frenzy. But when he hears the sad story of her death, and learns how she had been misled by the artful centaur, he sees at once that his doom is sealed, and resigns himself to his fate. He now exacts from his son a promise, under dreadful penalties, that he will convey his body, already more dead than alive, to the brow of Oeta, dear to Jove,[1] and there build a funeral pyre, place him upon it, and, without a tear, set it on fire and consume him to ashes. He further extorts from his son a promise to marry the captive maiden, the daughter of Eurytus, the love of whom had been the cause of his present calamity — a promise which the son gives only in implicit obedience to the command of his father, and to avoid his curse, leaving the responsiblity with him (1245–1253):

" *Hyl.* And would my father teach an impious deed?
Herc. It is not impious if it be my pleasure.
Hyl. And canst thou, then, with justice, thus command me?
Herc. I can; and call the gods to prove my truth.
Hyl. Then I will do it, nor resist thee more;
Appealing to the gods, thy will constrained me:
I cannot err if I obey my father."

The passage involves, it will be seen, the question of the higher and the lower law — a question which is often raised in the Greek tragedies, and which, between the gentle Hyllus and the mighty Hercules, seems to be decided against the higher,[2] but which we shall see

[1] Cf. above 200, 436, 754, et passim. We see everywhere among the Greeks the same disposition to worship in groves and high places, which so often led the Israelites into the idolatrous practices of their heathen neighbors.

[2] Hyllus yields his own convictions of right to the authority of his father.

meeting with quite another solution from the uncompromising and high-souled Antigone.

Now Hercules has only one more favor to ask, and that is, to hasten the funeral pyre, since:

> "This is my rest from ills, this my last end."

Hyllus reluctantly consents, distinctly laying all the blame on the gods (1261 sqq.):

> "Ascribe the injustice to the gods;
> They gave him being — bear the name
> Of fathers, yet can view his pangs unmoved."

And the drama ends with this brief moral from the chorus:

> "Ye have beheld the mighty fall,
> Beheld these recent woes, unnumbered, strange;
> But all were wrought by Jove.
>
> Οὐδὲν τούτων ὅ,τι μὴ Ζεύς."

The filial love and obedience of Hyllus commend him to our regard. He was a pattern son; but he was more pious towards his father, and more gentle even towards his erring mother, than he was reverential to the gods or obedient to the dictates of his own conscience. The woman's love and charity of Deianira, her conjugal fidelity and submission to the will of her unfaithful lord, and the speechless agony with which she goes away to find her last consolation, and her best vindication in death, reflect the essential features of many a tragedy in real life. But we sorrow over the darkness of the age which knew no better remedy than suicide

His first answer is, that he would rather die than marry her who was the occasion of his mother's death and his father's calamity, a deed which none would do, who was not smitten as with a plague by the avenging deities: ὅστις μὴ 'ξ ἀλαστόρων νοσοῖ, 1237.

for heavy calamities; while we deplore the blindness of human nature, which not unfrequently brings ruin on itself in the very endeavor to shun the ills of life. The choral songs in this piece are not of the highest order of poetical or moral excellence, though they breathe the simplicity and purity befitting virgins.

The leading character of the drama is the least perfect, and attaches to himself the smallest measure of our sympathy. The physical hero[1] of a barbarous age, battling incessantly with wild beasts and savage men, he has all the faults of Samson and many more, without all his virtues or extenuating circumstances. He was anything but a Nazarite in regard to wine and strong drink. If the lying messenger may not be believed when he represents him as expelled in a state of intoxication from the banquet of Eurytus, the manner in which the story is received, to say nothing of the inebriated Hercules of other dramas,[2] shows that the story was not, in itself, incredible. One Delilah at a time was not enough for Hercules; though, in that respect, he was no worse than his father. With all his weaknesses and imperfections, the son of Manoah was superior, morally and religiously, to the son of Jove; and though there are not a few circumstances of grandeur attending his tragical end, yet the apotheosis of Hercules on Mount Oeta can scarcely be compared in moral sublimity with the self-sacrificing and triumphant death of Samson at Gaza, who slew more of his enemies and the enemies of his country and his God in his death than he slew in his life.

[1] Compare his lamentation over his wasted muscles (1090 sq.) with that of Milo, for whom Cicero expresses so much contempt. De Senec. ix. 27.

[2] Cf. Eur. Alc. 799 sq.

But neither his relationship to Jove, nor his numerous sacrifices, can save him from the retribution due to his sins; and in the righteous providence of the supreme, the injured wife is made the unintentional instrument of that retribution; her robbed and wounded affections, the medium through which that retribution is visited on his head. The retributive government of the most high, his universal providence, and his particular care over his children (though they are children by natural or rather unnatural generation, and not by creation, still less by spiritual regeneration), the inspiration and divine authority of oracles, the acceptableness of vows and bloody sacrifices, and the divine appointment of afflictions to all of mortal race, especially to all who are raised up to be great public benefactors, are among the theological lessons which seem to be involved in the plot of the Trachiniae, or directly inculcated in the dialogue.

Perhaps the myth of Hercules may contain an unconscious prophecy; gross indeed, darkened by ignorance, and defiled by sin, but still a prophecy of a yet higher truth and a still deeper mystery: The son of Jove could be made perfect only through suffering; he could find life only in death, rest only by passing through life-long labors and a tragical end. While he dwelt on earth he was an exile and a wanderer, often a sufferer and a servant; and it was only through the purifying power of suffering that he reached his apotheosis. If the Logos is the light of every man that cometh into the world, why may we not refer to him all the truth and goodness there is in the heroes and sages of the ancient heathen world, as well as in the prophets and kings of Israel; and see in the former as well as in the latter, types and forerunners of the Messiah, whose office it was to awaken ideas and felt wants, which could be realized only in him who was "the desire of all nations!"

PHILOCTETES.

The Philoctetes has one point of close contact with the Trachiniae, and also one point of close resemblance. For setting fire to the funeral pile on Mount Oeta — a service which Hyllus shrunk at last from performing in person — Philoctetes was rewarded with the possession of the bow and arrows of Hercules. On the way to the siege of Troy he lands with the other Grecian warriors on the island of Chrysa, to offer sacrifices to the god of the island, and there receives a deadly wound from the bite of a serpent, the guardian of the sacred enclosure; and the Greeks, disturbed in their sacrifices by his cries of anguish, and moved also by the offensive odor of the wound, convey him to an uninhabited portion of the isle of Lemnos, and there leave him to perish or to support himself as he can by his famous arrows. In the tenth year of the war, taught at length by the prophecies of Calchas and Helenus that Troy cannot be taken without the arrows of Hercules, they send Ulysses and Neoptolemus, son of Achilles, to bring them, with their present owner, to the camp. Ulysses would fain take the bow and arrows by fraud, and then carry off the archer himself by force. Neoptolemus falls in for a time with the plan of the inventful Ulysses; but after he has got possession of the arrows he relents, refuses to succeed by such base means, and actually restores the arrows to their rightful owner, when Hercules appears, reconciles Philoctetes to the plan, and sends him voluntarily to aid in completing the siege of Troy. The arrows of

Hercules, and the reappearance of that hero on the stage, are the point of contact of which we spoke.

The point of resemblance is the intolerable physical suffering, to which the principal character is subject, and the paroxysms of which are exhibited on the stage. But here the resemblance ceases with the mere external suffering. The spirit of the sufferers is entirely different: Hercules longs for death, and demands the co-operation of his friends in hastening his fiery apotheosis. Philoctetes clings to life, though forsaken of all his friends (and even after he has been robbed of his faithful bow), and drags out an existence of ten long years, nursing all the while an incurable wound, obtaining a precarious subsistence by shooting the birds that chanced to come near his den, and then crawling with extreme pain and difficulty to the spot where they fell.

Besides the sympathy we feel for the patient toil and suffering of Philoctetes, and the painful interest which attaches to his Crusoe-like struggle to prolong life, the chief charm of the piece is the fine ethical contrast between the artful and unscrupulous son of Laertes, who holds and practices the jesuitical doctrine that the end sanctifies the means, and the frank, brave, and generous son of Achilles who scorns lying, hates all disguise, and though he attempts for a time to walk in the crooked ways of his comrade, ere long breaks the shackles and acts out his own noble nature. This nice discrimination of character, like that which distinguishes the modern drama and romance, and the Shakespearean perfection of the plot, without sacrificing, however, one iota of the simplicity so characteristic of Grecian tragedy, have made this a favorite play with most modern readers.

We cannot dwell on the opening scene in which Ulysses unfolds the web of artifice and falsehood by which he proposes to inveigle the unhappy wretch of his arrows; and then, with the ingenuity of the arch tempter, plies Neoptolemus with arguments and motives, once, for a brief portion of a day, to be false to himself and to that father who hated falsehood as the gates of hell (Hom. Il. ix. 312), and aid him in the execution of the plot. The reply of Neoptolemus is worthy of his parentage, and worthy of immortal remembrance among the noblest utterances of human lips:

> "If but to hear such words offends mine ear,
> Son of Laertes, how I loathe the actions!
> I stand prepared to seize the man by force,
> But not by falsehood; on one foot sustained,
> 'T were strange if he could match our manly might.
> Yet know, O prince, I deem it nobler, far,
> To fail with honor than succeed by baseness."

But the artless youth is no match for the man of wiles, and soon yields to the tempter's sophistries and the tyrant's plea — alleged necessity. Ulysses goes away offering the prayer (134, 135):

> "May Hermes, god of wiles, be now our guide,
> And conquering Pallas, queen of rampired towns,
> Whose favoring presence evermore preserves me;"

while Neoptolemus labors to justify himself and reconcile the choir by the "flattering unction" that Philoctetes is but suffering the just punishment of his impiety.

Philoctetes is now seen dragging his wounded foot towards his solitary cave amid the rocks and trees, and shrieking for anguish. He welcomes the Grecian costume in which they are clad, and anxiously inquires their errand. Neoptolemus tells him the story, partly true and partly false, in which he had been instructed by Ulysses, interweaving with it not a little of the history of the war and the fortunes of the heroes, and eliciting from Philoctetes comments on the character of those heroes, together with the touching tale of his own misfortunes. The death of Ajax and Antilochus calls forth complaints from a heart oppressed by its own griefs, and almost despairing of divine justice (428–430):

> "Ah, whither, whither must I look, since these
> Have perished, and the vile Ulysses lives;"

while, on the other hand, the safety of Thersites provokes the more rebellious comment (446 sqq.):

> "Aye, fit he should; for nothing vile is lost;
> Such the gods visit with peculiar care.
> How shall I judge or how extol the gods,
> Proved, by the actions I would praise, unjust!"

And these remarks receive the partial assent of Neoptolemus, though in less impious language:

> "War never sweeps away
> The vile and worthless, but destroys the good."

As Neoptolemus at length rises to depart, professedly to his own land, offended by the injustice of Ulysses and the Atridae brothers, Philoctetes importunes him by his sorrows and adjures him by Jove, the suppliant's aid (*πρὸς αὐτοῦ Ζηνὸς ἱκεσίου*, 484) to take him with him. This prayer is seconded by the chorus, who bid him beware of the Nemesis of the gods (518), if he refuse. With seeming reluctance the request is at length granted, and Philoctetes retires to take a last farewell of his home that is not a home (*ἄοικον ἐσοίκησιν*, 534). As he returns bringing the herb that soothes his wound, and the much-coveted irresistible arms of Hercules, he is seized by sudden and dreadful paroxysms of pain in his foot, during which he entrusts the arms to the care of Neoptolemus, adjuring him by the gods, not to yield them to any other hands, and charging him also to propitiate envy (*τὸν Φθόνον δὲ πρόςκυσον,*[1] 776); that is, to deprecate the jealousy of the gods, lest those arms should become a source of many woes to him, as they had been to their former possessors; as if the posession of so great a prize were a good fortune so superhuman, as might well excite the envy of heaven. After a succession of pangs so unwonted that they seem to the sufferer ominous of impending evil, he finds relief at length in sleep, and the chorus sing a brief and beautiful ode to Sleep as the sorrow-soothing, life-blessing (*εὐαίων*), healing (*παιών*) power (827 sqq).

While he sleeps the conflict begins in the breast of his captor; and when he awakes and the time comes for action, the son of Achilles is paralyzed. The wretched man is now entirely at his mercy. The way is clear to take him on board the ship by fraud, and then by force convey him to Troy. But he cannot do the base deed (902, 903; 908, 909):

"All must be ill,
When man the bias of his soul[2] forsakes,
And does a deed unseemly."

"Great Jove direct me! shall I twice be proved
A villain: first concealing sacred truth,
Then uttering words of falsehood?"

Truth and honor at length prevail. He frankly reveals to the exile the purpose of the voyage, and urges

[1] Cf. Aesch. Prom. 935: *οἱ προσκυνοῦντες τὴν Ἀδράστειαν σοφοί*; and Ps. ii. 12; "Kiss the son, lest he be angry," etc. The Greek word means worship, kiss the hand to, etc

[2] *Τὴν αὐτοῦ φύσιν*, 902.

him by every motive of duty and interest, of patriotism and piety, to go with free consent, and help to finish the siege of Troy. But resentment for his wrongs is too deep. He refuses, demands back his bow, paints in lively colors the baseness of the fraud that has been practised upon him; and, as if he had nothing to expect from human justice or divine compassion, calls on the rocks and trees to witness the wrong and sympathize with him in his calamities.

Unable to withstand the appeal, the generous son of Achilles is about to restore the bow to its rightful owner, when the master of the plot rushes in from his concealment, and forbids the surrender, pleading the divine will in justification of his course (989, 990):

> "It is Jove,
> Yes, Jove, supreme controller of the land;
> Jove thus hath willed, and I but do his will."

"Detested wretch," answers Philoctetes, pleading at once his own cause and the character of the gods (991, 992):

> "Detested wretch! what falsehood dost thou frame,
> The gods alleging; thou dost tax the gods
> With lies, to gloss thine own dissembling guile!"

And in the dialogue which ensues, he gives vent to his sense of justice and his religious faith, in the following strain of mingled sarcasms, arguments, and curses (1032 sqq.):

> "How can ye serve the gods in prayer? how slay
> The votive victims, if I share your bark!
> How pour libations due? Such was the plea
> On which ye first expelled me. Curses on ye!
> Ye who have wronged me thus, yourselves shall meet
> An equal doom, if Heaven cares aught for justice.

I know, I know it does; for never else
Would ye have voyaged for a wretch like me,
Had not a goad from heaven itself constrained you."

Ulysses bids him welcome to remain. The arms of Hercules are all they want. With them, perchance, himself can gain the prize which heaven intended for Philoctetes, but which he rejects. Neoptolemus waives his decision till the ship is ready, and they have offered prayers and vows to the gods (1077), in the hope that time and divine power will yet change the purpose of Philoctetes.

Meanwhile the conflict is fearful in the mind of the exile, aggravated by occasional spasms of physical pain, and expressed, now in argument with the chorus, now in pathetic apostrophes to the crags and caverns, wild beasts and birds. The chorus, loyal at once to their earthly and their heavenly lords,[1] argue thus (1116):

"The doom, the doom of Heaven![2] No treacherous scheme,
Framed by my hand, hath wrought thee this.

One moment, he bids them go and leave him to his fate. The next, he adds (1187):

"Go not, I pray, by Jove, who adds the curse."
Μή, πρὸς ἀραίου[3] Διός, ἔλθῃς ἱκετεύω.

Resolved at length, he asks but one boon, a sword or an axe, that he may put an end to his life, and go to his father in Hades (1210).[4]

Ulysses and Neoptolemus now reappear on the stage,

[1] The chorus consists of the sailors in the ship of Ulysses and Neoptolemus.

[2] πότμος δαιμόνων, 1116.

[3] Compare what is said of the goddesses Arae, in the Theology of Aeschylus.

[4] Compare the expression "gathered to his fathers," so often applied to patriarchs and pious kings in the history of the Old Testament.

in impassioned dialogue: the latter intent on restoring the bow to its owner; the former remonstrating with him, arguing the inexpediency of his course, and threatening him with the vengeance of the Greeks; to which the latter replies, in a high tone of ethical philosophy, not always found in public men, or even in ethical systems, that justice is better (stronger) than expediency; and that, with justice on his side, he fears not his threats. The Greek is worthy to be placed on record, and to be written in the heart of every scholar (1246; 1251):

Ἀλλ' εἰ δίκαια, τῶν σοφῶν κρείσσω τάδε.
Ξὺν τῷ δικαίῳ τὸν σὸν οὐ ταρβῶ φόβον.[1]

Then turning to Philoctetes, and finding him more resolved than ever not to go willingly to Troy, he gives him the bow. Ulysses rushes in to prevent, threatens to recover it by force; and is threatened in turn with the drawn bow in the hand of its owner. But Neoptolemus lays his hand upon him and entreats him, by the gods, to forbear. The hero's heart now opened by generous treatment, Neoptolemus again plies him with arguments: tells him — invoking Jove, the god and guardian of oaths (*Ζῆνα ὅρκιον*),[2] to witness his unsullied truth — that he is now suffering the penalty of divine providence (*ἐκ θείας τύχης*, 1326) for treading with rash foot on hallowed ground; and he never can be cured till, of his own free will, borne to Troy, he is healed by the sons of Esculapius; in proof of which he cites the prophecy of Helenus, the best of prophets (*ἀριστ-*

[1] Compare Shakespeare, Henry VI: "Thrice is he armed who hath his quarrel just." And Julius Caesar: "There is no terror, Cassius, in thy threats," etc.

[2] Cf. 1289, where he swears by "the sacred majesty of most high Zeus," — ἁγνὸν Ζηνὸς ὑψίστου σέβας.

τόμαντις, 1338). Philoctetes is much moved, hesitates for a season, but at length refuses to submit to such dishonor, and calls on Neoptolemus to fulfil his pledge, and conduct him home. Neoptolemus, finding argument unavailing, consents; and bidding the exile lean on his shoulder, is already on his way to the ship, when, in an emergency worthy the interposition of a god, *dignus vindice nodus*, Hercules appears from his celestial seat (*οὐρανίας ἕδρας προλιπών*, 1414), bringing the mandate of Jove, revealing to him the speedy fall of Troy, bidding him bring the spoils to his pyre, and charging him, last of all and most of all, to be ever pious towards the gods (1440–1444):

> "Once more must Troy be taken by my arms;
> And oh remember, when her lofty towers
> Are laid in ruins, to revere the gods.
> Second to this all else great Jove esteems.
> True piety alone defies the grave;[1]
> Let mortals live or die, this blooms forever."

He yields immediately to the voice of the god. A few words of farewell to his rocky home, and of prayer for a safe voyage, and they set out forthwith for the shore, whither great Destiny impels him, and the advice of friends, and the all-conquering deity, who brought it to pass.

> Ἔνθ' ἡ μεγάλη μοῖρα κομίζει,
> Γνώμη τε φίλων, χὠ πανδαμάτωρ
> Δαίμων ὃς ταῦτ' ἐπέκρανεν.

In the former part of this tragedy, the ethical element prevails over the theological. The right and the expedient are set over against each other. Duty and interest, truth and sophistry, strive for the mastery. Gratitude

[1] Οὐ γὰρ ηὑσέβεια συνθνήσκει βροτοῖς.

and resentment, desire of revenge and love of society, fear of pain and love of life, struggle for the ascendency. The human heart is laid open, and its springs of motive, action, and passion are laid bare, with a skill not unworthy of our own Shakespeare.

But as the drama draws towards a close, religious motives assert their native supremacy. The divine plans and purposes move on steadily and irresistibly towards their accomplishment. The light of prophecy shines on the future; and at length heaven opens and the son of Jove descends in person to disclose the will of the gods, and to make willing the appointed human instrument. May we not see here, in the light of revelation, what was imperfectly revealed to the consciousness of the poet or his audience, a dim foreshadowing of these great truths of Christian theology? God has foreordained whatever comes to pass. Yet even these foreordained events can be accomplished only through appointed instrumentalities. Those instrumentalities may be despised and rejected by men; but in due time they will be brought out, though it be from the deepest obscurity, and exalted to the highest honor. They may be unwilling; but they shall be made willing, in the day of God's power. They may appear too feeble to achieve the appointed work; but they shall be mighty through God. And, if need be, God himself will interpose by prophecy, and oracles, and messengers from heaven. Men have always believed in revelations, of some kind or other, from God; and though these have been but dim shadows, they foretell a substantial reality; if you pronounce them all counterfeits, they imply the genuine coin. And where you find the pure metal bearing this oft-counterfeited form and image, the presumption is that it is the genuine coin. When you find that which purports to be a revelation from God for all mankind, which meets not only the general expectation of a revelation, but answers to all the highest aspirations, the purest intuitions, and the deepest longings, of the race, there is certainly a strong presumption that it came down from heaven.

AJAX.

In Ajax, Ulysses is again a prominent actor, exhibiting the same character as in Philoctetes, the tragic Ulysses being generally an exaggeration, if not also a misrepresentation, of the leading traits in the much-scheming hero of the Odyssey and Iliad. Here, as in the Odyssey, he is under the special guidance[1] and guardianship of Athena, who appears on the stage, not like Hercules in Philoctetes, to reveal the future and bring the drama to a magnificent close; but at the beginning of the piece, conversing familiarly with her favorite, like another, though a wiser and more powerful self, acquainting him with facts which no mortal eye had seen, interpreting to him the mysterious conduct of Ajax, and instructing him in those arts and wiles of which he was himself already the acknowledged master — in strict accordance with the scriptural doctrine, "to him that hath shall be given, and he shall have more abundantly." It is a point which has been much disputed among critics, whether Athena is seen by the bodily eye or only by the mind of Ulysses; Hermann, Lobeck, and some others, maintaining the former opinion, but the latter being the prevailing sentiment among scholars. There is great weight in the

[1] Cf. 35: σῇ κυβερνῶμαι χερί.

names on the other side; still this latter is the most obvious interpretation of the language of Ajax (14 sqq.):

Ὦ Φθέγμ' Ἀθάνας, φιλτάτης ἐμοὶ θεῶν,
Ὡς εὐμαθές σου, κἂν ἄποπτος ᾖς, ὅμως
Φώνημ' ἀκούω, καὶ ξυναρπάζω φρενί.

"O accents of Minerva, to my soul
Dearest of powers immortal, how mine ear
Thy welcome voice perceives, and with my mind
I grasp the sounds, though thou art viewless still."

However that may be, it is admitted on both sides, that the goddess is seen by the audience, sustained aloft by stage-machinery; and she carries on an extended dialogue with Ulysses, and a briefer one with the frenzied Ajax.

The scene is before the tent of Ajax, on the plain of Troy. The time is shortly after the death of Achilles, whose arms, awarded to Ulysses by the Atridae brothers, have incensed Ajax to madness; and, in a fit of frenzy, blinded and made sport of by Athena, he turns his hands against the unoffending flocks, mistaking them for the Greeks; and, after dealing dreadful slaughter among them, he drives home the rest in triumph as captives, selecting two rams as Agamemnon and Ulysses, whom he reserves for further torture and a more ignominious death. Athena glories in these frantic deeds, as all the result of her agency:

"I urged him still, and lured to evil toils
The man, misled by frenzy's impulse wild:"[1]

[1] This frenzy is designated by various names, as μανιάσιν νόσοις here, 59; θεία νόσος, 186; and ἄταν οὐρανίαν 196: and these maddening paroxysms, this plague from the gods, this judicial blindness from heaven, involves him in ἕρκη κακά, in evil toils. Compare the "evil net." (Eccl. ix. 12). Tecmessa adds below (953), that Athena does it all for the sake of Ulysses.

She invites Ulysses to look on his fallen rival, and enjoy that sweetest of all laughs, a laugh over a fallen foe (79); a sentiment not much in the spirit of the golden rule, though uttered by the daughter of Jove and the goddess of wisdom. He looks on, while the goddess plays with her victim and mocks him in his madness, winding up with the triumphant exclamation:

> "Thou seest, Ulysses, Heaven's resistless might!"

He is moved, first, to pity, at seeing even his enemy thus yoked up with fatal blindness (*ἄτῃ κακῇ*, 123); and then he is led to reflect, that such might easily become his own lot:

> "I see that we who live are nothing more
> Than a vain image and a fleeting shade."[1]

To which she adds this moral lesson, suggested by the life and fall of Ajax (127 sqq.):

> "This then observing, dare not thou to breathe
> High words of swollen pride against the gods;
> Nor boast presumptuous, if in martial deeds
> Or treasured wealth thou pass thy fellow man.
> A day o'erthrows, a day to light restores
> All mortal things; and still the heavenly powers
> Regard the lowly, while they loathe the proud."

We understand better the reason for this warning, and the moral of the whole dramá, when, towards its close (760 sqq.), we learn, indirectly, from the mouth of the prophet Calchas, that Ajax, though of mortal race, has entertained thoughts not becoming a mortal. When he set out for the Trojan war, his father had given him this parting counsel:

> "Seek, my son, in fight
> To conquer, but still conquer through the gods."

[1] Εἴδωλ' ἢ *κούφην σκιάν*, (126). Cf. Aesch. Prom. 447; Job. viii. 9; Eccl. viii. 13; Ps. cxliv. 4 et passim.

But he made this arrogant and impious reply (766 sqq.):

> " Father, with heavenly aid a coward's hand
> May grasp the prize of conquest; I confide
> To win such trophies e'en without the gods."

Again, when in the midst of the fight, Athena incited him, in common with the others, to battle against the enemy, he replied in language dreadful and not to be spoken (δεινὸν ἄῤῥητόν τ' ἔπος, 773):

> " O queen, to other Argives lend thine aid;
> No hostile might shall break where Ajax stands."

And now she laughs at his calamity, because he has despised her reproof.

While the frenzy still remains upon the unhappy Ajax, and none but Ulysses, under the teaching of Athena, understands fully what he has done, or why he has done it, the chorus (consisting of sailors who followed him from Salamis) mourn over his madness, and impute it to a stroke from Jove (πληγὴ Διός, 137), or Artemis, or Enyalius (Mars), for some neglected sacrifice; at any rate, some plague from the gods (θεία νόσος, 186) — for surely he could not have done such a deed in his own right mind — and they pray that Zeus and Phoebus will avert the spread of the evil report. Tecmessa, the captive concubine of Ajax, now joins with them in their lamentation over his fall, recounts to them what she knows of the events of that dreadful night, and represents him as uttering dreadful words, taught him by some δαίμων, and no man (243).

Meanwhile Ajax recovers from his paroxysm, and awakes to the sudden consciousness that he is the sport of angry gods and the scoffing of unfriendly men. He prays for darkness and the shades of Erebus to receive him, for these are indeed his brightest light (ἰὼ σκότος, ἐμὸν φάος κ. τ. λ., 394, etc.). He calls on his comrades to slay him, and intimates his purpose to take his own life, justifying that purpose by such arguments as these (473 sqq.):

> "It shames a man to seek protracted life,
> Who sees no limit to encircling woes.
> I count the man most worthless who would feed
> His wavering soul with vain delusive hope:
> To live with glory, or with glory die,
> Befits the noble."

Tecmessa entreats him in pity to her woes, and in love to their son,[1] and conjures him by *Ζεὺς ἐφέστιος*, the guardian of domestic ties, not to take his life. Ajax, not yet fully cured of his impiety, declares that he owes no reverence to the gods (590). After breathing out hatred to his enemies and impiety towards the gods for a time, he seems to be somewhat softened by the words of his wife and the sight of his son, and professes his intention to seek the baths of the seashore, that he may wash away his pollution (λύμαθ' ἁγνίσας ἐμά, 655) and escape the weighty anger of the goddess, the gorgon-faced, invincible daughter of Zeus (656 cf. 450); and on his way thither he will hide, where none but Night and Pluto will ever see it more, the hated sword, which he received from Hector at the close of their single combat, and which, from that day to the last fatal night, has been his constant curse. Moreover, he will yield obedience to the powers that be; and, as change is the law of nature (a law which the poet beautifully illustrates through his lips, 670 sqq.), so he will henceforth change his whole course (666, 667):

[1] The passage resembles in pathos the parting address of Andromache to Hector, Hom. Iliad, vi. 407, sqq.

> "Henceforth we 'll pay meet reverence to the gods,
> And learn submission to the sons of Atreus."[1]

And the chorus break forth into a song, accompanied by the dance, at the marvellous change and happy reconciliation.

It is only a feint, however, to escape observation and find opportunity to execute his fixed and fatal purpose. Instructed by the prophet Calchas, his brother Teucer sends a message to prevent Ajax from leaving the house. But the messenger arrives too late. He has already gone out. Tecmessa and the choir, half distracted, seek him in every direction, but find him already fallen on his sword. The choir lay the blame on Ulysses and the sons of Atreus. But the submissive and pious Tecmessa responds (950; 970):

> "It had not fallen thus, but heaven decreed."
> Οὐκ ἂν τάδ' ἔστη τῇδε, μὴ θεῶν μέτα.

> "'T was by the gods he perished, not by them."
> Θεοῖς τέθνηκεν οὗτος, οὐ κείνοισιν, οὔ.

And she consoles herself with the assurance that his death, though sad to her and sweet to his enemies, was yet more joyous to himself:

> "The death
> He prayed for, wished for, now hath closed his woes."

Contrary to the usual law of the Greek drama, the suicide takes place on the stage, while the wife and the choir are seeking in vain to find him; and it exhibits some characteristic, some instructive features. Ajax has now but one favor to ask of Jove; and that is, that he will send Teucer to give him due burial, that his body

[1] The same association of duty to God and to civil rulers as occurs often in the Scriptures; cf. 1 Pet. ii. 17.

may not be a prey to dogs and birds. He next invokes infernal Hermes guide of souls (*πομπαῖον Ἑρμῆν χθόνιον*, 833), to put him well to sleep by a speedy and easy death. Much of his dying breath is poured out in prayers, and curses on the heads of his enemies (835 sqq.):

> "I next invoke to aid me those dread powers,
> Forever virgins, and of mortal wrongs
> Forever conscious, swift in keen pursuit,
> The awful Furies,[1] to attest my doom,
> By the base sons of Atreus basely slain,
> And plunge the traitors in an equal fate.
> As they behold my blood by mine own hand
> Poured forth, so be their best-loved children's hands
> Imbrued in theirs — thus self-destroyers too.
> Come ye avenging Furies, swift and stern,
> Quaff their warm blood, nor spare the peopled host."
>
> *Ἴτ', ὦ ταχεῖαι ποινιμοί τ' Ἐρινύες,*
> *Γεύεσθε, μὴ φείδεσθε, πανδήμου στρατοῦ.*

Then imploring the Sun to bear the tidings to his aged father and mother, he welcomes death, bids farewell to earthly scenes, and dies with these words on his lips:

> "The rest will I say to those below in Hades."
>
> Τὰ δ' ἄλλ' ἐν Ἅιδου τοῖς κάτω μυθήσομαι.[2]

The lamentation of Teucer over the dead body, is worthy of notice as expressive of his full belief in an overruling Providence, in contrast with the scepticism which is implied as more or less prevailing in the minds of others (1034 sqq.):

[1] *ἀεί θ' ὁρώσας πάντα τὰν βροτοῖς πάθη*
σεμνὰς Ἐρινῦς τανύποδας (836, 837).

[2] The reader will not fail to observe how the expectation of a conscious existence after death is constantly implied, as in Aeschylus, so in Sophocles. Philoctetes wishes to go and see his departed father; and here Ajax expects soon to converse with the inhabitants of the unseen world.

"Did not the Furies forge that slaughtering sword,[1]
And Hell's dread monarch, ruthless artist, frame
That belt?[1] These things, I deem, and all the events
Befalling mortal man, are by the gods
Always assigned. To these, whose mind dissents?
Let him enjoy his thoughts: but these are mine."

Herein, doubtless, the poet expresses his own believing, and at the same time tolerant spirit; and both in opposition to a spirit which he saw widely prevalent around him. The higher classes were inclined to scepticism, while the masses at Athens were believing, but intolerant of any departure from the religion of the state. Sophocles has a settled faith in the providence and government of the gods; but be is willing that others should enjoy, with equal freedom, their own religious opinions.

After the death of Ajax, which is the natural catastrophe of the drama, the piece is still prolonged through some four hundred verses (from one quarter to one third of the whole), in a strife between Teucer on the one hand, and the sons of Atreus on the other, touching the burial of the body, which is finally terminated in favor of his burial, by the intervention of Ulysses, who is too politic to sanction any gratuitous or unprofitable crime. Menelaus charges Ajax with treason, and argues at some length the necessity, to the state and to the maintenance of law and order, that he should be made an example. Teucer denies, in the first place, that Ajax was ever subject to the Atridae, and then pleads the higher law of heaven (1125 sqq.):

[1] The sword which Hector gave Ajax, and the belt which Ajax gave Hector; the former of which Ajax plunged into his own breast, and the latter bound Hector to the car of Achilles, 1027 sqq.; cf. Hom. Iliad, vii. 363. See also 665, where Ajax himself, in view of the same fact, gives his assent to the truth of the proverb: ἐχθρῶν ἄδωρα δῶρα κ' οὐκ ὀνήσιμα.

"Conscious of right,
The soul may proudly soar.
Men. Is it right, then, right
To grace with honor the base wretch who slew me?
Teuc. Slew thee! Oh wondrous, — slain, and yet alive!
Men. The gods preserved my life; in his intent I died.
Teuc. Thou dare not, then, despise the gods,
Thus by the gods preserved."

As Menelaus retires, and Teucer, with the wife and child, hastens to effect the interment, Agamemnon appears to enter his imperial prohibition, repeats his brother's reasoning, and heaps threats and abuses on the head of Teucer; and Ulysses interposes to plead, not so much the cause of Ajax and Teucer, as the welfare of the army, the honor of the commander, and the eternal laws of heaven (1343 sqq.):

"Thus to degrade the chief would shame thyself:
Not him alone, but heaven's eternal laws
Wouldst thou contemn. Unjust it is to wrong
The brave in death, though most abhorred in life."

Ulysses prevails. Teucer thanks him, though still imprecating dire curses on the head of the sons of Atreus from the revered fathers of Olympus, unforgetting Erinys, and unfailing (literally, fulfilling) Dike (1389 sqq.):

Τοιγάρ σφ' Ὀλύμπου τοῦδ' ὁ πρεσβεύων πατὴρ,
Μνήμων τ' Ἐρινὺς, καὶ τελεσφόρος Δίκη
Κακοὺς κακῶς φθείρειαν,[1] κ. τ. λ.

Preparations are made for the burial — the hollow trench (κοίλην κάπετον), the ablution of holy water (λουτρῶν

[1] *Evilly destroy those evil men*; cf. Matt. xxi. 41: κακοὺς κακῶς ἀπολέσει αὐτούς. This formula, so frequent in classical and sacred Greek, is not mere paronomasia, but an apt expression of the great law of justice and fitness. Campbell well renders it: He will bring those wretches to a wretched death.

ὁσίων), the arms which cover the body, and which are to be buried with it; and the scene closes where all earthly scenes, sooner or later, close upon all of mortal race, with those honors which friends pay to friends gathered around their graves.

The voice of nature, which is the voice of God, has taught men in all ages and nations, however rude, to render certain offices, rights, duties, dues,[1] to their departed friends; and these have almost always been such as not only to honor their memories, but such as imply more or less clearly a belief in their continued existence after death, with the same essential nature and character, if not also with the same identical wants, and in the very same pursuits as during the present life.

The Greeks and Romans deemed these rites essential to the repose of the soul, nay, to its very entrance into the world of spirits. Hence the burial of the dead was esteemed the most sacred duty of surviving friends. The stranger even was pronounced inhuman who would not throw earth upon a dead body which he might chance to find unburied; and though it was the keenest vengeance which an enemy could inflict upon a fallen foe not to suffer him to be buried, yet for an enemy to carry this vengeance too far were to provoke the vengeance of heaven. When Paul preached the doctrine of the resurrection on Mars' Hill, the Athenians mocked. Yet in their own view there was a mysterious connection between the burial of the body and the repose of the soul; and in this idea, as well as in the care with which they, in common with all nations, preserved

[1] Τὰ δίκαια, νομιζόμενα, προσήκοντα, κτεριζόμενα, funera justa, etc., are among the expressions used by the Greeks and Romans to denote these dues.

the entire body or the ashes of the dead, we see an "unconscious prophecy" of the resurrection. Do no evil to the dead (1154); speak no evil of the departed, for they are with the gods, and under their special protection: these sentiments are written everywhere in Greek literature; in the laws of legislators, in the maxims of philosophers, in the writings of scholars, and in the hearts of the people. The Iliad of Homer and the Ajax of Sophocles could not come to an end till the minds of the readers or hearers were put to rest respecting the burial of those whose right of interment had been called in question. And this question is the central point and subject matter of that drama of Sophocles (Antigone) which won for him the highest honors in the gift of the Athenian people.

Certain criminals who had been put to death by the state were deprived of the right of burial, as an additional punishment. Suicide did not incur this dreaded penalty, though sometimes the hand which had done the deed was cut off and buried by itself, as it were in unconsecrated ground. Indeed, the frequency of suicide is one of the striking features of the Greek drama,[1] and a marked characteristic of Grecian and Roman as compared with Christian civilization. If not more frequent among the masses, it was less condemned, nay, more approved in the higher classes. It was not only celebrated by poets, but justified by moralists,[2] and it was expected of heroes, if they could not live honorably, to die honorably by their own hand. Christianity in-

[1] There are suicides in more than half the extant dramas of Sophocles, and in some of them repeated instances.

[2] Even Plato's authority was claimed for, as well as against, suicide by different disciples, though it seems to us to be clear and decisive against it.

spires its genuine disciples with a higher appreciation of the sacredness of life, a deeper reverence for the authority of God, a more awful dread of appearing unbidden before his judgment seat; and above all, a more submissive, humble, cheerful, childlike trust in the all-wise, all-good providence of a heavenly Father.

Defective as are the morality and the theology of Ajax — burlesque as it almost seems to be, on heroism and on divinity — still it teaches forcibly one great lesson which is most sedulously inculcated in the Scriptures; and that is the helplessness, the littleness, the nothingness of great men when they set themselves in opposition to the laws and government of God; and the folly of wise men when they imagine they can be anything, or do anything, independent of the blessing of heaven. Nothing short of the arrogant self-conceit and daring impiety of Ajax could have reconciled the taste or the moral feelings of an Athenian audience, or of modern readers, to see him tossed about in the hands and blown about by the breath of Athena, like the feeblest prey in the paws of a sporting lion.

ELECTRA.

The four remaining tragedies are all upon those fruitful themes of tragic interest, the houses of Pelops and of Labdacus. And here we come upon ground occupied in common by the three masters of Greek tragedy. The Choephoroe of Aeschylus, the Electra of Sophocles, and the Electra of Euripides, are all on the same subject — the vengeance of heaven on Clytemnestra and Aegisthus for the murder of Agamemnon, of which Orestes was the appointed instrument, and for which Electra had waited till impatience had changed almost to despair. Their different methods of treating the same high theme afford a fine opportunity for comparing these great masters.

Euripides, partly from the necessity of avoiding the track of his predecessors, and partly from faults inherent in his nature, has failed in his Electra. There are not wanting in it lofty sentiments and single passages of great power. But on the whole he has almost burlesqued this grandest of tragic themes by his unbefitting trivialities. Aeschylus, by introducing the tomb of Agamemnon on the stage, and carrying the purposed vengeance into speedy execution, has given a sublime exhibition of the irresistible decree of destiny and the overwhelming march of divine justice; though in the scarcely less grand portrait which he has drawn of Clytemnestra, justifying her murderous deed, and claiming to be herself also the executioner of justice, as well as in the appearance of the Furies to Orestes, and the bewildering madness which comes over him, he represents Loxias and the Furies, wisdom and vengeance, as for the time in conflict. Sophocles transfers the conflict to the breast of mortals, where joy and grief, hope and despair, faith and scepticism, false security and fearful forebodings, in alternate billows go over the soul, while divine justice moves on tardily and stealthily, but surely, to the infliction of the penalty which meets the harmonious approval of heaven, earth, and the powers beneath. "Aeschylus makes the Furies, so to speak, personifications of an impulse, which wreaks itself upon the violator of natural order, whether he is engaged on the side of justice or not—of a blind power, which, like the fiery furnace in Scripture, burns the ministers of the highest authority. Sophocles places the whole plot in the hands of divine intelligence, leaves the Furies but a very subordinate part, and does not imagine that any atonement is demanded from Orestes for a deed which the god has justified."[1] The punishment of the wicked is delayed in Sophocles, till faith and hope have almost expired in the bosom of Electra, but agreeably to the solution of this mystery of divine providence in Plutarch's admirable treatise,[2] this delay is only that they may be deceived with false hopes of impunity, and that, in the very moment of their seeming triumph, justice may overtake them in a form and manner more befitting their crimes. The conception is bolder in Aeschylus, the poetry grander, and the theology more awful in its sublimity; but Sophocles surpasses his rival in the harmony and beauty of his religious sentiments, not less than he does in the dramatic interest which he excites by his marvellous succession of contrasts, his power in delineating character and the varied workings of the passions, and his skilful management of all the details of the plot.

The scene opens with a dialogue between Orestes, Agamemnon's son, and the old servant who snatched him in infancy from the hands of his murderers, and bore him to an asylum in foreign lands, and who now, after pointing out to him the objects of chief interest in the plain of Argos, brings him to the palace of his fathers, and thus strikes the key-note to the whole piece (10 sqq.):

> "This is the home of Pelops' race, defiled
> With frequent murders; on thy father's death,
> From thy true sister's hand receiving thee,

[1] Woolsey's Preface to the Electra of Sophocles.
[2] De Sera Numinis Vindicta.

I bore thee hence, preserved thee, trained thee up
To man, — avenger of thy father's blood."

Orestes, in reply, details his own plan for surprising, and thus destroying, the murderers of his father, in obedience to the command of the oracle, and in righteous retribution for the treachery with which Agamemnon was slain (32 sqq.):

"When to the Pythian oracle I came
A suppliant, asking how I should exact
Just retribution for my father's blood,
Phoebus, as thou shalt hear, this answer gave:
That I, devoid of arms or martial host,
Should strike by stratagem the righteous blow."

The audience are thus put in possession of a clew to the mazes of the plot, through which poor Electra is left to wander without any such guidance or support. While Orestes offers prayers to the gods of his country and his sires, for success in the work, which, sent by the gods, he comes to accomplish, as a purifier (*καθαρτής*, 70) of his father's house, Electra is heard moaning within the palace; and as they retire to do, first, the will of Loxias (*μηδὲν πρόσθεν ἢ τὰ Λοξίου*, 82), and to offer libations and garlands of hair on the tomb of Agamemnon, she comes upon the stage, gives vent to her sorrows, like the hapless nightingale; and in the following dreadful imprecation, invokes the avenging powers (110–120):

"Ye dark abodes of Dis and Proserpine,
Thou Hermes, guide to hell, thou awful Curse,
And ye dread Furies, offspring of the gods,[1]
Who on the basely murdered look,
On those who mount by stealth the unhallowed couch:

[1] πότνι' Ἀρὰ, σεμναί τε θεῶν παῖδες Ἐρινύες.

Come aid me, and avenge the blood
Of my beloved sire,
And give my absent brother to mine arms.
Alone no longer can I bear the weight
Of this o'erwhelming woe."

A choral dialogue ensues between Electra and the chorus of noble women; in which they express their sympathy and strive to comfort her, among other consolations, with the assurance that a god of justice still reigns, and will, sooner or later, punish the wicked (174 sqq.):

"Still in yon starry heaven supreme,
Jove, all-beholding, all-directing, dwells —
To him commit thy vengeance."

At the same time a graphic picture is drawn of the crime, as if it were a frightful living form, begotten of Fraud, brought forth by Lust, and originated by some unknown dreadful power (197–200):

Δόλος ἦν ὁ φράσας, Ἔρος ὁ κτείνας,
Δεινὰν δεινῶς προφυτεύσαντες
Μορφὰν, εἴτ' οὖν θεὸς εἴτε βροτῶν
Ἦν ὁ ταῦτα πράσσων.

These lines will strongly remind the reader of the Scriptures of the passage in the epistle to James (i. 13–17), in which the apostle gives a similar genesis of sin; but distinctly answers in the negative the question in regard to the divine authorship of sin, which the heathen poet leaves unanswered.

Meanwhile, Electra complains, Aegisthus sits on the throne of her father, and insults the gods with libations at the hearth which he has sprinkled with that father's blood; Clytemnestra shares his bed, and joins with him in celebrating, with dance and offerings to the gods, the anniversary of the murder; while she is compelled to dwell beneath the same roof with the murderers, waiting in vain the return of Orestes.

Chrysothemis now comes forth from the palace with funeral offerings to the dead, and reproves her sister for not submitting, like herself, to the ruling powers and the necessities of their lot. Electra replies with great severity, charging her with weakness and falseness to her father's name. Chrysothemis endeavors to soften her asperity by disclosing the severities which Aegisthus threatens to visit upon her (Electra) when he returns home. The audience know that Aegisthus is to return home only to fall himself beneath the avenging stroke of Orestes, and they enjoy the contrast. But Electra knows it not. Still threats only brace her to resist the tyrant; only provoke her to the utterance of bitter scorn for her sister's cowardice. Failing to subdue her sister, Chrysothemis says she will go on her errand (405–410):

"*Elec.* What errand? Whither dost thou bear those off'rings?
Chry. My mother sends me, at my father's tomb
To make the due libation.
Elec. What! to him
Of all mankind her most detested foe?
Chry. And whom she murdered, since thou'lt have me say so.
Elec. By whom persuaded? Who hath counselled this?
Chry. From some nocturnal vision, as I deem."

Chrysothemis relates the vision. It is rumored that she saw Agamemnon again before her, returned to the light of life; that he took again his ancient sceptre, the sceptre of Aegisthus now, and planted it in the earth, and there sprung from it a blooming branch, which overshadowed all the land of Mycenae.[1] Electra sees

[1] In Aeschylus, it will be remembered, Clytemnestra has a dream of the

in the vision the shadow of the returning Orestes, and begs her sister not to offer the hateful libations [1] of her mother, but cast them to the winds, and lay upon the tomb, instead, a lock of hair from the head of each of the sisters, and the belt of Electra; and then kneeling down beside it, pray for the avenging interposition of their father from below,[2] and the coming of their long-expected brother. Chrysothemis consents, and goes away to execute the plan. The choral song which succeeds is full of confident predictions of speedy vengeance (472 sqq.):

"If true prophetic skill be mine,
If aught of wisdom's ray divine,
Soon shall avenging justice here
Her own dread harbinger appear;
With hand of might and threatening brow,
She cannot, will not, linger now;
But soon, my daughter, shall pursue
The track of guilt, and punish too."

The antistrophe repeats the same idea in other words (488 sqq.):

"With many a foot of matchless speed,
With many a hand of deadly deed,
Erinys, veiled in ambush now,
With brazen tread, shall track the foe."

And the epode concludes with a reference to the guilt

same purport, but the sign is different. She dreamed that she gave her breast to a dragon in the cradle of her son, and suckled it with her blood. This diversity of form with identity of substance illustrates the manner in which the poets felt at liberty to deal with the fables of the Greek mythology.

[1] *δυσμενεῖς χοάς*, 440. These offerings are spoken of below (447) as *λυτήρια τοῦ φόνου*, intended to ransom or expiate the murder. Cf. 1490, where Electra says that to give the body of Aegisthus to the dogs and birds were the only adequate *λυτήριον τῶν πάλαι κακῶν*.

[2] In 459, 460, Electra declares her full belief that Agamemnon was concerned in sending the ill-boding dream to Clytemnestra.

of Pelops in slaying Myrtilus, and the woes which have ever since followed his devoted race (508 sqq.)

> "Since Myrtilus, in ocean deep,
> Was headlong hurled to death's cold sleep,
> Hurled from his radiant car of gold,
> With insult fierce and uncontrolled,
> Nor woe hath passed, nor dire disgrace,
> Unfelt by this devoted race!"[1]

Clytemnestra, herself, now comes upon the stage; and, in a conversation with Electra, justifies her act, as in Aeschylus, though with less daring; representing it as done in righteous retaliation for the sacrifice of her daughter Iphigenia. Electra, in reply, explains the dire necessity of that sacrifice, as a satisfaction to the hunting-goddess Artemis, offended at the slaying of a stag in her sacred grove; and though beginning with the deference due to the relation, yet her indignation kindles as she speaks, and she ends with renouncing all filial regard for a mother who has not only stained her hands with a husband's blood, but shamelessly published the motive, by taking a murderous paramour to that husband's bed. Clytemnestra imprecates the vengeance of Artemis, her tutelary goddess, on the unnatural daughter, and then (having begged of Electra to desist from such ill-omened words, at least while she brings her offerings to the gods, a favor which Electra willingly grants, in the confidence that offerings made by such blood-stained hands can only provoke the displeasure

[1] The language of this chorus (472–515) is strong and impassioned. The epithets are singularly apt and expressive. Observe, for instance, the *πρόμαντις* Dike; the *πολύπους, χαλκόπους, πολύχειρ* Erinys, and the description of the unhallowed, incestuous strugglings of a murderous marriage (*ἄλεκτρ' ἄνυμφα μιαιφόνων γάμων ἁμιλλήμαθ'*), attacking those whom it ought not.

of heaven), she pours forth prayers to tutelary Phoebus, that he will confirm or avert the doubtful import of her dream, according as it is propitious or adverse; concluding with this beautiful tribute to the divine omniscience (657 sqq.):

> "What still remains unsaid, though I be mute,
> Is known, I deem, to thee, a potent god:[1]
> Nought can be hidden from the race of Jove."[2]

At this moment, and, as the blinded Clytemnestra thinks, in answer to her prayers, the old servant enters, announcing, according to the preconcerted plan of deception, the death of Orestes. While he sets forth in lively detail the narrative of Orestes, overthrown in the chariot-race and slain on the very eve of a splendid triumph,—a detail fitted to work powerfully on the sympathies of friends and foes,—Electra gives herself up for lost; the chorus lament the utter extinction of the house of Pelops; and Clytemnestra, though touched by a momentary pang of maternal sorrow, yet drinks in the tale with ill-concealed satisfaction, and, on the whole, concludes, that the doom he met became him well. To which Electra answers (792):

> "Hear, thou avenger of the recent dead;
> Hear, Nemesis!"
>
> Ἄκουε, Νέμεσι τοῦ θανόντος ἀρτίως.

While Clytemnestra, with her fears all lulled preparatory to the approaching catastrophe, goes within the palace to reward the old servant for his good news, thus with her own hand admitting and welcoming the avenger, Electra remains deploring the destruction of all her hopes, and the chorus half reprove and half minister to her despair, in such strains as these (823 sqq.):

[1] δαίμον' ὄντ'. [2] τοὺς ἐκ Διός.

"Where are the vengeful bolts of Jove,
Or where the beaming sun,
If deeds like these beholding, still
Such deeds they calmly hide ?"

As Electra thus despairs and refuses to be comforted, Chrysothemis returns from the tomb of Agamemnon, rejoicing in the assurance that Orestes has already come, as is proved by the libations of fresh-flowing milk, the garland of flowers, and the locks of fresh-cut hair which she found upon the tomb, and which could have proceeded from no other source. But so far from gladdening the despairing heart of her sister, her own heart falls from the heights of hope and joy to the depths of sorrow and despair, at the positive assurance, derived from an eye-witness, that Orestes is no more. Yet gathering courage from despair, Electra resolves herself to execute the stroke of vengeance, and invites, but invites in vain, the co-operation of the timid and passive Chrysothemis, who hears unmoved, or moved only to pity, her sister's mad appeals to a sense of duty to the dead, and the desire of undying fame ; while that sister, in turn, steeled by adversity and despair, casts off the remonstrances of sisterly affection, seconded by the counsel of the choir, and resolves to do the deed alone. And in the succeeding chorus, even the choir, carried away by sympathy with such heroism and such misfortunes, cannot withhold their approval of her love of honor and her fear of Jove (1085 sqq.) :

"Waging with guilt eternal war,
That on thine honored name might rest
A double meed — approved by far
At once the wisest daughter and the best.

. . . .

In every law divine
Which blooms with holiest awe above,
A steadfast piety was thine, —
The love of honor and the fear of Jove."

At the same time they express their confidence that:

"If Themis reigns on high,
And Jove's blue lightnings rend the sky,
Ere long shall vengeance crush the guilty pair."

To complete the pathetic scene, Orestes now enters in disguise, with an attendant bearing the urn which purports to contain the ashes of the deceased brother. Electra takes the urn in her hands, and, in a strain of unaffected pathos scarcely to be equalled in the whole range of elegiac literature, mourns the sole, sad relic of all they loved and all they hoped on earth. The scene is too much for Orestes. Despite of his plans for concealment, he is constrained to make himself known to his sister, whom he convinces of his identity by showing his father's seal; and then a scene of joy succeeds, which contrasts powerfully with the previous mourning, and which finds utterance not in the cold iambics of the usual dialogue, but in the strophe, antistrophe, and epode of choral songs from the lips of the rejoicing brother and sister. This untimely rejoicing is prolonged till the old servant, who has been keeping watch within the palace, comes out and reproves them, and summons them to immediate action. Orestes yields his hearty assent, saying as he enters (1374, 1375):

"Let us speed
Within, adoring my paternal gods,
All, who within this vestibule abide."

Justice now delays no longer. The plot hastens to its consummation. Electra beseeches Apollo whom she has often served with such as she had (ἀφ' ὧν ἔχοιμι), and now entreats with such as she has (ἐξ οἵων ἔχω, 1379), that he will be a helper in these righteous measures, and thus show men what penalties the gods award to impiety. The chorus see, and summon others to see, the avenging Orestes enter the palace, guided by Hermes, the god of stealth, and followed by the Furies, those hounds of retribution, from whose pursuit there is no escape (ἄφυκτοι κύνες). And soon from within are heard the shrieks and cries for mercy of the dying Clytemnestra. And her death is celebrated by the chorus: now the curses are fulfilled, the dead live again; the long-slain shed the blood of their slayers.

Meanwhile Aegisthus, who has heard in the street the tidings of Orestes' death, comes home exulting, and mocks Electra, by demanding of her the details of such welcome news. Electra, whose office it is to cherish his false security till he falls into the hands of Orestes, "palters with him in a double sense,"[1] describing the fate of Clytemnestra in language which he understands of Orestes. He commands to open the gates and let all Argos and Mycenae see the blasting of their hopes in Agamemnon's son; and blinded to the last, he draws near to the supposed body of Orestes, saying (1466 sqq.):

> "O Jove, a sight I view that well hath chanced—
> If thus to speak be lawful; but my words,
> If Nemesis be present, I recall."

Nemesis was indeed present, and heard his indecent joy at the supposed death of a near relative, and re-

[1] The reader will excuse the repetition of these words of our great English dramatist. They express better than any other language a frequent characteristic of the tragic style.

turned at once the poisoned chalice to his own lips. The veil is removed; he sees the lifeless body of Clytemnestra, and soon falls himself beneath the avenging stroke of him at whose fancied death he came exulting, on the same fatal spot on which he had slain the unsuspecting Agamemnon.

Contrary to the plot of both the other masters, but with that correctness of taste which almost never errs, Sophocles has made the death of Clytemnestra precede that of Aegisthus; thus letting the mother fall beneath the first uncalculating stroke of her children's vengeance, while the more cool and deliberate slaying of Aegisthus forms the closing scene, on which the mind dwells with unmixed satisfaction.

The Electra furnishes the best example in the Greek drama of that perfect adaptation of punishment to crime which is called "poetic justice." Of course this nice adjustment is not often seen in the distribution of rewards and punishments in real life. Yet there are not wanting examples, both in secular and sacred history,[1] which suffice to show that the principle which so commends itself to the aesthetic and the moral nature of man is recognized in the providence and government of God, and so constitute a presumptive argument from analogy, answering to the intuitive convictions of the human soul, that this principle will be fully carried out in the retributions of the life to come.

The same tragedy which develops the doctrine of

[1] Herodotus' history of the Persian wars, and indeed his whole history, is a great prose drama, written to illustrate the same moral as that of the book of Esther and the history of the Old Testament generally. That moral, stated generally, is providence, and specifically it is the doctrine of a divine nemesis in human affairs.

retributive justice in a manner so congenial to the aesthetic and the ethical nature of man contains also a distinct recognition of another principle deeply rooted in the human soul, — the principle of expiatory and vicarious sacrifices of one human being as a substitute and a satisfaction for the sins of others.

Artemis is offended by the slaying of a stag in her sacred grove, or rather by some boastful words uttered by Agamemnon when he slew it (569). Adverse winds detain the Grecian fleet in port at Aulis, and they can neither set sail for Troy nor return home till they have propitiated the goddess. This propitiation, as they are instructed by the voice of oracle or seer, can be effected only by the sacrifice of Agamemnon's daughter, as a compensation (*ἀντίσταθμον*, 571) for the slain stag. The father resisted, and for a time refused to offer the sacrifice. But there was no other means of escape (*λύσις*, 573) from the anger of the goddess and the winds that imprisoned them in the harbor. At length, though much against his will (*βιασθεὶς πολλά*); he yielded. The unwilling victim was brought and sacrificed.[1] The angry goddess was appeased; the adverse winds became favorable, and the host set sail for Troy. The mother treasured up in her memory the dreadful sacrifice, and, many years after, alleged this rending of her affections in justification of her crimes. She argues that Agamemnon had no right to offer her daughter to

[1] According to Euripides (Iph. in Taur.) and some other authorities, Iphigenia was rescued by the goddess herself, when on the point of being sacrificed, and conveyed in a cloud to Tauris, where she became the priestess of Artemis; while a stag (or, as others say, some other victim) was offered in her stead, thus bearing a striking resemblance to the sacrifice of Isaac, as related in the book of Genesis. But Sophocles makes Electra say in so many words that Agamemnon sacrificed her (*ἔθυσεν αὐτήν*, 576).

make satisfaction for the Greeks (*Ἀργείων χάριν τίνων*, 534), nor instead of Menelaus his brother (*ἀντ' ἀδελφοῦ Μενέλεω*, 537), on whose account the voyage was undertaken. The pure-minded, earnest Electra justifies her father on the ground of unavoidable necessity, and casts the blame, if blame there be, on the goddess, who demanded the sacrifice, saying: Ask the huntress Artemis as a satisfaction for what (*τίνος ποινῆς*, 564) she restrained the favoring winds at Aulis? Reason about the justice of it as we may, men have never been able to get rid of the idea of expiatory and vicarious sacrifice. History—Grecian, Roman, and barbarian—is full of it. In one form or another it pervades or underlies all religions, be they Pagan, Mohammedan, Jewish, or Christian. And the law of vicarious sacrifice is almost universal in nature. Throughout the mineral, vegetable, and animal kingdoms the higher organizations and forms of life are nourished by the destruction or decay of the lower. Life springs from death, and the nation is saved, the race is rescued and reclaimed, the species is propagated, multiplied, and improved by the sacrifice of the individual. The corn of wheat must fall into the ground and die before it can bear much fruit. But it is only in the gospel of Christ that we see the great propitiatory sacrifice for a sinful race provided by the holy love of the Universal Father, made by the willing and joyful obedience of the Son of Man, who is at the same time the Son of God, and accepted with admiring and adoring gratitude by believing souls, as a necessary "satisfaction for the ethical nature of both God and man."

ANTIGONE.

In its leading characters the Antigone bears a strong resemblance to the Electra. The central figure in each, on whom all eyes are fastened, and who gives name to the piece, is a young woman who stands up for the right in opposition to the ruling powers, and is willing to sacrifice herself in the performance of a duty which she owes to her kindred, to justice, and to the gods. In each, the heroine, who is made of sterner stuff, and possesses the martyr-spirit, is contrasted with a sister of more complying disposition, the representative of ordinary womanhood. Antigone is offset by Ismene, as Electra is by Chrysothemis, and is exalted to a higher pitch of heroism and self-sacrificing devotion by the contrast. But Electra has the sympathy and support of the chorus, which is made up of noble women, like herself; while the chorus in Antigone, consisting of Theban senators and courtiers, after a few feeble attempts to withstand oppression, yield a servile submission to the tyrant, and leave the more manly, more heroic woman to stand up, unfriended and alone, against despotism, clothed with the forms of the law and the powers of the state. Moreover, Electra has a brother to lean upon, who takes the active part in the work of vengeance, while Antigone, although she has a lover who pleads her cause, is forbidden by female delicacy to ask his co-operation, or even to mention his name; and so she goes alone, to perform with her own hand, the prohibited rights of sepulture to her brother. This, however, she is the better able to do, because there is no room for doubt or conflict in her own bosom. Electra, in avenging her father's death, is obliged to lift her hand against the life of her mother. The ties of nature bind her to both her parents. The claims of filial duty might well impel her in opposite directions. But in Antigone, however plausible the pleas by which the ruling powers justify their action to their own consciences, it could not but appear to her a clear case of wrong to the dead on one side, and of duty to the dead on the other. Whether, therefore, we consider the holy cause in which she is enlisted, or the solitary grandeur in which she resists the mandates of the government, Antigone carries with her our undivided sympathy, and rises to a moral sublimity that finds its parallel only in the annals of martyrdom, in which tender and delicate, yet heroic and devoted, women have ever borne a conspicuous part.

Not the least interesting feature to modern readers — and doubtless a point of chief interest to the writer also and his contemporaries — is the conflict between human government and divine authority; in other words now familiar to our ears, the conflict between the lower and "the higher law," which lies at the foundation of the plot, and makes itself prominent in the dialogue. Creon is an eloquent advocate of the divine right of kings to do wrong, and of that still more subtle and demoralizing heresy: "Our country, right or wrong." Antigone asserts the eternal and immutable supremacy of the law and government of God with a clearness and force which should put to the blush the professedly Christian, but practically atheistic, politicians and divines, who deny the existence in political affairs of any higher law than the law of the land — of any will paramount to the will of the people.

After the defeat of the confederate chiefs and the

death of the two brothers, rival claimants to the throne of Oedipus, which Aeschylus has sketched with such a masterly hand in his Seven against Thebes, Creon, who as nearest of kin has now succeeded to the throne, awards sepulchral honors to Eteocles; but forbids, under the severest penalties, the burial of Polynices, as a traitor to his country. Antigone, in open disobedience to the inhuman mandate, performs the last sad offices to her unhappy brother, and falls beneath the vengeance of the king. But the blow recoils, with overwhelming force, upon the whole family of the oppressor. The law of the land seizes on its victim; but divine justice soon overtakes the maker and executioner of the law. Warned by providence and awakened to a sense of his guilt and folly by visible tokens of divine displeasure, he begins to retrace his steps. But it is now too late. The storm has already gathered; and now it bursts, and not only strikes down the guilty, but involves also the innocent who are connected with the guilty; nay, it strikes the personally guilty chiefly through those members of his family who are personally innocent.

Here, not only the conclusion, as in Ajax, but the whole plot, turns on the sacredness of the right of burial — sacred in the sight of the gods, as well as in the eyes of men; and here too, as in Ajax, Trachiniae, and Oedipus, suicide is the last resource of those who find the ills of life too heavy to be borne.

The opening scene between the two sisters is pathetic, and almost painful, especially in the want of sympathy and sisterly tenderness between those who now have no earthly resource but their love for one another. But it is of dramatic rather than theological interest.

Creon, on whom the sceptre has now devolved, next

appears before the councillors of the state, who constitute the chorus; and after a preface, in which he justifies his course by the most plausible reasons of patriotism and state policy, to which he is willing to sacrifice even the ties of friendship and relationship, he makes public proclamation forbidding the burial of that son of Oedipus who, in asserting his right to the throne, had dared to levy war in foreign lands against his own country. The chorus, who had just been celebrating the fall of the confederate chiefs beneath the walls, now, as in duty bound, acknowledge Creon's right to rule over the dead as well as the living (214). Scarcely has the proclamation gone forth from his lips, when a messenger arrives, bringing intelligence that some one has already dared to sprinkle dust over the dead. The chorus venture humbly to raise the question, whether this may not be a divinely ordered deed (*θεήλατον τοὔργον τόδε*, 278). But Creon sternly rebukes the thought that the gods can honor one so accursed; and from this time the chorus are little more than politicians, courtiers, echoes of the king. In the spirit of an Asiatic despot, Creon threatens death to the messenger himself, if he does not detect the guilty person; and the chorus, in place of the high-toned moral and religious sentiments which such tyranny and impiety should elicit, goes off into a splendid lyric declamation (332–375) on the marvellous inventive powers of mankind,[1] the gods of this lower world, and the conquerors of all but death.

The messenger now returns, bringing with him the young Antigone, and relates how when the guard had

[1] Very like, perhaps the original of, Hamlet's celebrated panegyric: "What a piece of work is man." See also Eccl. vii. 29: "They have sought out many inventions."

removed the slight covering of earth that had been cast upon the body, — an act of impiety which was followed by whirlwinds and sweeping clouds of dust, the visible tokens of heaven's displeasure, — she had been detected in again scattering dust and pouring libations on the dead. When asked by Creon if she knew the royal command, she frankly avows her intentional disobedience. When further asked how she dared to disobey, she makes this heroic, this martyr-like, this almost inspired answer (450 sqq.):

"Ne'er did eternal Jove such laws ordain,
Or Justice, throned amid the Infernal Powers,
Who on mankind these holier rites imposed.
Nor can I deem thine edict armed with power
To contravene the firm unwritten laws
Of the just gods; thyself a weak, frail mortal!
These are no laws of yesterday: they live
Forevermore, and none can trace their birth."

Creon declares that, though sprung from his own sister, Antigone shall suffer the full penalty of her disobedience; and crowning cruelty with impiety, (for Jupiter is already making mad whom he intends to destroy), he gratuitously adds (486 sqq.):

"Were she sprung from one
Dearer than all whom Hercian Jove defends,
She and her sister shall not now evade
A shameful death."

Antigone bids him hasten his tyrannical will; enough for her is the holy praise of having done her duty to her brother (510 sqq.):

"*Cre.* Doth it not shame thee to dissent from these?[1]
Ant. I cannot think it shame to love my brother.

[1] The Chorus.

Cre. Was not he too, who died for Thebes, thy brother?
Why then dishonor him to grace the guilty?
Ant. The dead entombed will not approve thy words.
Cre. Yet he wronged his country:
The other fought undaunted in her cause.
Ant. Still death[1] at least demands an equal law.
Cre. Ne'er should the base be honored like the noble.
Ant. Who knows if this be holy in the shades?[2]
Cre. Death cannot change a foe into a friend.
Ant. My love shall go with thine, but not my hate.[3]
Cre. Go, then, and love them in the tomb;[2] but know,
No woman rules in Thebes while Creon lives."

Ismene enters, and is charged with being an accomplice of Antigone. With true womanly fortitude and beautiful sisterly affection, she consents to share the guilt, if her sister does not refuse. But Antigone, whose heart is steeled, even against her sister, by the terrible process through which she has passed, scorns a friend who loves only in words, and denies her sister's right, though tenderly pleading for it now as a privilege, to die with her whose life has long been devoted to the dead. Ismene now turns to Creon (who thinks that of the two maidens, the one has gone mad, and the other was born so), and pleads for the life of Antigone, urging especially that she is the affianced bride of Creon's son. But Creon answers that she is already dead, and Hades shall put a stop to the intended nuptials. And the chorus, as if her doom were fixed, descant at length on the wretchedness of families on which there rests an hereditary taint or curse (583 sqq.):

"But when a house is struck by angry Fate,
Through all its line what ceaseless miseries flow!

[1] ὅ γ' Ἅιδης. [2] Κάτω.

[3] The flexibility and expressiveness of the Greek in this verse is inimitable; οὔ τοι συνέχθειν, ἀλλὰ συμφιλεῖν ἔφυν (523).

I see the ancient miseries of thy race,
O Labdacus, arising from the dead
With fresh despair; nor sires from sons efface
The curse some angry power hath riveted
Forever on thy destined line."

This curse, however, is not irrespective of the character and conduct of the individuals. Their own folly and madness conspire with divine vengeance: *Ἄτη*, *Ἄνοια*, and *Ἐρινύς* reap, together, the bloody harvest, and the imperishable, irresistible might of Jove presides over all (601 sqq. cf. 584):

Κᾆτ' αὖ νιν θεῶν φοινία τῶν
Νερτέρων ἀμᾷ κοπὶς,
Λόγου τ' ἄνοια καὶ φρενῶν Ἐρινύς, κ. τ. λ.

Grand, worthy almost of some Hebrew prophet, is the description of the unsleeping, undecaying power and dominion of Jove (606–614):

" Spurning the power of age, enthroned in might,
Thou dwell'st mid heaven's broad light.
This was in ages past thy firm decree,
Is now, and shall forever be:
That none of mortal race on earth shall know
A life of joy serene, a course unmarked by woe,"

The chorus do not seem to be aware that they are thus not only deploring the calamities of the house of Oedipus, but foreshadowing those which are soon to fall upon the family of Creon. And yet more distinctly, though still unconsciously, do coming events cast their shadows before, as the chorus descant, in the conclusion of their song (615 sqq.), upon the delusive power of hope, and the blinding force of passion, changing evil to apparent good, in the eyes of him whom the god is hurrying to destruction.

As the chorus conclude this unconscious prophecy, Haemon, the son of Creon and the affianced husband of Antigone enters; and, with a filial deference which contrasts beautifully with the unfeeling, unparental sternness of his sire, pleads, not so much his own cause, or that of his affianced bride, as the character, reputation, and well-being of his father. The son now takes up the doctrine of the higher law, while the father, as the advocate of the lower, lays down the doctrine of implicit obedience to the powers that be, in all things whatsoever, whether right or wrong (667; 737–745):

Καὶ σμικρὰ, καὶ δίκαια καὶ τἀναντία.

"*Haem.* That is no state, which crouches to one despot.
Cre. Oh thou most vile!
Wouldst thou withstand thy father?
Haem. When I see
My father swerve from justice.
Cre. Do I err,
Revering my own laws?
Haem. Dost thou revere them,
When thou wouldst trample on the laws of heaven?"

The unnatural father at length proceeds so far as to threaten to put to death the bride of Haemon before his own eyes. Haemon declares that shall never be, but he will leave his father's sight forever. As he goes away, the chorus express their fears that he may perpetrate some act of rashness. But Creon, blinded by pride and passion, says: let him do it; still he shall not save Antigone (773 sqq.):

"To a spot
By mortal foot untrodden, will I lead her,
And deep immure her in a rocky cave,
Leaving enough of sustenance to provide
A due atonement, that the State may shun

Pollution from her death.[1] There let her call
On gloomy Hades, the sole power she owns,
To shield her from her doom ; or learn, though late,
At least this lesson : 't is a bootless task
To render homage to the powers of hell."

A chorus succeeds, celebrating the irresistible power of love (781) :

Ἔρως ἀνίκατε μάχαν.

And then Antigone is brought in, under guard, and she and the choir bewail, in responsive strains, like Jephthah's daughter and her companions, her unhappy lot, to be wedded only to death ; or, what is worse, to live, Niobe-like, petrified with grief, tears ever flowing down her rocky cheeks. The chorus, however, do not admit that she is an innocent sufferer :

" Deeply, my daughter, hast thou sinned
Against the exalted throne of right."

And they even add sentiments worthy the lips of their master Creon :

" Religion bids us grace the dead ;
But might, when regal might bears sway,
Must never, never be contemned."

Creon at length breaks off the lamentation, by hurrying her away to a living death, to which she goes expostulating with the gods and struggling with her own doubts of divine justice (921 sqq.) :

" Which of your laws, ye Powers, have I transgressed ?
Yet wherefore do I turn me to the gods ?
If acts like these are sanctioned by the gods,
I will address me to my doom in silence."

The next chorus still expatiates on the irresistible

[1] How like the ceremonial scruples of the Jews, when they were intent on shedding the blood of their innocent victim (John xix. 28).

power of destiny, as illustrated in its victims from Danae to Antigone (986, 987):

> Ἀλλὰ κἀπ' ἐκείνα
> Μοῖραι μακραίωνες ἔσχον, ὦ παῖ.

The blind old prophet Tiresias (the same who denounced on Oedipus his doom in the presence of Creon) now breaks in upon Creon himself like one of those sudden and awful appearances of Elijah to the king of Israel, and strives to arrest him in his career of madness. In the exercise of his holy calling as a prophet-priest, he has seen frightful omens: birds with dissonant cries tearing each other, and the hallowed fire on the altar casting out the offerings as unholy; and he interprets these omens dire as tokens of the divine displeasure at the king's unrelenting refusal to permit the burial of the son of Oedipus. At the same time addressing him kindly as his son, and reminding him that to err is human, he calls upon him to remedy the error by retracing his steps, as now he may, while it is not yet too late (1025 sqq.):

> Ἐπὴν δ' ἁμάρτῃ, κεῖνος οὐκ ἔτ' ἔστ' ἀνὴρ
> Ἄβουλος οὐδ' ἄνολβος, ὅστις ἐς κακὸν
> Πεσὼν ἀκεῖται, μηδ' ἀκίνητος πέλει.

But the king is still unrelenting. He charges the prophet with bribery, criminates the whole race of prophets as a venal race, and even dares, indirectly, to defy the avenging bolts of heaven by declaring that, though Jove's eagles should carry the dead body to the throne of Jove himself, not even the fear of such pollution (*μίασμα*) should induce him to permit the burial, for he knows well that no mortal can pollute the gods (1044):

Ἐὺ γὰρ οἶδ᾽ ὅτι
Θεοὺς μιαίνειν οὔτις ἀνθρώπων σθένει.

Now the king has received his last warning. The minister of god has made his last effort to save him. And now the insulted prophet, not without some apparent mixture of personal resentment, proceeds to denounce upon him the just recompense of his crimes according to the ancient *lex talionis:* life for life — one dead from his own family for the dead whom he has wronged and dishonored (*νέκυν νεκρῶν ἀμοιβὸν ἀντιδούς*, 1067). And since he has intermeddled with matters with which neither he nor the gods above have any proper part, the powers beneath, the after-destroying Erinyes of Hades and of the gods (*ὑστεροφθόροι . . . . . Ἅιδου καὶ θεῶν Ἐριννύες*, 1075) are already lying in wait to avenge upon him the invasion of their prerogatives.

No sooner has the prophet departed than the king begins to stagger under the weight of the curses that have fallen upon him; and yielding now to the counsels of the choir, he takes measures for the immediate reparation of his wrong, since the curses of the gods are swift-footed to cut off (*συντέμνειν*[1]) the evil-minded. But it is already too late to repair the mischief. He sends his attendants, with all speed, to release Antigone. But it is too late. He hastens himself to bathe and bury the body of Polynices, imploring Pluto and Proserpine to restrain their anger. But it is too late. The chorus intercede with Bacchus, the patron god of the city, and Phoebus, the son of Jove. But it is too late. Prayers and efforts are now unavailing. While they yet utter the language of prayer a messenger comes

[1] Cf. Rom. ix. 28: συντέμνων ἐν δικαιοσύνῃ.

and announces that all is lost.[1] Antigone has made way with herself by a noose woven from her own dress; and Haemon, embracing her lifeless body, lies weltering in his own blood. Eurydice, the wife of Creon, hears the overwhelming news, and without uttering a word, goes away to follow the example of her only son. And while Creon is lamenting the death of that son, and cursing his own folly as its cause, a second messenger comes to him announcing the death of his wife, and that she died imprecating curses on his head as the murderer of their child. He takes all the blame to himself, and prays for death, bereft as he is by his own blind folly of friends and resources, with all adverse in the present, and an intolerable fate overhanging him in the future. And the drama closes with this reflection of the chorus summing up the moral lessons of the piece:

> "There is no guide to happiness on earth,
> Save Wisdom; nor behooves it us to fail
> In reverence to the gods. High-sounding vaunts
> Inflict due vengeance on the haughty head,
> And teach late wisdom to its dark old age."

Some critics have strenuously maintained that the Antigone was intended to censure alike the transgressor of human statutes and the violator of divine laws. Both laws do indeed claim their victims. But the moral lesson gathered from the piece by the chorus applies directly to the arrogance and impiety of the aged Creon (*γήρᾳ τὸ φρονεῖν ἐδίδαξαν*). Moreover, as we have before remarked, the sympathies of the audience are with

[1] The poet has put into the mouth of this messenger words of high import and remarkable conciseness touching the perpetual obligations of truth; ὀρθὸν ἡ 'λήθει' ἀεί (1195). They chime well with the higher law doctrine of the tragedy.

Antigone. Her death is viewed as a calamity, in which she is involved by the curse on her family; while Creon confesses with his own lips, that the ruin which has fallen upon his entire family is the just punishment of his own evil counsels (1269). The transgressor of human statutes, even though he acts in obedience to his own conscience, transgresses at his peril.[1] But the violator of divine law, even though in obedience to human statutes, incurs a more dreadful and inevitable doom. The perpetual and unchangeable supremacy of the divine law over all human laws and constitutions, is the instructive lesson which the poet has bequeathed to the ages in this immortal drama.

The Antigone is the only drama of Sophocles, we might almost say the only poem of ancient Greece (leaving brief lyrics out of the question), in which love between the sexes — pure, unwedded love, like that which forms the staple of modern poetry and romance — holds any important place. And here it is not the cardinal point in the plot, or the main-spring of the action. It is not even the sole cause of the suicide of Haemon. The unnatural cruelty and injustice of his father furnishes the immediate impulse to that fatal act. And Antigone, the heroine of the play, while she bewails her virginity with a tragic pathos worthy of Jephthah's daughter, and a frankness little in accordance with modern notions of female delicacy, never once alludes to the young prince to whom she had been betrothed. This suggests one of the most remarkable contrasts between the literature of ancient and modern times. Is the controlling power of woman in modern

[1] Cf. Hickok's Moral Philosophy, Part Second, Chap. viii.

society, and the never-failing charm of love in modern literature — is it owing to race or to religion? Is it the offspring of Teutonic blood, or is it the fruit of Christianity, elevating the sex, purifying the relation, frowning on unchastity with a severity of which we find no trace among Greeks or barbarians, and appropriating purity and fidelity in the marriage state as the sacred symbol of the union between Christ and the church, and of the normal relation between God and the human soul?[1]

OEDIPUS TYRANNUS.

The two Oedipuses and Antigone are so closely connected in the subject matter, in the characters, and in the continued operation of the same moral causes, that some have even called them a trilogy; though it is quite certain that they were composed at wide intervals of time, and not performed together; the Antigone, which is the last in the supposed trilogy, having been written the earliest of all the extant tragedies of Sophocles, the Oedipus Tyrannus about the middle, and the Oedipus Coloneus the last, and not exhibited on the stage till after the death of the poet. Following the order of time and causation in the connected series, we should have reserved the Antigone to the last. But Antigone so resembles Electra, that we could speak of it most easily and concisely in that connection. And the two Oedipuses form a bilogy (if we may be allowed the coinage of a convenient though unauthorized word), so complete in itself and so in harmony with the con-

[1] Compare Antig. 909 sqq., where Antigone sets the fraternal tie above the filial or the conjugal, with Eph. v. 25–31, and even with such passages of the Old Testament, as Gen. ii. 24.

cluding epoch of the poet's life, that we cannot consent to let even Antigone come after them in our analysis.

The preliminary history of Oedipus is too familiar to require repetition. Doomed before his conception to be the murderer of his father, and thus the avenger of the crimes of his ancestors; begotten by that father in the recklessness of intoxication, against a solemn resolution not to approach his mother; exposed immediately after his birth by that mother, in the mountains and forests of Cithaeron; found there by one of the shepherds of the king of Corinth, whose wife, being childless, prevailed upon her husband to adopt him as their son; brought up till manhood as heir-apparent to the Corinthian throne; fleeing his adopted home to avoid the doom (revealed to him by an oracle) of killing his supposed parent, and in that very flight falling in with his real father, and, in a quarrel by the way, unintentionally putting him to death; coming to Thebes just in time to rescue the city from the devouring Sphinx, and receive the kingdom as a free gift at the hands of the grateful people; honored with the hand in marriage of the late queen, and blessed (?) by her with sons and daughters; reigning with wisdom and in the hearts of a willing and obedient people, who look up to him as their father — down to the opening scene of the tragedy he is, in his own estimation and to all human appearance, among the most fortunate of men.

But the wisdom which baffled the Sphinx and saved the people, is not sufficient to baffle the Fates and save himself. Every step he has taken to escape his destiny, has only brought him nearer to his inevitable doom. Every round of the ladder by which he has climbed to the throne is stained, though unawares to himself, with blood and crime. His very prosperity has not only awakened the jealousy of the gods, but it has in some measure hardened his own heart; so that he will not go down altogether innocent and undeserving to his ruin. All the critics, from Aristotle downwards, have remarked the consummate skill with which the poet has adjusted the character of Oedipus: with so large a measure of good in it as to enlist our sympathy strongly in his misfortunes, yet not so free from the taint of pride and evil passion that our moral sentiments are shocked when we see him suffer. He is neither a god nor a demon. Mentem mortalia tangunt. And as we behold this solver of enigmas and saviour of his people, this imperfect yet, on the whole, wise and good king, drawn as if by fascination within the circle of the destroyer; like the parent bird, moved at first by love of her offspring, then fluttering with fear, and finally screaming with anguish, but still by all her fluttering and fear borne continually nearer the fatal centre; as we see every measure which he uses to gain light involving him in thicker darkness, and every struggle which he makes to extricate himself plunging him deeper in the mire,—we behold a striking illustration of the doctrine of holy writ, that "the foolishness of God is wiser than men, and the weakness of God stronger than men." We see, also, one of those examples of imputed guilt, of hereditary crime and calamity, which are not unfrequent in the history of the world, which the Scriptures describe as the visiting of the iniquities of the fathers upon the children unto the third and fourth generation of those that hate God, and which, however mysterious, however apparently irreconcilable with our ideas of divine justice, in themselves considered, manifestly serve an important purpose in the natural government of the world, by the fearful lessons which they teach of the evil consequences of sin as affecting, perchance, generations yet unborn; and, if our sense of justice is offended, it is at least partially reconciled by the intuitive conviction that, so far as there is partial injustice to any individual, it will, sooner or later, meet with full reparation — that the Oedipus Tyrannus will be followed by the Oedipus Coloneus, if not in this life, yet surely in the next.

A wasting pestilence has fallen upon the city, Thebes (as we learn from the opening dialogue between Oedipus and the priest of Zeus), which is consuming the fruits of the earth, the herds of cattle, and the race of men, and enriching Hades with groans and lamentations. The people instinctively impute it to the anger of the gods; for unsophisticated minds are at the farthest possible remove from that philosophical scepticism, or atheistic materialism, which severs natural from all connection with moral causes; and with their religious leaders they betake themselves with prayers and offerings to the altars, especially of Zeus, Athena, and Apollo. They gather in crowds with suppliant branches about the altar in front of the palace, and look to their king (the very person who is the occasion of their sufferings — affecting picture of human ignorance and helplessness) as, next to the gods and under their teaching, able to find some way of reconciliation and deliverance (33, 34):

'Ανδρῶν δὲ πρῶτον ἔν τε συμφοραῖς βίου
Κρίνοντες, ἔν τε δαιμόνων ξυναλλαγαῖς.[1]

[1] The same word so often used in the Scriptures to denote reconciliation to God.

Oedipus comes forth and assures them of his sympathy, nay, his sleepless anxiety, and informs them that he has already sent his brother-in-law, Creon, to the Pythian oracle to learn what he must do; and when he learns, he will not fail to do it. While he yet speaks, Creon appears crowned with laurel, and announces as the will of the god that they must remove the polluting curse of the land (*μίασμα χώρας*, 97), by exiling the murderers of Laius, or expiating his blood by shedding theirs (*φόνῳ φόνον πάλιν λύοντας*, 100). After making some inquiry into the facts attending the murder (which took place just before the affair of the Sphinx, as he learns without once being reminded of his own slaying a royal personage at that time), Oedipus responds that, with the help of Apollo, he will do all in his power to avenge at once the land and the god; and he will labor to disperse the defilement (*μύσος*, 138) for his own sake also; though he little suspects how nearly it concerns himself. The chorus, aged and venerable men, trembling at the unknown import of the oracle (which they call the oracle of Zeus, though proceeding from the healing Delian god at Delphi), invoke the interposition of Athena, Artemis, and Apollo, triple averters of death (*τρισσοὶ ἀλεξίμοροι*, 163), also father Zeus, and Bacchus, the patron-god of Thebes, to smite Ares the fire-bearing god [1] and drive him from the country. This choral prayer ended, Oedipus makes proclamation of his intentions, inviting all who have any knowledge of the murder to make it known, with the assurance that, if guilty themselves, they shall in that case suffer only exile; but denouncing the direst woes on the man who

[1] The priest of Zeus calls the Pestilence by the same name, *πυρφόρος θεός*, 27.

should harbor the murderer, even though himself should be the man (236–243; 249–251):

> "This man, whoe'er he be, let none that owns
> Our sceptre and our sway presume to grant
> The shelter of a house; let none accost him;
> Let none associate with him in the vows
> And victims of the gods, or sprinkle o'er him
> The lustral stream; let all, from every roof,
> Chase far the dire pollution, as the word
> Of Phoebus, by his oracle, enjoined.
> Yea, on myself, if, conscious of the deed,
> I grant the wretch asylum in my house,
> The same dread curse in all its vengeance fall.[1]"

But to those who co-operate with him in the discovery, may the allied justice (Dike) and all the gods ever grant their favoring presence.

The chorus, thus laid under a curse (*ἀραῖον*, 276), declare their ignorance of the deed, and advise Oedipus, in this matter known only to the gods, to have recourse to the seer Tiresias, the royal seer whose vision is most nearly the same with that of royal Phoebus (*ἄνακτ' ἄνακτι ταὔθ' ὁρῶντ'*,[2] 284). Oedipus replies, that in this too he has already anticipated their suggestion and sent two messengers for the prophet. The prophet soon arrives. The king addresses him with the utmost reverence, as one who revolves (literally, dispenses—*νωμῶν*,[3] 300) everything on earth and in heaven, the

[1] In his fatal blindness, as if possessed by some higher power, and compelled in mockery to foreshadow with his own lips the whole dreadful future, he says that he will toil for Laius, as for his own father.

[2] Cf. Dan. v. 11: "Wisdom, like the wisdom of the gods, was found in him," etc.

[3] As if "the man of God," were in the place of God himself, and did what he predicted, cf. Jer. i. 10: I have this day set thee over the nations and over the kingdoms, to root out and to pull down and to destroy and to throw down, to build and to plant.

only guardian and preserver of the state, and entreats him to disclose his knowledge, whether derived from birds or by any other method of divination, and so deliver the city. The whole dreadful truth seems to flash at once upon the mind of the prophet. He deplores the possession of wisdom that is not profitable to the possessor, as the prophets of the Old Testament and the New found the book of prophecy bitter in their souls,[1] and begs to be sent home at once, since it will be better both for him and the king. Oedipus, seconded by the chorus, adjures him not to withhold the knowledge he possesses. Tiresias charges them with folly and refuses. Oedipus is at length provoked, and declares his suspicion that the prophet himself was an accomplice in the deed. The prophet turns instantly upon him, pronounces him the unhallowed polluter (*ἀνοσίῳ μιάστορι*, 353) of the land, and bids him execute on himself his dreadful curse. Oedipus threatens punishment for such treasonable words. Tiresias replies, that he has nothing to fear if there is any power in truth (369):

Εἴπερ τί γ' ἐστὶ τῆς ἀληθείας σθένος.

The king taunts the prophet with utter blindness of the mind as well as all the senses. The prophet answers, that that reproach will soon return with all its force upon the king. The king says, a blind man cannot harm him. The prophet answers, it is not a blind man he has to fear; but Apollo, whose concern it is, can maintain the credit of his own oracles.

Oedipus, who seems honestly to regard his wisdom and his power, both so soon to fail him, as objects of envy to those around him, charges Tiresias with being

[1] Cf. Ezek. ii. 10; Jer. xx. 14–18; Rev. x. 10.

suborned by Creon, at whose instance he had sent for him, and inquires where the boasted wisdom of the prophet was when he, the ignorant Oedipus, solved the riddle of the Sphinx. Tiresias now throws off all restraint, declares that he is a servant of Loxias, not of Oedipus or Creon, and predicts in full, though still in somewhat enigmatical terms, the woes that are soon to overwhelm Oedipus and his family, bereft, blinded, and driven from the land by the δεινόπους 'Αρά of his own father and mother. At the same time he throws out incidental hints touching his parentage, which, with all his skill in solving enigmas, Oedipus cannot understand.

The prophet gone, the chorus take up something of his spirit, and exult over the now certain and speedy punishment of the murderer, overtaken and overwhelmed by the ever-living, hovering oracles that proceed from Delphi, centre of the earth, by the unerring Fates (Κῆρες ἀναπλάκητοι, 472), and by the son of Jove armed with fire and lightnings; though they are still slow to accept any intimations against their sovereign who had been found so wise and friendly to the state in the matter of the Sphinx.

In the ensuing interview between Oedipus and Creon, the monarch carries his suspicions, or rather his charges and threats, to such a height of injustice, as to prepare, and in some measure reconcile, the spectators to his fall. Jocasta, the wife of Oedipus and the sister of Creon, interposes to allay their strife. The choir also, or the choir-leader in its behalf, takes part in the dialogue, and begs of Oedipus not to charge with crimes unproved a friend "who calls the gods to witness for his truth;" but to reverence him who, before was not a child, and now is great, since he is under oath

(680 sqq.).[1] The king goes so far as to reflect upon the loyalty of the chorus. The choir-leader calls the sun, the god, leader of all gods (*πάντων θεῶν θεὸν πρόμον*), to witness his innocence, praying that he may perish without god and without friend (*ἄθεος ἄφιλος*, 661), if he harbors an unloyal thought. The king at length yields the life of Creon to the entreaties of Jocasta and the chorus, but still hates him and frowns him from his presence in an unforgiving spirit, which elicits from Creon the prophetic answer (673–675):

> "Even in relenting art thou stern; thy wrath,
> Too far indulged, most fearful. Souls like thine
> Are the just authors of their own remorse."

In the endeavor to pacify her husband, Jocasta proceeds to show how little reliance can be placed on any pretended oracles among men, by relating the oracle which had predicted that Laius should fall by his own son; whereas their only son had been left to die, in infancy, on the mountains, and Laius had fallen by the hand of foreigners, where three ways met. This incidental, chance allusion to three ways, awakens, at length, the recollections and the fears of Oedipus; and thus her own lips confirm the truth of the oracle in the very attempt to prove it false. On further inquiry, the time and place are found to agree with his own encounter on the way to Thebes. The description of Laius and his attendants, also, answers to his own recollections; and a slave, sole survivor of his train, who, at his own earnest request when Oedipus was crowned, had been allowed to retire to some rural charge, is sent

[1] This idea of being bound by an oath or curse is expressed in three different ways in the connection, *ἐν ὅρκῳ*, 653; *ἀραῖος*, 644; *ἐναγῆ*, 656.

for to make the matter sure. Meanwhile Oedipus relates to his wife his early history at Corinth, his flight from home to avoid the killing of his parent, and his encounter at the three corners between Corinth and Thebes, trembling the while with apprehension, lest he had, unwittingly, pronounced upon himself a dreadful curse. But Jocasta still blindly insists, that even if Laius fell by the hand of Oedipus, he could not have fallen by the hand of his own son; so that the oracle, she argues with bitter and impious madness, is false at any rate, and unworthy of the slightest regard; to which conclusion the deluded Oedipus also gives, at least, a partial assent (*καλῶς νομίζεις*, 859). But the chorus, so far from falling in with this sceptical reasoning, gives utterance to these lofty strains, in vindication of eternal truth and eternal law (863–872):

> "Oh, be the lot forever mine
> Unsullied to maintain,
> In act and word, with awe divine,
> What potent laws ordain.
> Laws spring from purer realms above:
> Their father is the Olympian Jove.
> Ne'er shall oblivion veil their front sublime,
> Th' indwelling god is great, nor dreads the waste of time."

> Μέγας ἐν τούτοις θεὸς
> Οὐδὲ γηράσκει.

And this sublime strophe is followed by a full and dark picture of the daring impiety that will universally prevail, if men loose their reverence for divine truth and justice, ending in the concise and expressive line (910):

> Ἔρρει δὲ τὰ θεῖα.

Overcome by the fears of her lord, which she cannot allay, Jocasta goes to the altar of Apollo, with garlands and incense, and prays the god to bring them some righteous deliverance. But when a messenger arrives from Corinth announcing the death of Polybus, the supposed father of Oedipus, the evil spirit of unbelief and impiety returns upon her with increased violence (946–949):

> "Vain oracles,
> Where are your bodings now? My Oedipus,
> Fearing to slay this man, forsook his country:
> Now Fate, and not his hand, hath laid him low."

And Oedipus again falls into the same snare into which his Eve has already fallen before him (964 sqq.):

> "Ha! is it thus? Then, lady, who would heed
> The Pythian shrine oracular, or birds
> Clanging in air, by whose vain auspices
> I was foredoomed the murderer of my father?"

The unhappy pair are now ripe for ruin. From these heights of presumption they are to be hurled, in a moment, to the depths of despair; and the very messenger who has raised them to such a pitch of exaltation is to dash their hopes and occasion their fall. In order to relieve Oedipus of his only remaining fear, which is that he may yet defile the bed of his mother, the messenger informs Oedipus that he is not, in reality, the son of Polybus, but a foundling, whom he himself (the messenger) had rescued from an ignominious and cruel death, on the mountains of Citheron, to which rescue his very name (*Οἰδίπους*, or he of the swollen feet) bore testimony. Jocasta now sees, at a glance, the whole dreadful truth, and adjures her husband to investigate no further. But he is bent upon solving the mystery of his birth, which tortured him in former years, and insists on seeing the herdsman who had delivered the exposed infant into the hands of the Corinthian; and she goes away, in silence and despair, to put an end to her own life. The herdsman comes. It is the same aged servant who, when Oedipus was crowned, had fled the court in the vain hope of concealing the dreadful fact of which his breast was the sole repository. Between the chattering Corinthian and the frantic Oedipus his secret is extorted from him. Oedipus sees the frightful gulf of infamy and ruin which yawns before him and prays for darkness to hide it from him (1182–1185):

> "Woe! woe! 't is all too fatally unveiled.
> Thou light! Oh may I now behold thy beams
> For the last time! Unhallowed was my birth,
> In closest ties united, where such ties
> Were most unnatural; with that blood defiled
> From whose pollution most the heart recoils."

And then he leaves the stage.

The chorus bewail the sad destiny of mankind, "of vanity and woe combined," and deplore the fall of the sphinx-vanquishing Oedipus from the proudest height of earthly wisdom and glory to the lowest depth of ignominy, horror, and despair. A messenger now appears and gives a detailed account of the suicide of Jocasta, and of Oedipus, over her dead body, tearing out his own eyes with her golden clasps (1271–1274):

> "That never, never more
> Her should they see, the sufferings he endured,
> Or the dire deeds he wrought."

And while the messenger is yet speaking, Oedipus, having burst the palace gate, shows himself to public view, as the guilty murderer of his father, mother, and all his house; and when asked by the sympathizing chorus what god impelled him to such violence on himself, he replies (1329–1333):

> "'T was Phoebus, Phoebus, O my friends, above,
> Who wrought my doom of woe,
> My hopeless agony:
> But this dark deed no hand save mine hath dared."

The chorus intimate that he might better have died at once than pine in darkness. But he answers, that he could not endure the sight of his father and mother in the lower world (1371–1374):

> "Descending to the dead, I know not how
> I could have borne to gaze upon my sire,
> Or my unhappy mother; for to them
> Crimes dark as mine not death can e'er atone."

Oedipus is now morally and politically dead. The throne is, *ipso facto*, vacated, as palpably, as immediately, as if the king had deceased; and the wronged and suspected Creon succeeds to the sovereignty. Of him, who comes not to insult the fallen monarch, but to remove him to the palace from the public gaze, and from the light of the sun, Oedipus asks but one boon — exile. Taught by his predecessor's fall to respect the oracle, Creon replies that he must first ask the pleasure of the god. Oedipus now bethinks him of his daughters, commends them to the care of Creon, and when suffered to place his hands upon them, blesses Creon for the privilege, and breathes out his love and sorrow — sorrow for their inheritance of shame — in tones of disinterested and pathetic tenderness, which melt the heart of the spectator. Yielding to necessity, he now retires within the palace to await the disposal of the ruling powers on earth and in heaven; and the chorus express the moral of the tragedy in these concluding words, addressed to their fellow citizens:

" Sons of Thebes, my native city, this great Oedipus survey,
Who resolved the famed enigma, who, for virtue far renowned,
Naught of favor recked or fortune, with transcendent glory crowned.
Mark him now, dismayed, degraded, tost on waves of wildest woe.
Think on this, short-sighted mortal, and, till life's deciding close,
Dare not pronounce thy fellow truly happy, truly blest,
Till, the bounds of life passed over, yet unharmed, he sinks to rest."

God alone is happy; God alone is wise; God alone is great; God alone is good,—this seems to be the moral and religious lesson (expressed in the language of Christian piety) which the Oedipus is intended to inculcate. Not only is human power weakness, and human wisdom folly, but all human good is evil in comparison with the divine standard. Oedipus is an object of felicitation and envy in the eyes of men. He is the wise man of his age. But when he sets himself in opposition to the oracles of Apollo and strives to defeat the plans and purposes of heaven, we are astonished at the blindness and infatuation which mark his course. He is a good man in the view of the world. His people love and honor him as a good king; but, in his mysterious providence, the deity " plunges him in the ditch, and his own clothes abhor him." He finds himself stained with involuntary crimes, and loathes himself for his imputed guilt. To-day, like Job he sits on the throne the greatest of all the kings and princes of the age; to-morrow, like Job he sits in ashes, bereft of his power and forsaken by his friends, pitied if not despised by all who were wont to do him reverence. In the Oedipus at Colonus, we shall see whether like Job he in the end receives the double of all his former prosperity. Certainly in his terrible fall we see the same apparently blind, all-controlling, irresistible power which men call destiny, and which even Christians call mysterious and inscrutable providence.

OEDIPUS AT COLONUS.

With our sympathies thus enlisted in the fate of Oedipus, we are now prepared to follow him to the last scene of his life at Colonus. An interval of some years has passed away, his sons have grown up, the younger is in possession of his throne, the older at the head of confederate armies is marching to possess himself by force of the birthright which has been wrested from him; his daughters also, have arrived at maturity, and while both serve as props of his declining years, and eyes for him in his blindness, Antigone already manifests that peculiar fervor of feeling and strength which are more conspicuously displayed in the drama bearing her name, and which have rendered that name immortal. The Oedipus Coloneus is a natural sequel to the Oedipus Tyrannus. But there is more of contrast than of resemblance in the incidents, and in the situation of the leading character who gives name to both. The one is the compensation of the other. If fortune, or the fates, or the gods, or the laws of the universe (different names in Greek for essentially the same thing), or, to use an expression of our author which harmonizes and combines them all, if the god in them (*ἐν τούτοις θεός*, Oed. Tyr. 871) has heretofore dealt hardly with Oedipus, he is now to receive his compensation. If the sins of his ancestors have involved him, more through ignorance and necessity than of his own free will, in an unequal controversy with higher powers, he is now reconciled, and blessed with a departure from these scenes of earthly conflict amid supernatural tokens of divine favor. If Creon and his own sons have treated him selfishly and cruelly in the days of his humiliation, the sceptre of more than regal power is now in his hands; and it is now their turn to solicit and plead in vain. If his native city, Thebes, has too soon forgotten his services, and ungratefully banished him from the realm, she now supplicates in vain, and endeavors to compel, his return; while Athens, which grants him an asylum in his apparent helplessness, has thus unconsciously reared for herself a bulwark in her suburbs which her enemies shall never pass.

The Oedipus Coloneus of Sophocles brings us to the same asylum of human law, and the sanctuary of the same divinities as the Eumenides of Aeschylus. Oedipus in the former, like Orestes in the latter, comes to the sanctuary of the Furies at Athens for rest from his weary wanderings, for expiation of his involuntary crimes, for reconciliation to the retributive and avenging powers. Orestes is welcomed and protected by Athena, the patron-goddess of the city; Oedipus, by Theseus, its demigod hero and king. Athena summons the elders of her people to a court and council, and so institutes the Areopagus. Theseus takes counsel of the priests and at the altars of the gods. In both poets the proceeding is partly civil and partly religious. In both the human and the divine, the powers of earth and the powers of heaven, conspire to effect a reconciliation. In Aeschylus, the Furies appear in person, in that fiendlike form which we always associate with the name, pursue their victim like hounds hunting their prey, dance in chorus around him, and howl their curses on his head. In Sophocles, in accordance with the advancing refinement of the age and under the guidance of his own cultivated genius, they are invisible, and their dreadful power is only shadowed forth by the suppressed breath with which their name is mentioned, and the shuddering horror with which the beholders see Oedipus unwittingly invade their sanctuary. But in both, the vengeful powers are appeased, the Erinyes are transformed into the Eumenides, the wrathful deities into the gracious ones. And as in the Eumenides of Aeschylus they are conducted to their sanctuary with songs and rejoicings by the magistrates and the whole people; so in the Oedipus Coloneus, all nature sympathizes with the calm and sweet peace which has succeeded to the storm: the olive and the vine spring up in unwonted beauty about the sanctuary of the appeased Furies, and the nightingale sings perpetually in the branches. Of course, neither the spectators in the ancient theatre, nor the poet himself, saw in these conceptions all the breadth and depth of meaning which we find in them. They were "unconscious prophecies," "shadows of good things," which could be fully understood only when the substance had come, and the true light shone upon the world. But we cannot but see in them ideas, or germs of ideas, of profound moral and spiritual significance. Perhaps the primary aim of the poet was, in the language of Schlegel,[1] "to confer glory on Athens, as the sacred abode of law and humanity, where the crimes of the illustrious families of other countries might by a higher mediation be at last propitiated; and hence an enduring prosperity was predicted to the Athenian people." But as Schlegel him-

[1] Lectures on Dramatic Literature, Lecture iv.

self confesses, "when the rancor of these goddesses of rage is exhausted, it seems as if the whole human race were redeemed from their power."

At the opening of the drama, Oedipus is seen, aged and blind, leaning on the arm of Antigone, and entering the suburbs of Athens. The scene is thus described by her who is at once the staff and the eyes of her father (14–20):

> "O Oedipus,
> My much afflicted father, the high towers
> Which girt the city rise in distant view;
> The spot on which we stand I deem is holy:
> Where laurels, olives, vines, in one green shade,
> Are close inwoven; and within the grove,
> The nightingales make frequent melody.
> Rest, now, thy faltering limbs on this rude stone.
> Such lengthened wanderings ill befit thine age."

Scarcely has he taken his seat when he is warned to remove his feet, for it is holy ground, and must not be profaned by mortal footsteps (37; 39–43):

Ἔξελθ', ἔχεις γὰρ χῶρον οὐκ ἁγνὸν πατεῖν.

> "From mortal touch and mortal dwelling pure,[1]
> Is that mysterious grove; the awful powers,[2]
> Daughters of earth and darkness dwell within.
> *Oed.* By what most holy name should I invoke them?
> *Athen.* We call them in this land th' Eumenides,
> The all-beholding powers;[3] in other lands,
> By various lofty titles men adore them.

In answer to further questions, he is informed that the whole suburb is sacred to Poseidon, Prometheus, and Colonus, whose name it bears. When the Athenian with whom he holds this conversation withdraws to

[1] ἄθικτος οὐδ' οἰκητός [2] αἱ ἔμφοβοι θεαί, 39. [3] πάνθ' ὁρῶσας.

apprise the king, Oedipus addresses his prayers to the august powers of dreadful aspect (πότνιαι δεινῶπες, 84) and entreats them to receive him propitiously, in accordance with the oracle of Phoebus, which had predicted that his days should at length come to a peaceful end at the hospitable abode of the venerable goddesses (θεῶν Σεμνῶν ἕδραν καὶ ξενόστασιν, 90), amid thunderings, lightnings, and earthquakes, as signs from heaven (σημεῖα).

As the company of aged men draw near, who constitute the chorus, Oedipus screens himself in the thickest of the grove; and they, as they search for him, sing with trembling voice (117–134):

> "Who, who is this sad, aged wanderer?
> Doubtless of foreign land, or his rash foot
> Had never trod the grove
> Of those unconquered virgin powers,[1]
> Whose name we tremble but to breathe,
> Whose mystic shrine we pass
> With far-averted eye,
> And pondering, silent and devout,
> On happier omens there."

Oedipus comes forth at their call. With shuddering, they bid him beware, lest he bring upon himself a more dreadful curse than his present blindness; and, not daring to tread where he stands, they guide him with words, as he withdraws, step by step, and seats himself again on the sloping verge of the rocky pavement. As, in obedience to their demand, he discloses his name and race, they are still more appalled, and bid him quit the land forever. Antigone intercedes for her father, pleading for that peculiar respect due to the miserable,

[1] ἀμαιμακέταν κορᾶν.

which we call pity, but which the Greek tragedians call *αἰδώς*.[1] They reply (254–257):

> "Know, child of Oedipus, we pity thee,
> Nor gaze relentless on thy woe-worn sire;
> But we revere the gods, nor dare rescind
> The firm decision of our former mandate."

Oedipus responds by appealing to the far-famed piety[2] and humanity of Athens: vain boast, if a stranger is to be thus inhumanly banished for a name; palliates his crimes, as committed in retaliation and in ignorance, and adjures them by the gods, whom they profess to venerate, to spare him now that, in obedience to their will, he has withdrawn himself from the inner sanctuary of the Eumenides. Overcome at length by entreaties, and overawed by something supernatural in the air and words of the mysterious stranger, they consent to wait the final sentence of their king.

Meanwhile Ismene, Antigone's gentle sister, arrives from Thebes, bringing news of the furious war which her brothers are waging for the throne; of a recent oracle which declared that he (Oedipus) whose downfall the gods had formerly willed, but whom now they purpose to exalt, holds in his hands the balance of power and victory; and that, for this reason, Creon is already on his way to bear him back to the borders of the State, that they may hold this now powerful arbiter in their possession, though they are still resolved that his tomb

[1] 247. cf. Aesch. Sup. 577 *δακρύων πένθιμον αἰδῶ*: tears of sorrow and pity (respect).

[2] *τάς γ' Ἀθήνας φασὶ θεοσεβεστάτας εἶναι*, 260. So below, 1006, Oedipus says, if any land knows how to honor and worship the gods, Athens excels in this. This explains the *δεισιδαιμονεστέρους* in Paul's address to the Athenians on Mars' Hill (Acts xvii. 22). Xenophon (Cyrop. iii. 3, 58) uses *δεισιδαίμονες* as a synonyme with *θεοσεβεῖς*.

shall not defile Theban ground. The indignation of Oedipus is roused by this new insult, added to the long neglect and injury with which he has been treated by his sons; and he imprecates destruction on them both, while he promises lasting benefit to Athens, if her citizens, with her tutelary gods, will now stand forth for his protection. Drawn towards him now by patriotism as well as compassion, the chorus instruct him how to propitiate (*θέσθαι καθαρμόν*, 466) the Eumenides: first, with three libations of honey and pure water, without wine, poured out upon the ground towards the rising sun; then with thrice nine olive branches, fresh-plucked, and planted on the spot which drank the libations; and then to offer this prayer (486, 487):

> "Propitious, so we call them, that, with minds
> Propitious, they their votary would receive
> And save."

Too blind and infirm to perform these rites himself, he devolves the duty on Ismene.

While the chorus are extracting from his reluctant lips some further confession of his calamities and involuntary crimes, Theseus arrives, and without waiting for petitions or any address, assures at once the anxious heart of the suppliant stranger with these comforting words (560–566):

> "Unfold thy wish; and arduous were th' emprise,
> When thou should'st ask my utmost aid in vain.
> I, too, was nurtured in a foreign land,
> As thou art now; an exile's woes to me,
> An exile's perils, are familiar all.
> Then never, never, from the stranger's prayer,
> Who comes like thee, relentless will I turn,
> Or needful aid withhold."

With the humility and yet the majesty befitting the double consciousness of what he is and what the gods intend to make him, Oedipus answers (576–578):

> "I come to offer thee this withered frame,
> A gift to sight unseemly; yet endowed
> With costlier treasures than the loveliest form;"

adding, that the value of the boon will be understood only when he is dead, and Theseus has attended to his burial. Previous to that, he has nothing to ask but protection against his unnatural sons and his ungrateful countrymen, who would fain bear him back by force, where once he would gladly have remained; but where now he is resolved never more to return. Theseus expostulates with him on the folly of such resentment in such wretchedness. But Oedipus is unrelenting. Athens is now his home and country; and when war shall arise between Athens and Thebes, as war will rise in the changeful course of human destiny, though now all is peace (621 sqq.):

> "Then this cold body, in the sleep of death
> Entombed, shall drink their[1] warm and vital blood,
> If Jove be mightiest still, and Jove-born Phoebus
> Retain his truth unbroken."
>
> Εἰ Ζεὺς ἔτι Ζεύς, χὠ Διὸς Φοῖβος σαφής.

Theseus pledges him protection, offering him an asylum here or in the palace, as he chooses. "Would to heaven," he answers (644):

> "Would to heaven
> I might attend thee; but the spot is here."

And when his fears return and agitate him, Theseus reassures him, declaring that his word is as sacred as

[1] Of the Thebans.

his oath ; that his name, alone, will suffice to protect him from insult; and, moreover, (664, 665):

> "If Phoebus hither was indeed thy guide,
> Without my feebler aid his arm can save thee."

The choral song, which follows, (668–719) celebrates the beauty of Colonus, in strains of poetry and eloquence, which betray the poet's love and admiration for his birth-place; and which, at the same time, remind the Christian reader of the glowing language in which the Hebrew prophets describe rejoicing nature under the reign of the coming Messiah.[1] We will not mar it by translation or synopsis. It is a glorification of Athens, which the patriotic and tasteful Athenians might well reward, as they did reward it, when he read it before his judges, by an instant acquittal and a more than regal triumph. But it seems to be also something more: piety joins with patriotism in celebrating Colonus, as not only the sanctuary of the Eumenides, but the favorite haunt of Aphrodite and the Muses (691, 692), and the sacred abode of Athena, Poseidon, and Zeus:

> "Morian[2] Jove, with guardian care,
> Watches, ever wakeful, there;
> And Athena's eye of blue
> Guards her own loved olive too."

Antigone breaks in upon the concluding strains of this magnificent song, by saying, that now the might and glory of Athens are to be put to the test. Creon approaches with his body-guard. He addresses the aged citizens of the country with respect; says he comes only to restore the wretched outcast to his native

[1] Isa. xxxv. 1, 2; lv. 12, 13, etc.

[2] That is, guardian of the μορίαι, or sacred olives.

land; and then turns his entreaties, not unmixed with compassion, to the unhappy Oedipus. Oedipus scorns his pity, withheld when it would have been gladly received, and extended only when it was no longer needed. He charges Creon not only with cruelty in times past, but with false pretences now, since it was not his intention to restore him to his home, but only to take him to the border. His body shall not go there; but his spirit shall ever dwell there as an avenging demon of the land (χώρας ἀλάστωρ οὑμός, 788) and his sons shall inherit of his kingdom only soil enough to die on (791–793):

> " Is not my presage of the doom of Thebes
> More sure than thine; yea, 't is e'en trebly sure,
> As drawn from truer prophets, Phoebus' self,
> And his dread sire, the all-controlling Jove."

Unable otherwise to bow his stubborn soul, Creon informs him that he has already seized one of his daughters (Ismene, who had gone away to prepare the offerings), and proceeds to take by force his only remaining support and solace. He even threatens to drag Oedipus himself from his asylum; and Oedipus defends himself by frightful curses. Summoned from the altar near by, where he had been offering a bullock to Poseidon, Theseus interposes, arrests Creon, sends forces at once for the recovery of the daughters, and censures, with dignified severity, the double crime, against the country and the gods, of forcing a suppliant from its altars. Creon endeavors to justify himself by expatiating on the crimes of Oedipus, which have forfeited even the right of asylum. This rouses Oedipus; he replies at much length; he confesses his crimes, but casts the responsibility on the gods (θεοῖς γὰρ ἦν οὕτω φίλον, 964), angry perchance at his race aforetime ; and he exculpates himself as only a foredoomed and involuntary murderer: how can I reasonably be held responsible for a deed which was involuntary (977):

Πῶς γ' ἂν τό γ' ἆκον πρᾶγμ' ἂν' εἰκότως ψέγοις;

and not only involuntary, but decreed and predicted before I was born or even conceived (973)? Questions going to the root of human accountability, which have always been asked in the world, and never fully answered.

While the king and his attendants are executing the mandates of justice, the chorus express their wish to join in the pursuit, and offer prayers for the right to Phoebus, Athena, and Zeus (1079, 1080; 1085–1091):

"Jove, Jove to-day will aid the right,
And I forebode a prosperous fight."

"Thou of the all-pervading eye,
In heaven by subject-gods adored,[1]
Jove, from thy radiant throne on high,
Send might and joy and victory,
To grace my country's lord!
Daughter of Jove, Athena, hear!
Thou Phoebus, lift thy fatal spear," etc.

The daughters are soon brought back, and Oedipus clasps them to his bosom. Theseus informs him that some person, kindred to him, is sitting at the altar of Poseidon, who begs the privilege of a few words with Oedipus. From the description, Oedipus recognizes his son Polynices, and at first refuses to see him; but the remonstrances of Theseus and the entreaties of Antigone, pleading not only the ties of nature but reverence for the gods, prevail to win his reluctant consent. Poly-

[1] ἰὼ θεῶν παντάρχα Ζεῦ παντόπτα, κ. τ. λ. (1085).

nices enters alone and in tears, deploring the misery he sees, confessing the wrong of which he has been guilty, and pleading for forgiveness (1266–1269):

"By the throne
Of mighty Jove, associate of his sway,
Sits gentle Mercy, judge of human deeds;
Let her be present at thy soul, my father."

Ἀλλ' ἔστι γὰρ καὶ Ζηνὶ σύνθακος θρόνων
Αἰδὼς ἐπ' ἔργοις πᾶσι, καὶ πρὸς σοί, πάτερ,
Παρασταθήτω.[1]

Oedipus maintains an awful silence. But Antigone encourages her brother at least to make known his wishes; and he proceeds. He has been deprived of the throne, his rightful inheritance, by his younger brother. The fell cause of all their feud was the avenging curse of their father. He has married the daughter of the king of Argos, and rallied, together with him, six other chiefs, a sevenfold force in all, for the recovery of his inheritance. And now he solicits his father's presence and blessing, since (1331, 1332):

"If faith be due to heaven's prophetic voice,
Whom thou shalt succor, them must victory grace."

For a long time Oedipus deigns no answer; but at length his resentment and indignation burst forth in reproaches and curses too frightful to repeat, too dreadful for a son to hear from a father's lips. Neither of his sons shall possess his throne. The blood of both shall stain the plain of Thebes. Such were the curses which he pronounced upon them before; and now he invokes again the Curses to come as his allies, and teach

[1] See what is said of Αἰδώς (mercy, pity) above, p. 348. Here she is personified, or rather regarded as a goddess, the sharer of the throne of the supreme; just as justice is represented below (1382).

his sons not to dishonor their parents. They therefore (the Curses, *'Αραί*) shall occupy the throne, which else had been his sons', "if ancient Justice sits associate with Zeus and Guardian of primeval laws" (1381, 1382):

Εἴπερ ἐστὶν ἡ παλαίφατος
Δίκη ξύνεδρος[1] Ζηνὸς ἀρχαίοις νόμοις.

"Thus I curse thee," he concludes, in language more dreadful than the curses of king Lear, "thus I curse thee; and I invoke the gloomy paternal darkness of Tartarus[2] to remove thee hence to thine own place;[3] and I invoke these goddesses, the Furies; and I invoke Ares, who inspired you with fearful hate" (1389–1392).

Horrible as these curses are, the chorus take it for granted that they will be fulfilled to the letter. Polynices bows in despair to his fate, and goes away resolved not to acquaint his confederates with his doom; but in silence to meet, with them, his destiny, asking only of his sisters, that when he has fallen he may not be robbed of interment with proper funeral rites. Antigone utters not a word of remonstrance against the maledictions of her father; but with true sisterly tenderness, beseeches her brother not to return to the war, since if he does, those maledictions — oracles she calls them (*μαντεύματα*,

1 Quite another sharer of Jove's throne from the Mercy (Αἰδώς) to whom Polynices makes his appeal (1268). The epithet παλαίφατος is applied especially to Justice, as here; to oracles, 454; and to providence Trach. 825: τᾶς παλαίφατου προνοίας, and means literally, *spoken long ago*. The primeval law especially intended in this connection must be that of honor to parents. Cf. Theol. of Aesch. pp. 209, 210, 237.

2 τοῦ Ταρτάρου στυγνὸν πατρῷον Ἔρεβος. The meaning of πατρῷον, *paternal*, is doubtful, some understanding Erebus to be represented as the father or guardian of Tartarus; and others (as Hermann and Wunder), supposing it to mean the darkness that envelops Laius, father of Oedipus.

3 Ἀποικίσῃ, lit. to remove from home to a colony or other residence. Plato uses it of the transfer to the Islands of the blest. Rep. 519C.

1425) — will come upon him as sure as the decrees of fate.

Now (as if, in giving utterance to these prophetic curses on the last male offspring of his accursed race, he had fulfilled his earthly destiny) Jove's thunders begin to peal in fearful echoes over his head. He recognizes them as the appointed signal of his death, and sends in haste to Theseus. The chorus, overwhelmed with fear and amazement, betake themselves to prayer. Theseus comes, calm, yet full of sympathy, to receive the last counsels and benedictions of Oedipus. Oedipus summons him to follow him (for the blind is now to be the guide of the seeing) to the spot where he is to die. That spot, never to be named to any human being, will afford a surer defence than spears and shields. There, also, he will disclose to his royal ear secrets which he would not reveal to his dearest friend, and which Theseus must communicate only to his successor, as he draws near the end of life. These secrets will render Athens impregnable against the Thebans. And now, led by an unseen hand (*Ἑρμῆς ὁ πομπὸς, ἥ τε νερτέρα θεός*, 1548), leading his daughters and the king of Athens towards the mysterious spot, he passes off the stage, while the chorus, trembling with awe and almost doubting if it is right to invoke the infernal deities, beseech Pluto, Proserpine, the Eumenides, and Cerberus himself, to grant the stranger an open (*ἐν καθάρῳ*, clear, 1575) and peaceful entrance to the regions below, that he may thus be recompensed for the many sufferings which, without his fault (*μάταν*, 1565), may have come upon him.

This prayer ended, a messenger enters and narrates at length the death of Oedipus: Having arrived at the threshold of the steep descent (τὸν καταῤῥάκτην ὁδόν, sc. Ἅιδου, 1590), with the help of his daughter, he bathed in pure water from the hill of Demeter, put on a new attire, instead of the filthy garments of which he had divested himself; and then, summoned by the thunder of infernal Zeus, he embraced his daughters and bade them an affectionate farewell. A brief silence ensued, and then a voice was heard which caused the hair to stand up on the head of every one who heard it; a voice calling distinctly for Oedipus to hasten his departure. Commending his daughters to the care of Theseus, he now sends them away with all attendants, and was left alone with the Athenian king. As soon as the messenger and those with him had recovered from their awe sufficiently to look behind them, the king was seen standing alone, and holding his hand over his eyes, as if to shade them from some sight too fearful to behold, and soon after worshipping in one and the same prayer the powers of heaven and earth (γῆν τε ἅμα καὶ τὸν θεῶν Ὄλυμπον, 1655). But what became of him, the wonderful, the illustrious stranger, no mortal knew but Theseus. He was not struck by the thunderbolt, nor swept into the sea, nor wasted by pain and sickness; some god conducted him away, or the earth opened its kind bosom to receive him. For such a man, remarks the messenger, is not to be mourned; but if any one is to be admired and envied in his death, that man is Oedipus.

The daughters now reappear bewailing their loss. But Theseus forbids them to mourn for one to whom grace is reserved in the lower world (χάρις ἡ χθονία ἀπόκειται,[1] 1753), for that were to provoke the divine

[1] Possibly this may mean only one who was pleased and happy in the

displeasure (νέμεσις γάρ). Antigone, with characteristic ardor and fearlessness, begs to see the place of her father's death. But Theseus declares, that is forbidden by the charge of Oedipus himself and by the all-hearing oath ("Ορκος) of Zeus, who heard what passed between them. And with true paternal kindness he unites with the chorus in comforting the orphan children, assuring them that all had happened according to the wishes of their father and the sovereign will of Jove.

Counterpart and kindred to the instinctive satisfaction with which we behold the perpetrator of many and great crimes, who has long gone unwhipped of justice, brought at length to condign punishment—counterpart and kindred to this, is the pleasure with which we see the unfortunate victim of untoward circumstances and adverse fates, who, without any particular crime or fault of his own, has been involved in heavy calamities, restored to his former prosperity and standing, or in some other way compensated, and more than compensated, for all that he had suffered and lost. The former is the satisfaction afforded by Electra, and many other tragedies, and also by the book of Esther. The latter is the pleasure derived from Oedipus and the book of Job. The Oedipus at Colonus is a pathetic and beautiful picture of one who had long been pursued by the avenging furies of his own involuntary crimes and the real crimes of his father's house, finding an asylum at last in the sanctuary of those Furies appeased and reconciled — one who had been crushed beneath the weight of imputed rather than personal guilt, the power of destiny, the injustice of men, and the apparent anger

manner of his death, though it more naturally refers to something reserved, laid up, in another world.

of the gods, dying in the possession of such power and estimation among men, and amid such manifestations of divine favor as fully to counterbalance all the inequalities and ills of life. The plot is manifestly constructed on the principle of such a compensation. This principle is distinctly recognized in the prayer of the chorus (1565–1567).[1] Oedipus receives "the double" as manifestly as Job, though in a very different time and manner. The recompense does not come till the very hour of his departure from the present life, when, of course, it cannot consist in his restoration to twice his original wealth and prosperity and kingly power. But it comes in a way no less striking and impressive. The Theban exile is invited and entreated to return to Thebes. But he refuses, and becoms a citizen, and more than citizen, of Athens — a counsellor, and no ordinary counsellor, of her demigod and founder-king. The dethroned monarch is still king, and more than king, at Thebes. He not only holds the sceptre, and gives it to whom he will; but victory or defeat to the contending armies, and life or death to the opposing chiefs, hang on his lips. The neglected and despised old man, who lately wandered alone, supported only by his loving, sorrowing daughters, while all others shunned him as if smitten with leprosy or plague, departs this life amid lightnings and thunders, commotions in nature, and voices from another world, such as, according to an idea quite current among the nations of antiquity, mark the exit only of prophets, lawgivers,[2]

[1] See page 356.

[2] This idea meets its realization in the mysterious death and burial of Moses (Deut. xxxiv. 1–6). So far from militating against the reality, the idea confirms it — leads us to anticipate it, so that we should be disappointed if there were no answering fact in the Scriptures.

the greatest benefactors of mankind, and the special favorites of heaven.

The exaltation of Oedipus to such a height of glory is almost as mysterious as his fall. The poet does not enter into the philosophy of it. He only gives us the facts. He sheds no light on the ground of the reconciliation. And as to the character of Oedipus, it is no better at Colonus than at Thebes. Certainly he is no saint, according to the standard of the New Testament, or even of the Old. He is almost as far from the meekness and godly fear of Moses as he is from the loving and forgiving spirit of Christ. He is almost as ignorant of himself as he is of the character and government of God; and his views of sin are as inadequate as his ideas of redemption and reconciliation. He is as unconscious of his personal need of forgiveness as he is destitute of the gospel requisites to be forgiven. How impersonal and impalpable are his conceptions of the powers above and the powers beneath. Near and peculiar as the relations are into which he is brought to them, how little is there that is clear, and how much less that is attractive and endearing about them. How dark and cold, how dim and distant, is the view of death and the passage to another world which we get in this nearest approach that Greek tragedy ever made towards a revelation of that passage, when compared with that which the Christian obtains as he stands by the cross of the penitent and forgiven thief, and hears the promise: "This day shalt thou be with me in paradise;" or as he looks on at the stoning of Stephen, and sees heaven opened, and the dying martyr, like his dying Lord, praying for the forgiveness of his enemies, and then rising, almost visibly, to the immediate presence of his Saviour, saying: "Lord Jesus, receive my spirit."

Longinus cites as a fine example of the sublime, the scene where Oedipus suddenly disappears, and Theseus remains alone, gazing after him with his hands over his eyes, which are almost blinded by the awful spectacle. In a poetical and critical point of view the passage deserves all the critic's commendation. But scenes of more spiritual sublimity, and at the same time scenes of sweet and serene beauty, in which heaven is brought down to earth, and God comes nearer to the presence, clearer to the vision and infinitely dearer to the hearts of men, are common occurrences in the actual experience of Christians who gaze after their departing Christian friends, as the disciples gazed after their ascending Lord, and hear them sing as they ascend: "O death, where is thy sting? O grave, where is thy victory?"

Religion holds a prominent place in Greek tragedy, as in some form or other it always has done and always will do in real life. The existence and providence of God, his universal government, and his eternal and immutable laws, with their unfailing rewards and inevitable penalties, are constantly recognized. This is the point, perhaps, in which the tragedies approach nearest to the unapproachable light and glory of the Scriptures; and too many who bear the name of Christians might refresh their convictions and elevate their conceptions of the supremacy of the divine law and the certainty of retribution, by a familiar acquaintance with the doctrine of the divine nemesis, as it stands out on the pages of Aeschylus, Sophocles, and Euripides. The frailty, ignorance, and imperfection of men are also confessed. The necessity of a revelation of the divine will by prophets and oracles, is universally acknowledged. Prayer is offered. An existence after death is implied. And the connection between this life and the next, the dependence of men on a higher power, and the necessity of obedience to a higher law, though sometimes called in question, are more often strenuously asserted.

Some ideas exist not only of a fall, but also of a recovery; some ideas, not only of a controversy between the gods and wicked men, but of the possibility (in some cases at least) and the blessedness of reconciliation. Such ideas are universal. They belong to man as man; and they lie at the foundation, not only of natural, but revealed religion.

But as they appear in the Greek tragedies, these ideas are too much ideas of the reason and the imagination; too little of the conscience and the heart. This is true, perhaps, generally, of the religion of cultivated nations; and true of too many nominal Christians. But it is emphatically true of the Greeks. Their religion was ideal, poetical, aesthetic, rather than real, practical, personal. There is more of the religious element in Sophocles than there is in Shakespeare; but there is far less of the ethical element. The conscience is less developed. The writer seems to know less of its nature and power; and his characters who are fit subjects for its compunctious visitings seldom or never writhe under its tortures. And those sublime utterances touching the retributive providence and government of God, which hold very much the same place in the Greek dramatist as the remorse of conscience does in the English, proceed, not from the criminals who are to experience the retribution, but from the chorus and the better characters, who look on, and expect it, or see it fall on others. The want of an enlightened, sensitive conscience, is the grand defect in the Greek character, as it is seen either in the literature or in the history of the people.

And we see a decided growth of this ideal tendency in passing from Aeschylus to Sophocles; owing partly, perhaps, to the genius of the individual poet, but partly, also, we must think, to the advancing culture of the people. It seems as if, as they advanced in time and progressed in the cultivation of literature and art, they receded from the fountain of moral and religious truth, and the ideas of the primeval revelation lost their vital power. In Sophocles, more than in Aeschylus, there is room for the feeling, in some passages at least, that the gods are powers or personifications, rather than persons. Law and providence are more nearly another name for destiny, though the god in them is still at times brought out with great distinctness. Worship approaches somewhat the modern pantheistic worship, though it is still far from the unreality and absurdity of the latter. Prayer is a sublime or beautiful song. A veil is drawn over the unseen world, and its awful retributions are but dimly projected on the confines of the present scene.

As a natural consequence of the prevalence of the imagination over the conscience, of the aesthetic over the moral, in the character of the Greeks, their ideas of holiness and sin, and hence also of reconciliation and redemption, are sadly defective. Here, however, all religions are defective in comparison with the religion of the Bible. Holiness and sin are new ideas, almost new words, in the Bible, so frequent is their occurrence, so profound is their significance, so over-awing their power. Other books talk of infirmities, vices, crimes—the infirmities of this man, the vices of that man, and the crimes of the few. The Bible convicts every man of personal sinfulness in the sight of a personal and holy God. The Hindoos worshipped might, in Juggernaut and other monstrous forms; the Assyrians, the powers of nature, as idealized in their winged lions and bulls; the Persians, light; the Egyptians, life; the Greeks, beauty—human beauty as the image of divine; the Romans, law—the law of the State, as the representative of the law of God.[1] The Jew and the Christian alone worship a God of holiness. "*Glorious in Holiness!*"—you will get no such idea of God as that, from all the poetry and philosophy of the ages.[2] Yet that is the idea conceived of God by the Hebrew lawgiver, a thousand years before Sophocles and Plato were born. And as the higher idea always involves the lower, so in this case holiness is at once the greatest might, the purest light, the highest life, the truest nature, the divinest beauty, and the most perfect law; while, over and above all these, it is the only proper standard of personal, moral, and spiritual character that can stand the test of all earthly temptations, and the more fiery trial of the final judgment.

The chorus, in the Greek tragedy, sing of the all-seeing, all-powerful Zeus, with his oracle-inspiring, Loxian son, and his wise and terrible daughter—the triple powers of heaven; and also of the avenging deities—the dreadful powers of hell; and as they sing, the actors and spectators tremble at their majesty and might. The

[1] Cf. Robertson's Sermons, First Series, Sermon xi.

[2] It is not denied that holiness is an attribute of the supreme god of the Greeks; but it is not his characteristic and his glory.

seraphim of the Old Testament, and the living creatures in the New, veil their faces before Him who was, and is, and is to come, and cry *Holy! Holy! Holy!* And prophets and kings, the wisest and best men on earth, overwhelmed by a sense of their comparative impurity, cry out "Wo is me! for I am a man of unclean lips, and I dwell among a people of unclean lips; for I have seen the King, the Lord of hosts!" And saints and angels in heaven, prostrate themselves before the throne, saying, "Thou alone art holy."

It is just this lively consciousness of sin, educated by all the history and prophecy and sacrifices and shadows of the Old Testament, and quickened into yet higher sensibility by the word and spirit of the New, which gives such a new and strange significance to the ideas, and the very words, Atonement, Reconciliation, Justification, Sanctification, and the whole plan of salvation which is revealed in the gospel of Christ. "The exceeding sinfulness of sin" is the logical and practical antithesis of a God "glorious in holiness." And when men see and feel their "exceeding sinfulness" in the presence of a thrice holy God, then they are prepared to appreciate the unspeakable preciousness of the Christian revelation, which brings to such men life, salvation, and comfort through the divine Trinity. Blessed, glorious gospel of the Father, the Son, and the Holy Ghost! How it shines brighter and purer in comparison with the brightest lights that have ever twinkled and faded in the long night of ages!